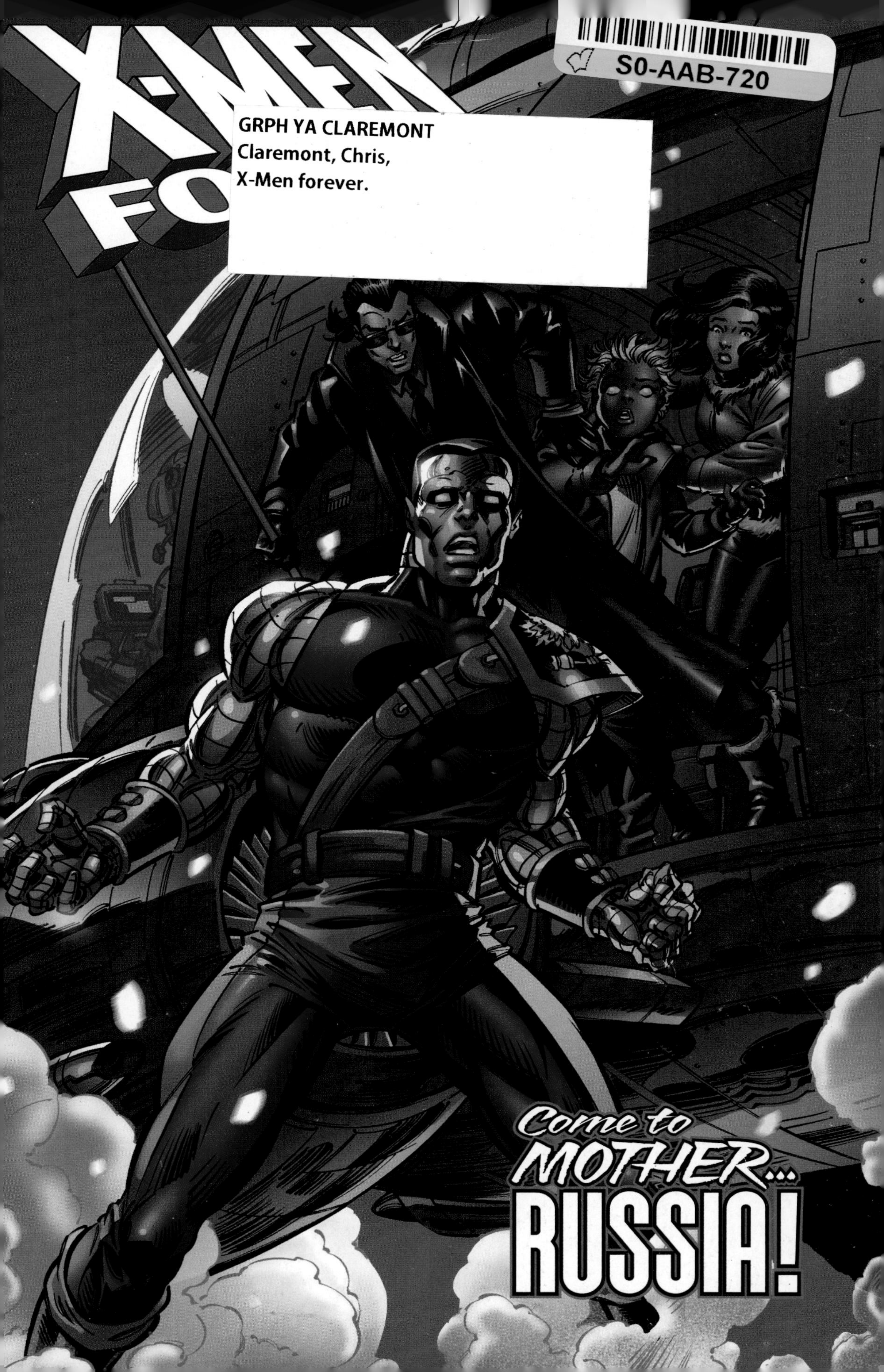
X-MEN FO
Come to MOTHER...
RUSSIA!

X-MEN FOREVER

Come to MOTHER... RUSSIA!

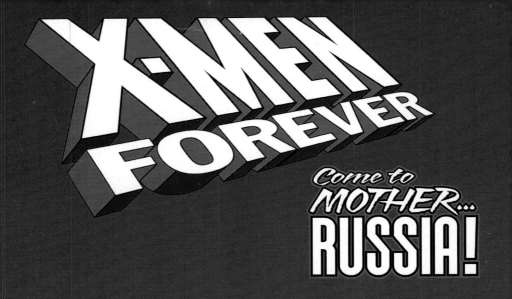

Writer:
CHRIS CLAREMONT

Penciler:
TOM GRUMMETT WITH PETER VALE (ISSUE #15)

Inker:
CORY HAMSCHER WITH AL VEY, GARY MARTIN & PETER VALE (ISSUE #15)

Colorist:
WILFREDO QUINTANA WITH SOTOCOLOR (ISSUE #14)

Letterer:
TOM ORZECHOWSKI

Cover Art:
TOM GRUMMETT, TERRY AUSTIN, CORY HAMSCHER, WILFREDO QUINTANA & MORRY HOLLOWELL

Assistant Editors:
CHARLIE BECKERMAN & MICHAEL HORWITZ

Editor:
MARK PANICCIA

Collection Editor: **JENNIFER GRÜNWALD** • Assistant Editor: **ALEX STARBUCK**
Associate Editor: **JOHN DENNING** • Editor, Special Projects: **MARK D. BEAZLEY**
Senior Editor, Special Projects: **JEFF YOUNGQUIST** • Senior Vice President of Sales: **DAVID GABRIEL**
Book Designer: **SPRING HOTELING**

Editor in Chief: **JOE QUESADA** • Publisher: **DAN BUCKLEY**
Executive Producer: **ALAN FINE**

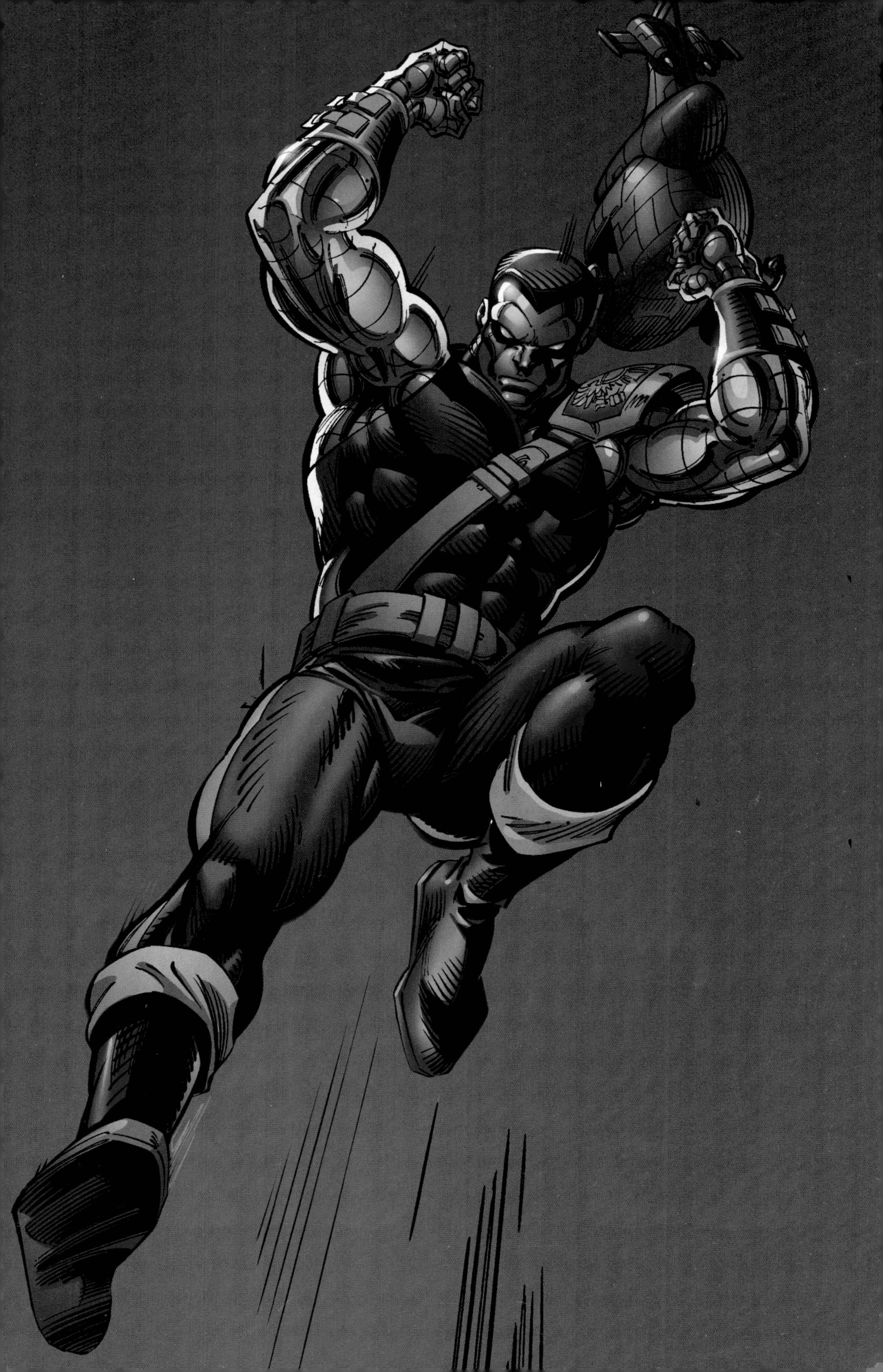

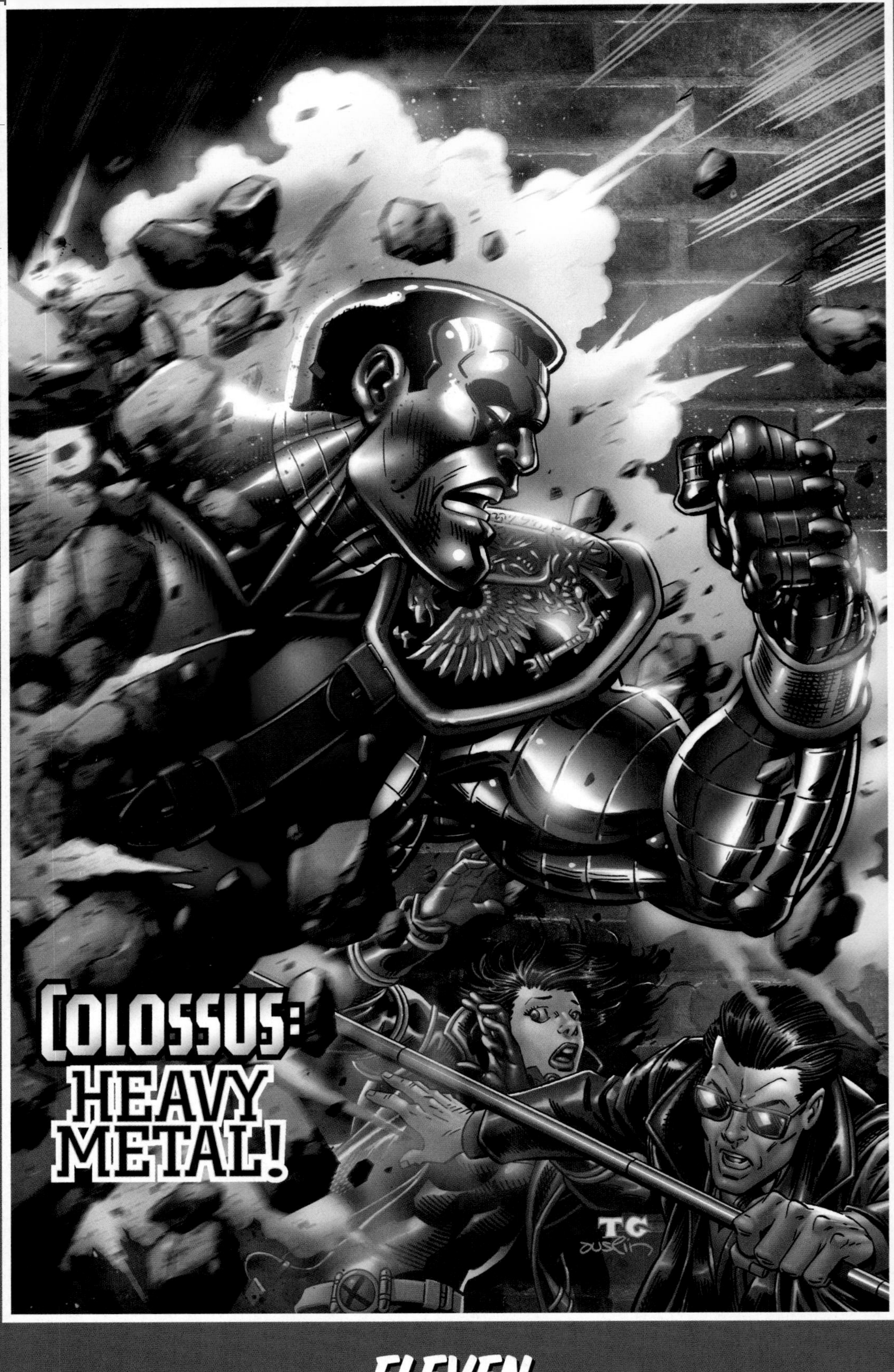
COLOSSUS:
HEAVY
METAL!
TG
austin

ELEVEN

Comics legend Chris Claremont had an epic 16-year run on ***X-MEN****, which concluded with* ***X-MEN: MUTANT GENESIS #1-3*** *in 1991. Now, in an unprecedented comics event, Claremont returns to his iconic run on the* ***X-MEN****.*

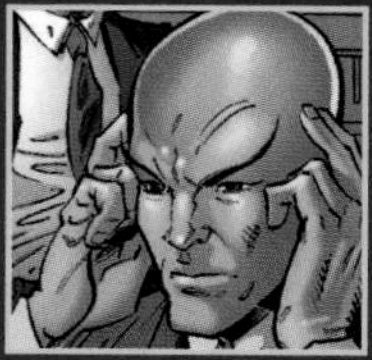

PROFESSOR X
Charles Xavier

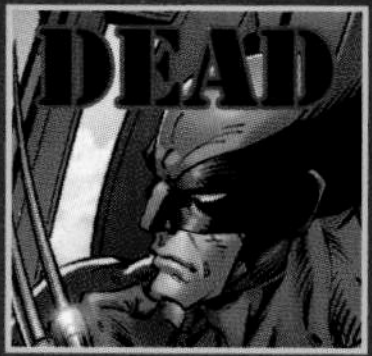
DEAD

WOLVERINE
Logan

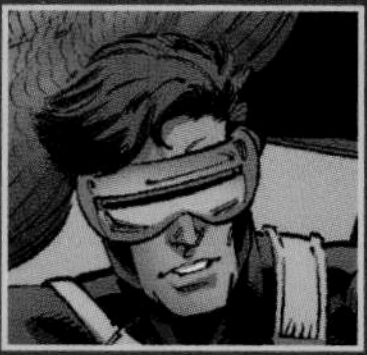

CYCLOPS
Scott Summers

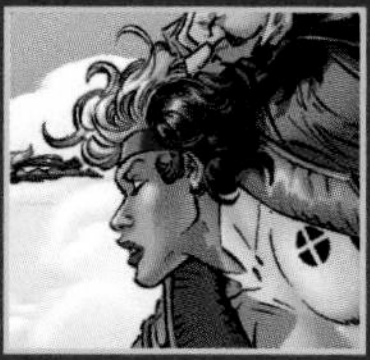

ROGUE
Anna Marie Raven

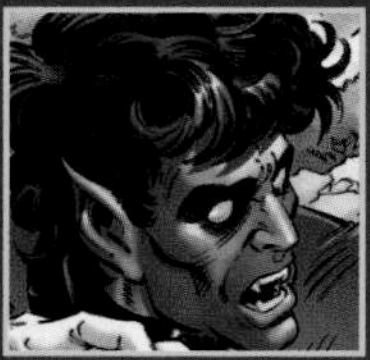

NIGHTCRAWLER
Kurt Wagner

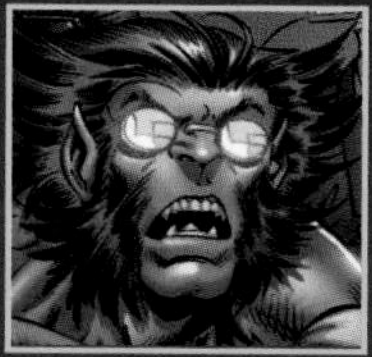

BEAST
Hank McCoy

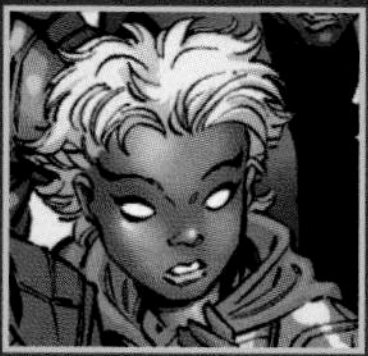

LIL' 'RO
Adolescent clone of Ororo Munroe?

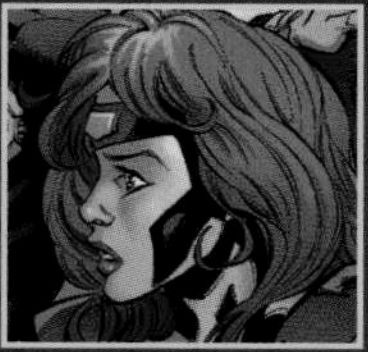

JEAN GREY

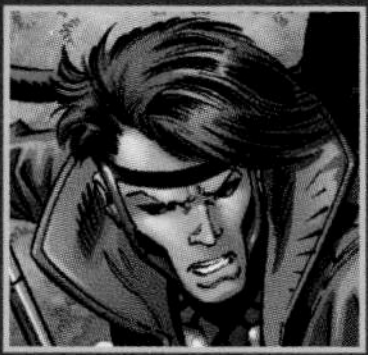

GAMBIT
Remy Picard

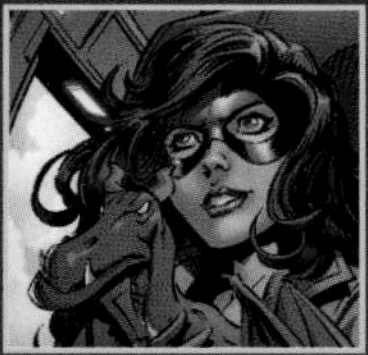

SHADOWCAT
Kitty Pryde

Previously, in

X MEN FOREVER

The X-Men have never had an easy road to travel, but lately things have been even worse. Storm, trusted team member and friend, revealed herself to be an imposter and murdered Wolverine, the one X-Man they never expected to have to say goodbye to.

The entire team was rocked to its core, but a few X-Men felt the sting more deeply than others: Kitty Pryde, who somehow "acquired" one of Logan's claws and whose personality has taken a much darker turn; Jean Grey, who shared a passionate, unconsummated love with Logan; and Sabretooth, one-time foe who has made an uneasy alliance with the team to find justice – or vengeance – for his son.

On top of this personal tragedy, the X-Men received the damning news that Professor Xavier had been hiding a terrible secret from the team. Through years of research, Professor Xavier discovered that the same genetic qualities that give mutants their extraordinary abilities also make them dangerously unstable. In summary: all mutants eventually burn out, and die young.

Before they could bid farewell to their beloved friend, part of the team had to fly out to South America, where they discovered that Sigrid "Ziggy" Trask, heiress to the Sentinel-creating Trask family, had reactivated the program with new metal monsters that target humans and mutants alike. Before they could complete this mission, however, Ziggy escaped, leaving a dangerous loose end for the team.

Once they returned, the X-Men and a group of Wolverine's many friends gathered to say a heartfelt goodbye to their fallen ally. One notable X-Man, however, was conspicuously absent…

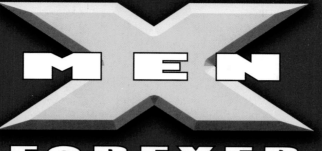

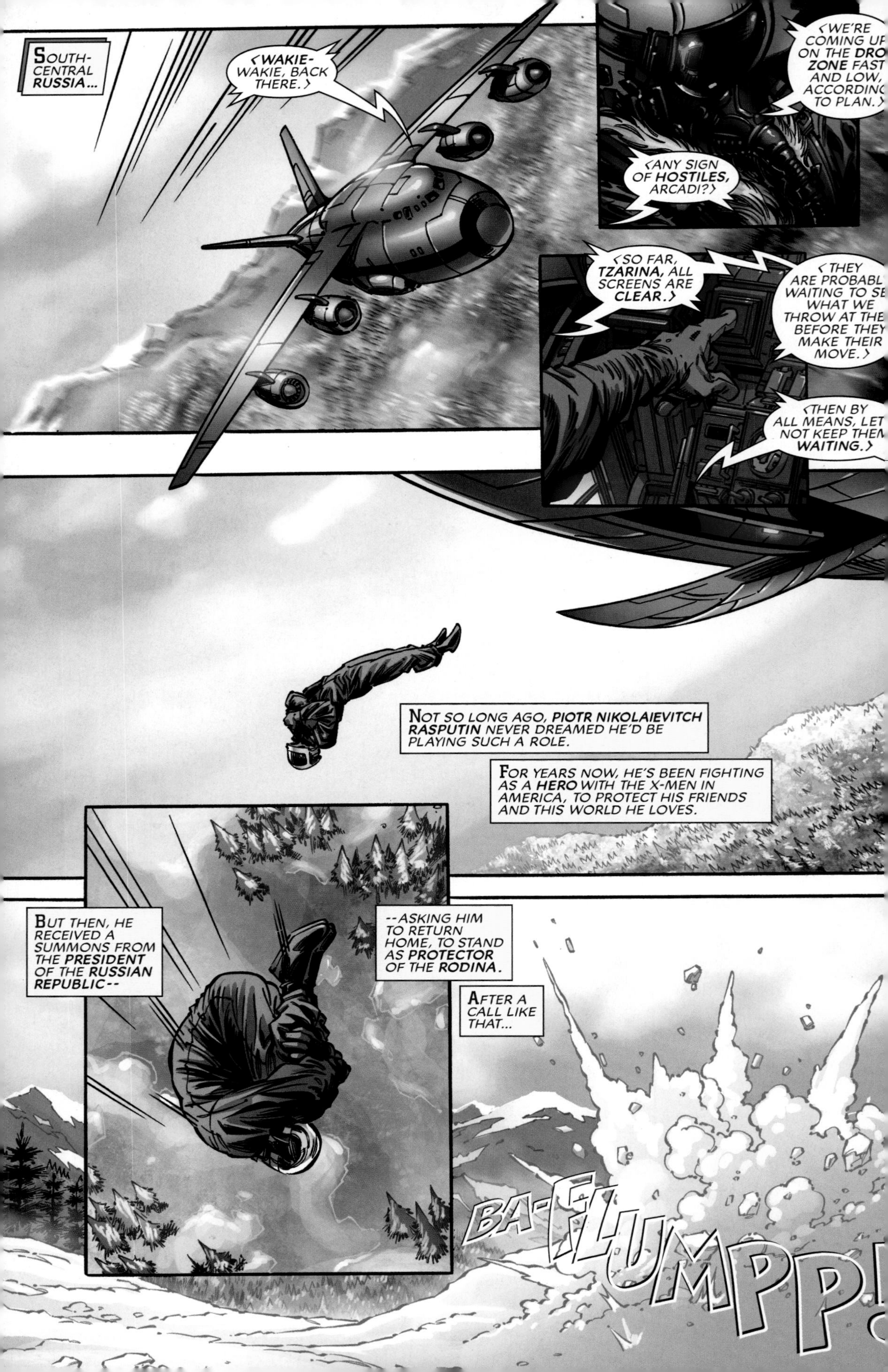
SOUTH-CENTRAL RUSSIA...
‹WAKIE-WAKIE, BACK THERE.›
‹WE'RE COMING UP ON THE DRO ZONE FAST AND LOW, ACCORDING TO PLAN.›
‹ANY SIGN OF HOSTILES, ARCADI?›
‹SO FAR, TZARINA, ALL SCREENS ARE CLEAR.›
‹THEY ARE PROBABL WAITING TO SE WHAT WE THROW AT THE BEFORE THEY MAKE THEIR MOVE.›
‹THEN BY ALL MEANS, LET NOT KEEP THEM WAITING.›
NOT SO LONG AGO, PIOTR NIKOLAIEVITCH RASPUTIN NEVER DREAMED HE'D BE PLAYING SUCH A ROLE.
FOR YEARS NOW, HE'S BEEN FIGHTING AS A HERO WITH THE X-MEN IN AMERICA, TO PROTECT HIS FRIENDS AND THIS WORLD HE LOVES.
BUT THEN, HE RECEIVED A SUMMONS FROM THE PRESIDENT OF THE RUSSIAN REPUBLIC--
--ASKING HIM TO RETURN HOME, TO STAND AS PROTECTOR OF THE RODINA.
AFTER A CALL LIKE THAT...
BA-FLUMPP!

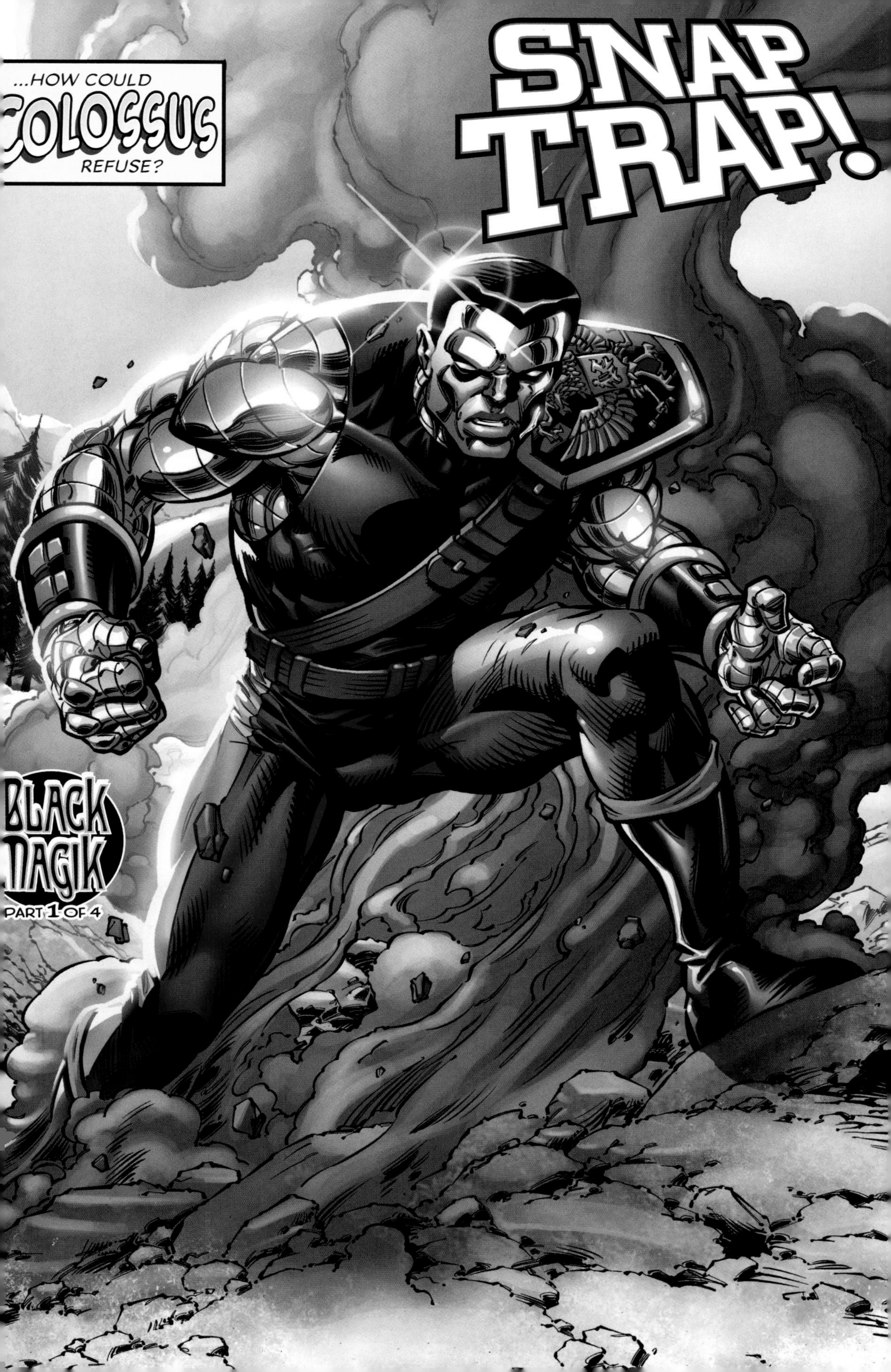
...HOW COULD COLOSSUS REFUSE?
SNAP TRAP!
BLACK MAGIK
PART 1 OF 4

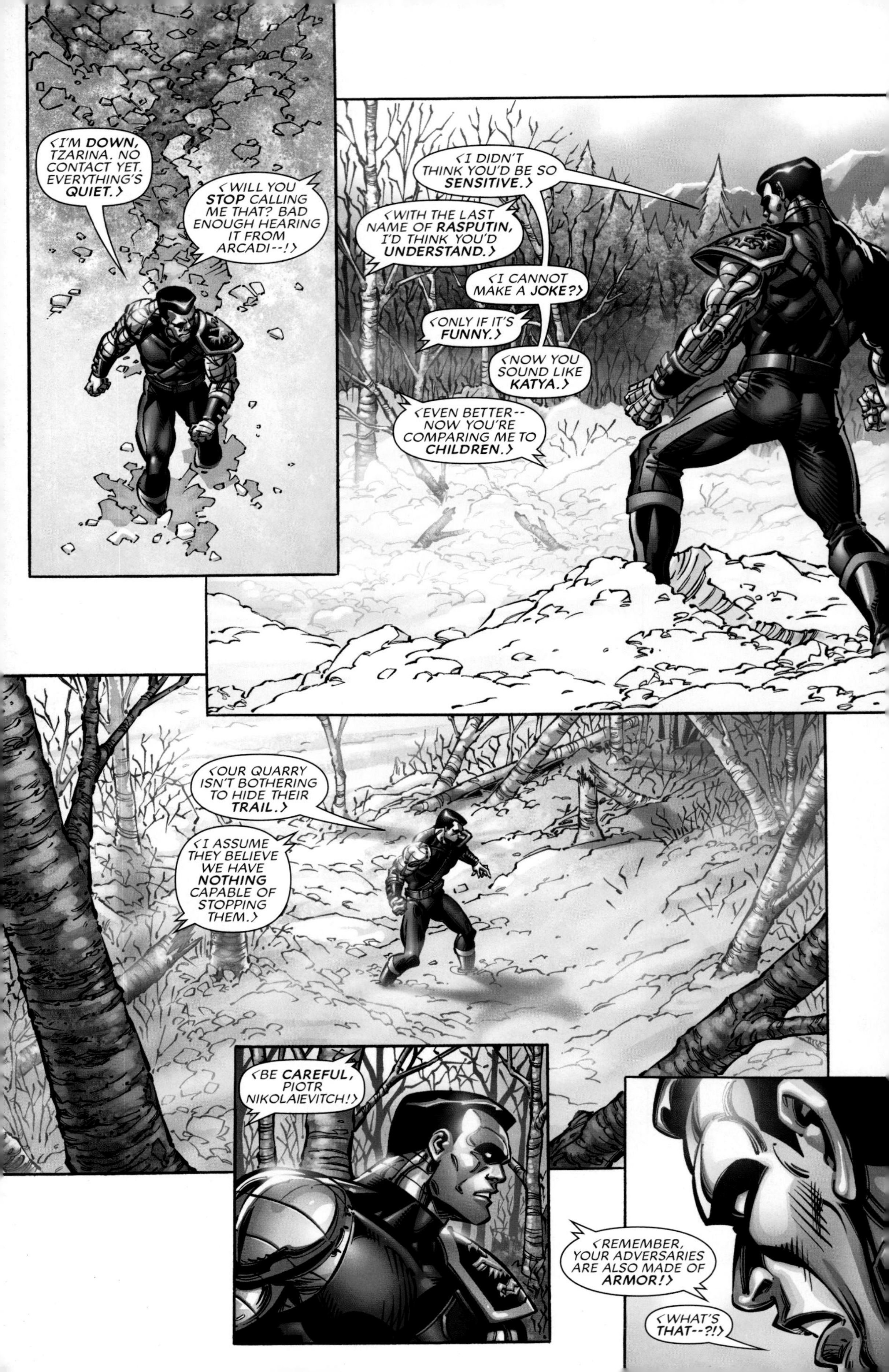

<I'M DOWN, TZARINA. NO CONTACT YET. EVERYTHING'S QUIET.>
<WILL YOU STOP CALLING ME THAT? BAD ENOUGH HEARING IT FROM ARCADI--!>
<I DIDN'T THINK YOU'D BE SO SENSITIVE.>
<WITH THE LAST NAME OF RASPUTIN, I'D THINK YOU'D UNDERSTAND.>
<I CANNOT MAKE A JOKE?>
<ONLY IF IT'S FUNNY.>
<NOW YOU SOUND LIKE KATYA.>
<EVEN BETTER--NOW YOU'RE COMPARING ME TO CHILDREN.>
<OUR QUARRY ISN'T BOTHERING TO HIDE THEIR TRAIL.>
<I ASSUME THEY BELIEVE WE HAVE NOTHING CAPABLE OF STOPPING THEM.>
<BE CAREFUL, PIOTR NIKOLAIEVITCH!>
<REMEMBER, YOUR ADVERSARIES ARE ALSO MADE OF ARMOR!>
<WHAT'S THAT--?!>

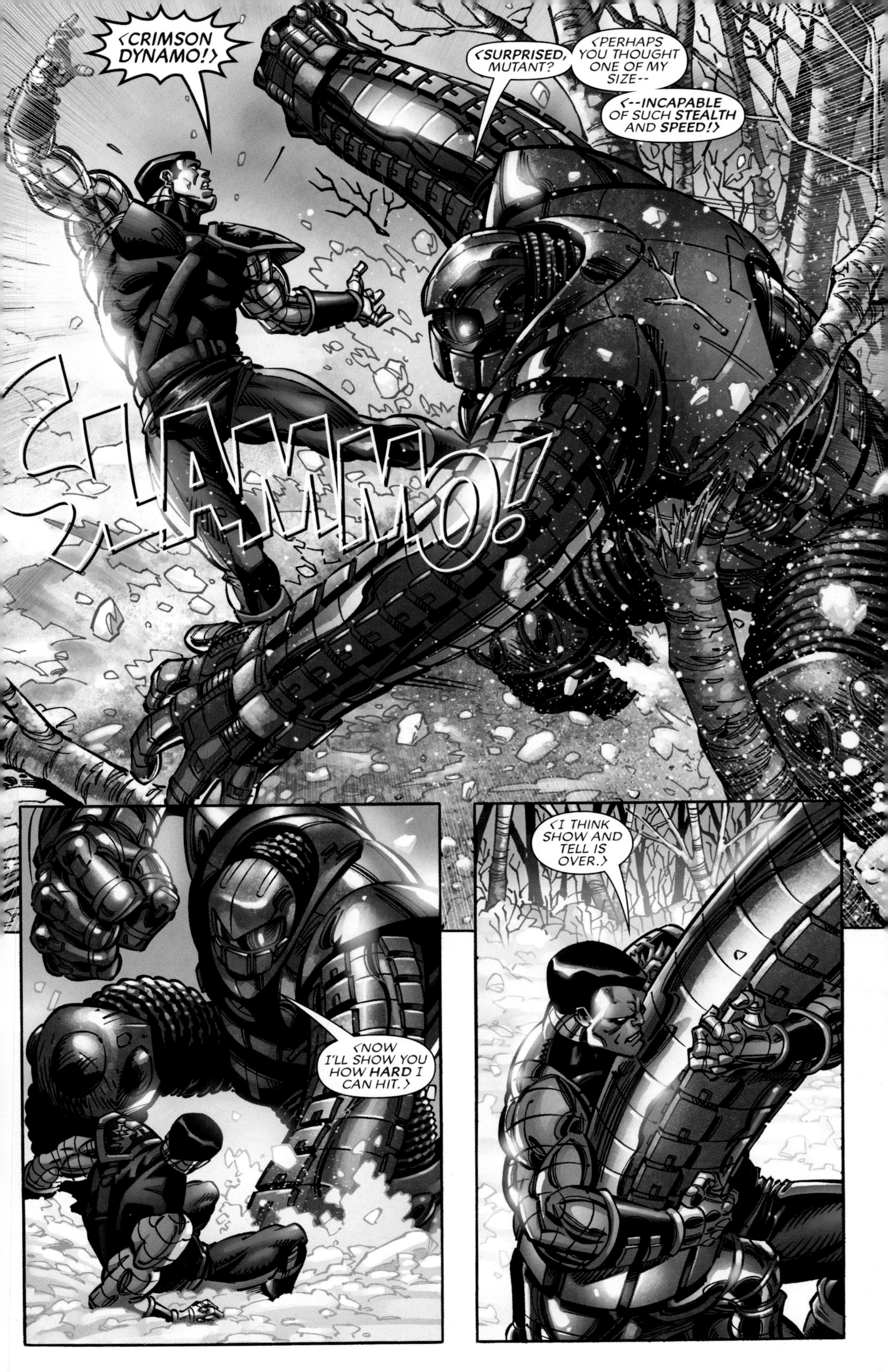
‹CRIMSON DYNAMO!›
‹SURPRISED, MUTANT?
‹PERHAPS YOU THOUGHT ONE OF MY SIZE--
‹--INCAPABLE OF SUCH STEALTH AND SPEED!›
SLAMMO!
‹NOW I'LL SHOW YOU HOW HARD I CAN HIT.›
‹I THINK SHOW AND TELL IS OVER.›

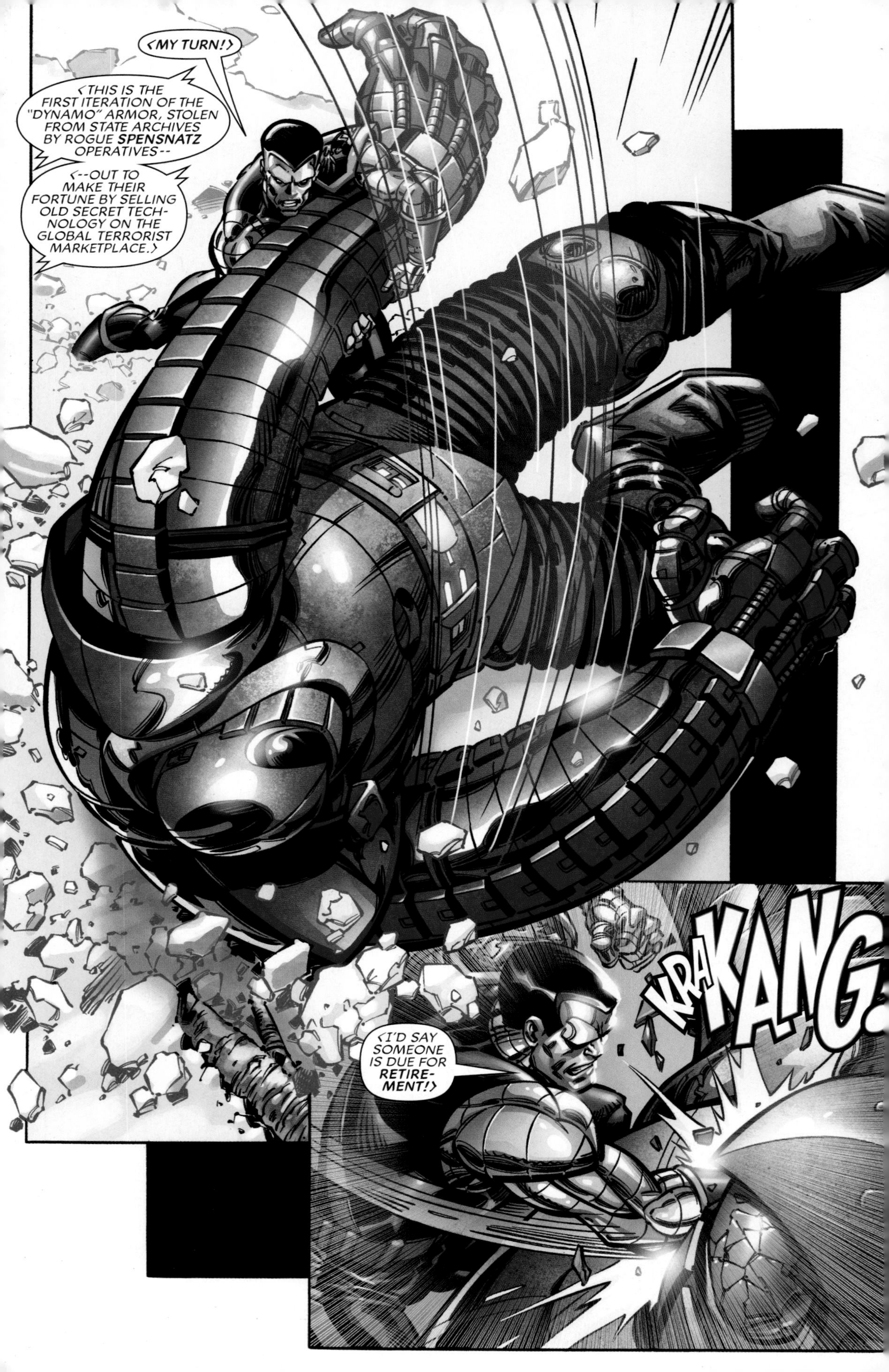
<MY TURN!>
<THIS IS THE FIRST ITERATION OF THE "DYNAMO" ARMOR, STOLEN FROM STATE ARCHIVES BY ROGUE SPENSNATZ OPERATIVES--
<--OUT TO MAKE THEIR FORTUNE BY SELLING OLD SECRET TECHNOLOGY ON THE GLOBAL TERRORIST MARKETPLACE.>
KRAKANG!
<I'D SAY SOMEONE IS DUE FOR RETIREMENT!>

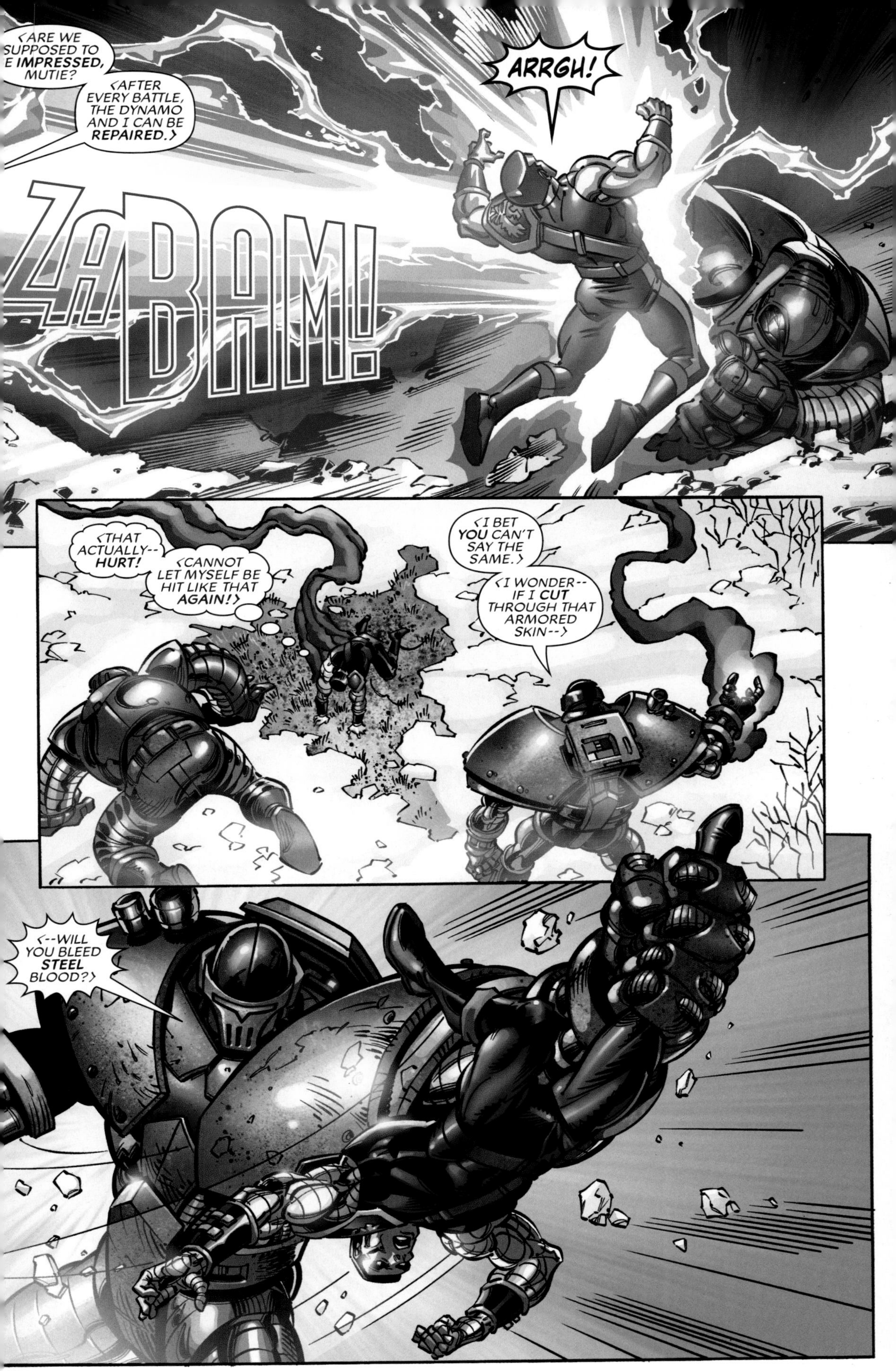

‹ARE WE SUPPOSED TO E IMPRESSED, MUTIE?
‹AFTER EVERY BATTLE, THE DYNAMO AND I CAN BE REPAIRED.›
ARRGH!
ZABAM!
‹THAT ACTUALLY-- HURT!
‹CANNOT LET MYSELF BE HIT LIKE THAT AGAIN!›
‹I BET YOU CAN'T SAY THE SAME.›
‹I WONDER-- IF I CUT THROUGH THAT ARMORED SKIN--›
‹--WILL YOU BLEED STEEL BLOOD?›

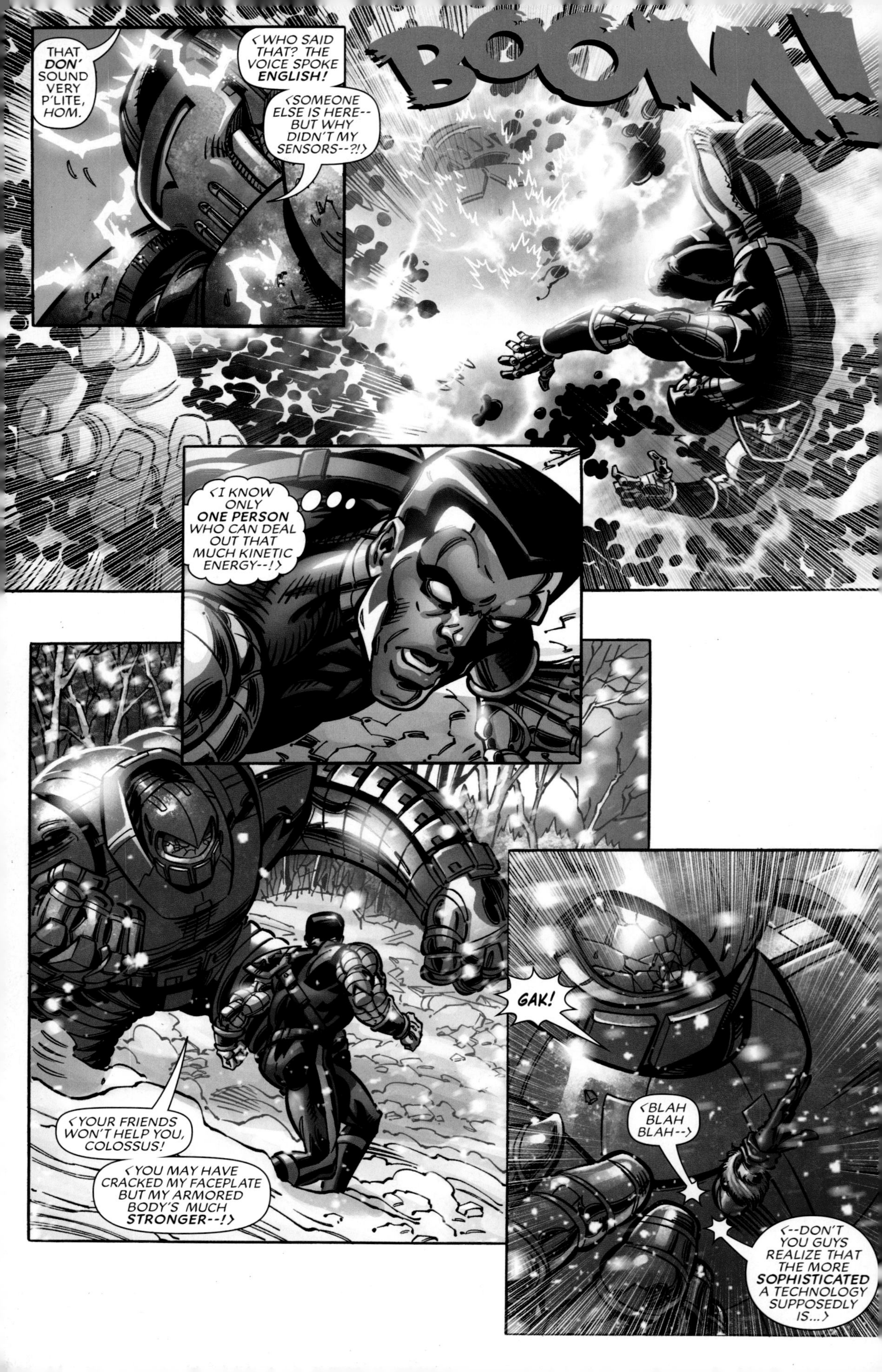
THAT DON' SOUND VERY P'LITE, HOM.
<WHO SAID THAT? THE VOICE SPOKE ENGLISH!
<SOMEONE ELSE IS HERE-- BUT WHY DIDN'T MY SENSORS--?!>
BOOM!
<I KNOW ONLY ONE PERSON WHO CAN DEAL OUT THAT MUCH KINETIC ENERGY--!>
<YOUR FRIENDS WON'T HELP YOU, COLOSSUS!
<YOU MAY HAVE CRACKED MY FACEPLATE BUT MY ARMORED BODY'S MUCH STRONGER--!>
GAK!
<BLAH BLAH BLAH-->
<--DON'T YOU GUYS REALIZE THAT THE MORE SOPHISTICATED A TECHNOLOGY SUPPOSEDLY IS...>

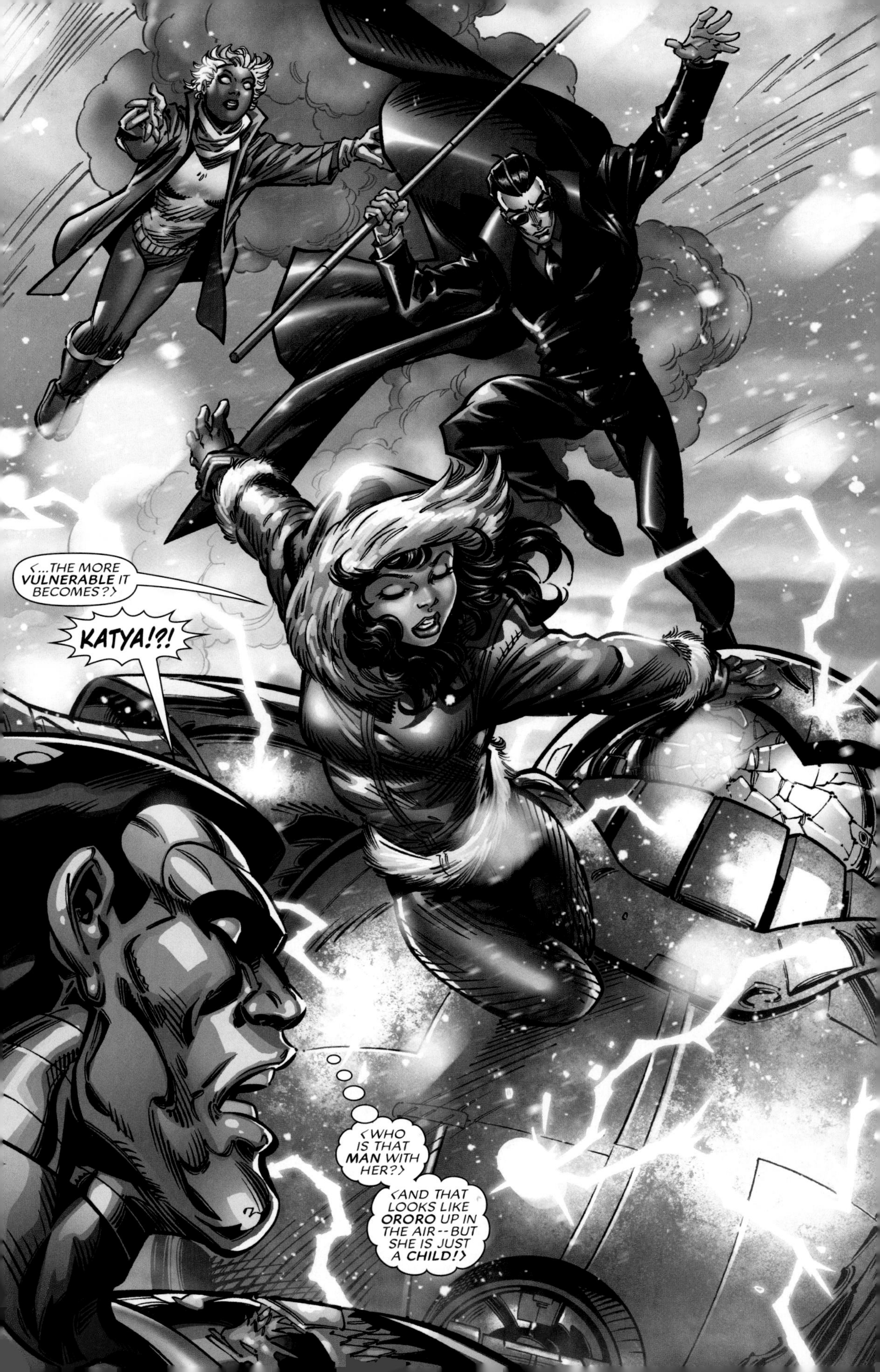
<...THE MORE VULNERABLE IT BECOMES?>
KATYA!?!
<WHO IS THAT MAN WITH HER?>
<AND THAT LOOKS LIKE ORORO UP IN THE AIR--BUT SHE IS JUST A CHILD!>

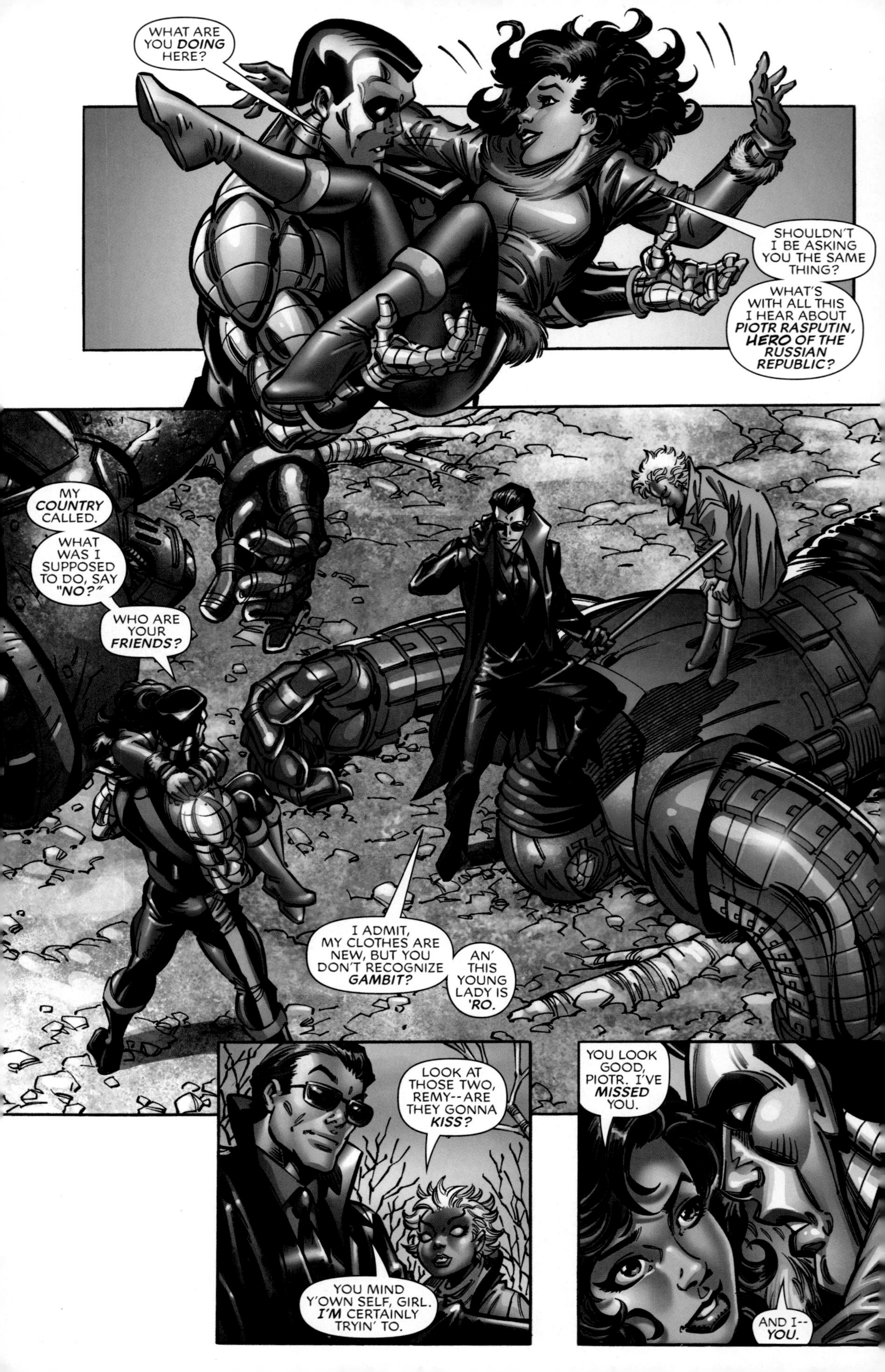
WHAT ARE YOU DOING HERE?
SHOULDN'T I BE ASKING YOU THE SAME THING?
WHAT'S WITH ALL THIS I HEAR ABOUT PIOTR RASPUTIN, HERO OF THE RUSSIAN REPUBLIC?
MY COUNTRY CALLED.
WHAT WAS I SUPPOSED TO DO, SAY "NO?"
WHO ARE YOUR FRIENDS?
I ADMIT, MY CLOTHES ARE NEW, BUT YOU DON'T RECOGNIZE GAMBIT?
AN' THIS YOUNG LADY IS 'RO.
LOOK AT THOSE TWO, REMY--ARE THEY GONNA KISS?
YOU MIND Y'OWN SELF, GIRL. I'M CERTAINLY TRYIN' TO.
YOU LOOK GOOD, PIOTR. I'VE MISSED YOU.
AND I-- YOU.

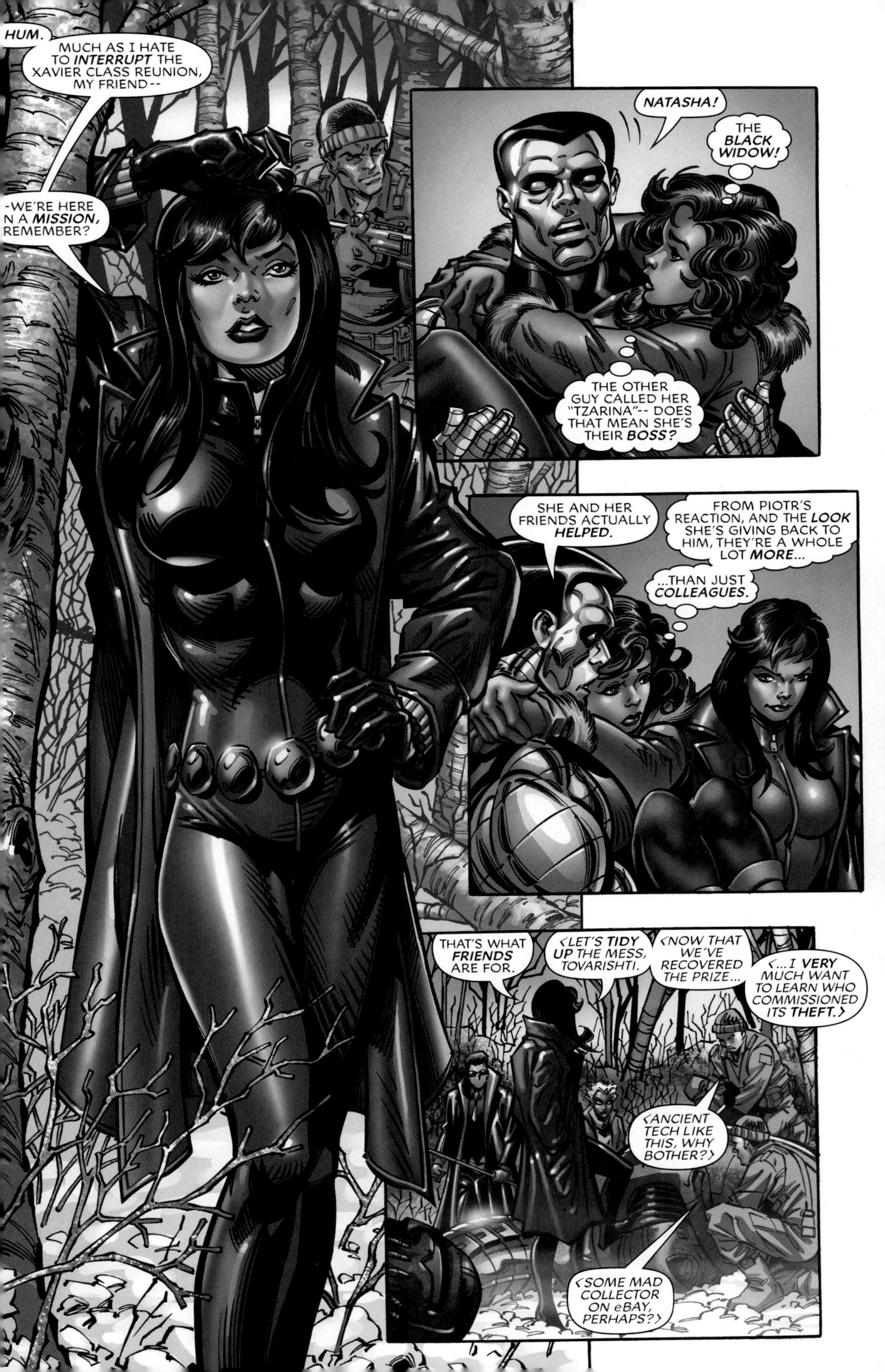
HUM.
MUCH AS I HATE TO INTERRUPT THE XAVIER CLASS REUNION, MY FRIEND--
-WE'RE HERE ON A MISSION, REMEMBER?
NATASHA!
THE BLACK WIDOW!
THE OTHER GUY CALLED HER "TZARINA"-- DOES THAT MEAN SHE'S THEIR BOSS?
SHE AND HER FRIENDS ACTUALLY HELPED.
FROM PIOTR'S REACTION, AND THE LOOK SHE'S GIVING BACK TO HIM, THEY'RE A WHOLE LOT MORE...
...THAN JUST COLLEAGUES.
THAT'S WHAT FRIENDS ARE FOR.
<LET'S TIDY UP THE MESS, TOVARISHTI.
<NOW THAT WE'VE RECOVERED THE PRIZE...
<...I VERY MUCH WANT TO LEARN WHO COMMISSIONED ITS THEFT.>
<ANCIENT TECH LIKE THIS, WHY BOTHER?>
<SOME MAD COLLECTOR ON eBAY, PERHAPS?>

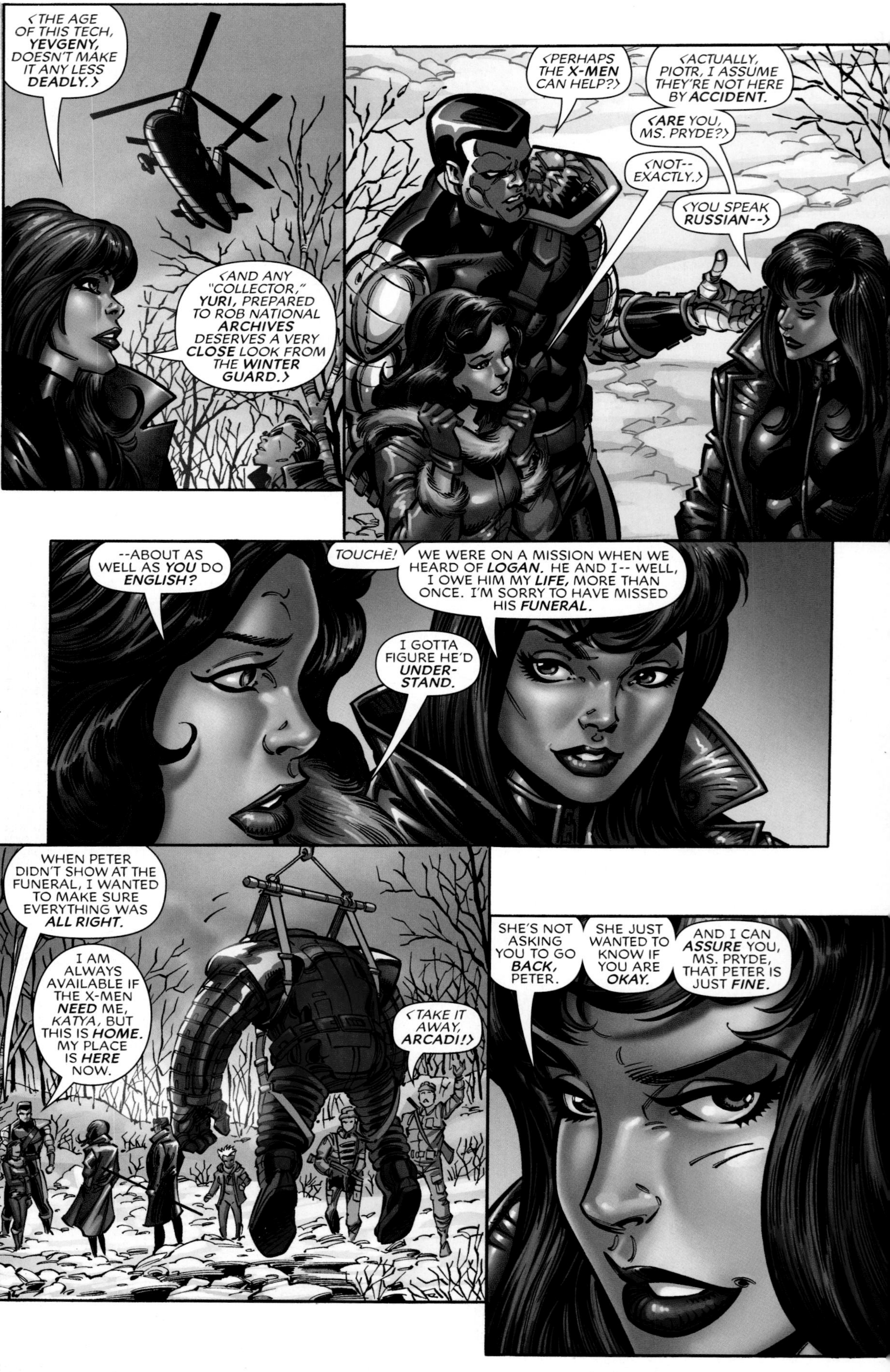

<THE AGE OF THIS TECH, YEVGENY, DOESN'T MAKE IT ANY LESS DEADLY.>
<AND ANY "COLLECTOR," YURI, PREPARED TO ROB NATIONAL ARCHIVES DESERVES A VERY CLOSE LOOK FROM THE WINTER GUARD.>
<PERHAPS THE X-MEN CAN HELP?>
<ACTUALLY, PIOTR, I ASSUME THEY'RE NOT HERE BY ACCIDENT.
<ARE YOU, MS. PRYDE?>
<NOT-- EXACTLY.>
<YOU SPEAK RUSSIAN-->
--ABOUT AS WELL AS YOU DO ENGLISH?
TOUCHÈ!
WE WERE ON A MISSION WHEN WE HEARD OF LOGAN. HE AND I-- WELL, I OWE HIM MY LIFE, MORE THAN ONCE. I'M SORRY TO HAVE MISSED HIS FUNERAL.
I GOTTA FIGURE HE'D UNDER-STAND.
WHEN PETER DIDN'T SHOW AT THE FUNERAL, I WANTED TO MAKE SURE EVERYTHING WAS ALL RIGHT.
I AM ALWAYS AVAILABLE IF THE X-MEN NEED ME, KATYA, BUT THIS IS HOME. MY PLACE IS HERE NOW.
<TAKE IT AWAY, ARCADI!>
SHE'S NOT ASKING YOU TO GO BACK, PETER.
SHE JUST WANTED TO KNOW IF YOU ARE OKAY.
AND I CAN ASSURE YOU, MS. PRYDE, THAT PETER IS JUST FINE.

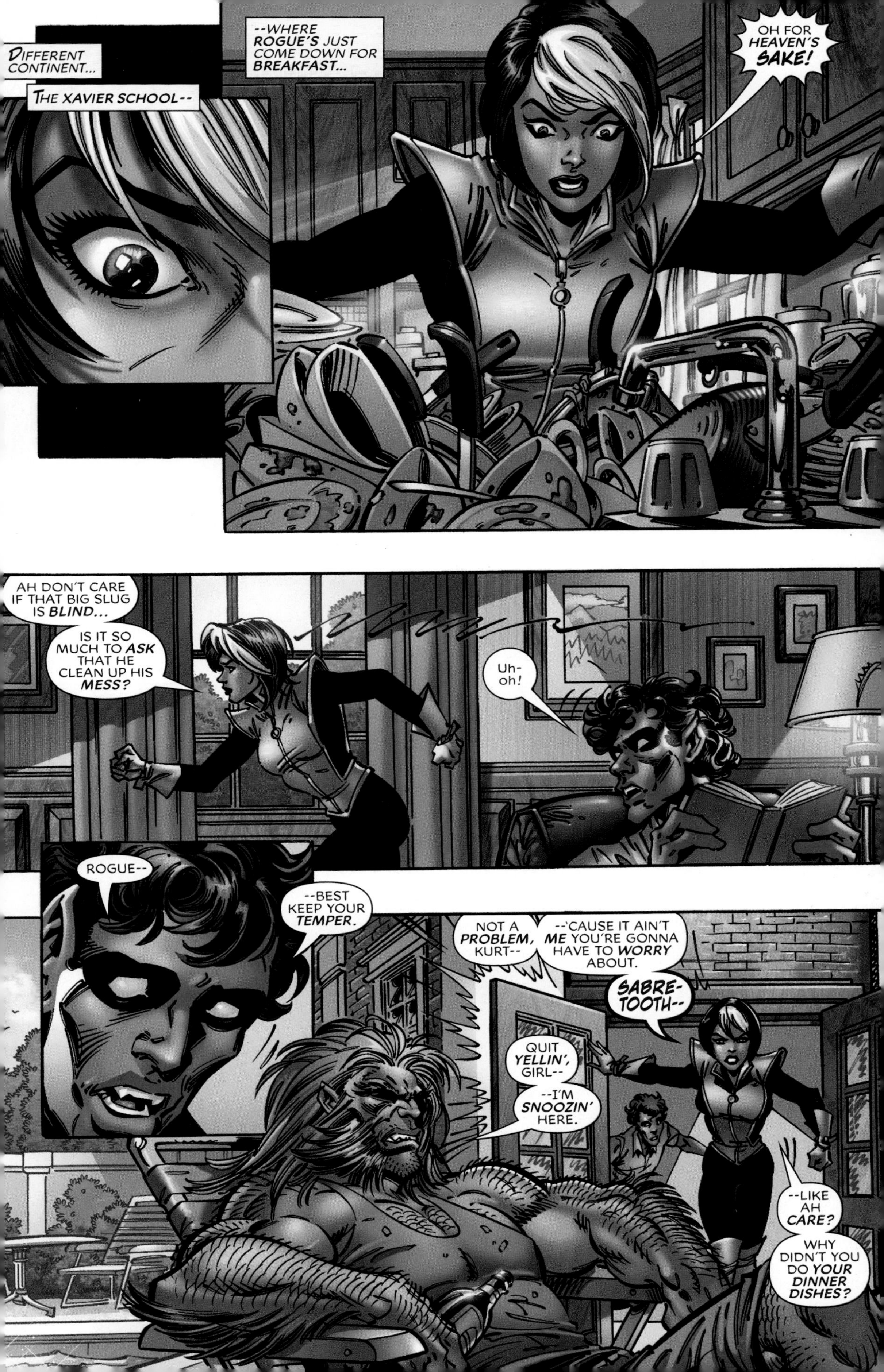
DIFFERENT CONTINENT...
THE XAVIER SCHOOL--
--WHERE ROGUE'S JUST COME DOWN FOR BREAKFAST...
OH FOR HEAVEN'S SAKE!
AH DON'T CARE IF THAT BIG SLUG IS BLIND...
IS IT SO MUCH TO ASK THAT HE CLEAN UP HIS MESS?
Uh-oh!
ROGUE--
--BEST KEEP YOUR TEMPER.
NOT A PROBLEM, KURT--
--'CAUSE IT AIN'T ME YOU'RE GONNA HAVE TO WORRY ABOUT.
SABRE-TOOTH--
QUIT YELLIN', GIRL--
--I'M SNOOZIN' HERE.
--LIKE AH CARE?
WHY DIDN'T YOU DO YOUR DINNER DISHES?

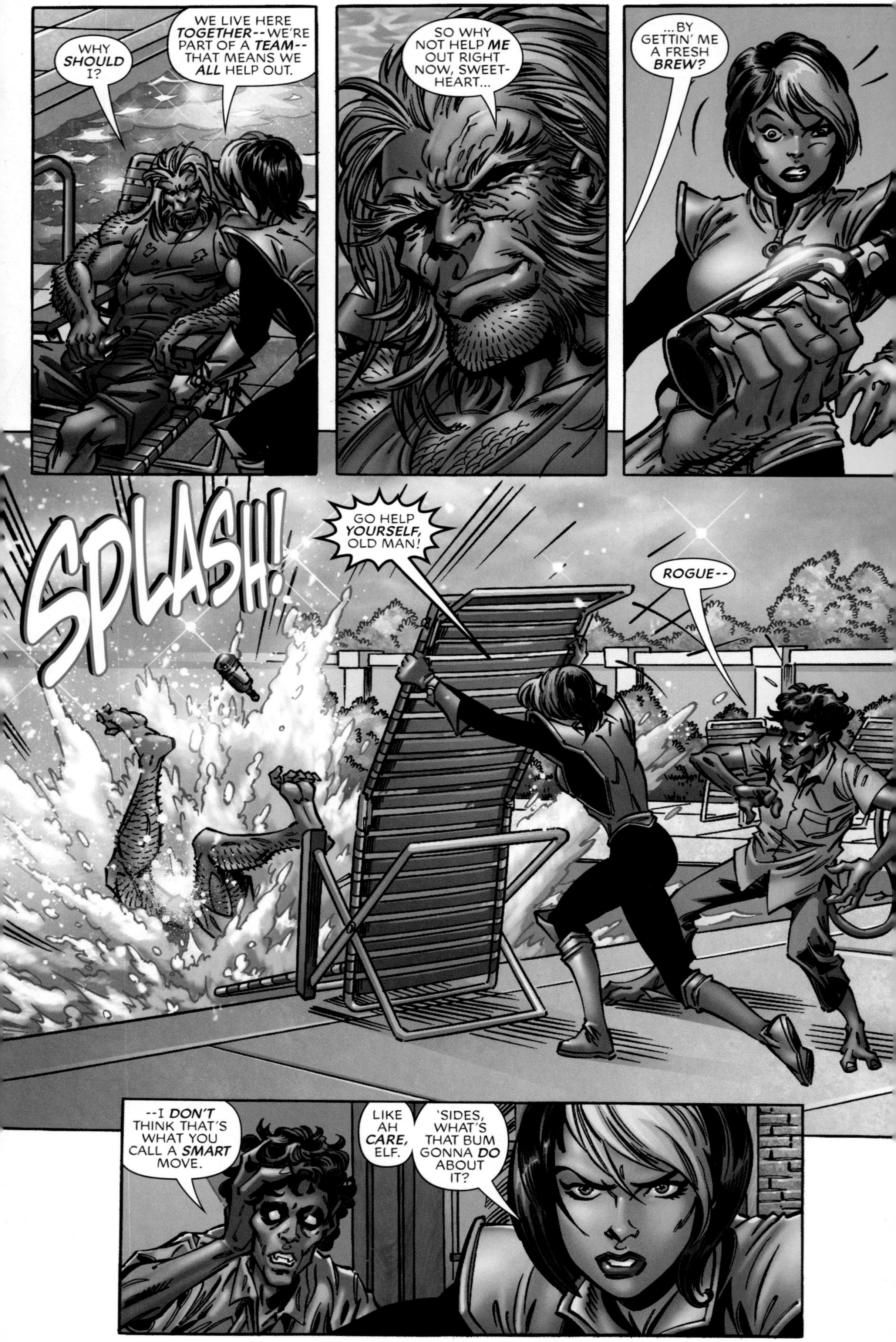
WHY SHOULD I?
WE LIVE HERE TOGETHER--WE'RE PART OF A TEAM--THAT MEANS WE ALL HELP OUT.
SO WHY NOT HELP ME OUT RIGHT NOW, SWEET-HEART...
...BY GETTIN' ME A FRESH BREW?
SPLASH!
GO HELP YOURSELF, OLD MAN!
ROGUE--
--I DON'T THINK THAT'S WHAT YOU CALL A SMART MOVE.
LIKE AH CARE, ELF.
'SIDES, WHAT'S THAT BUM GONNA DO ABOUT IT?

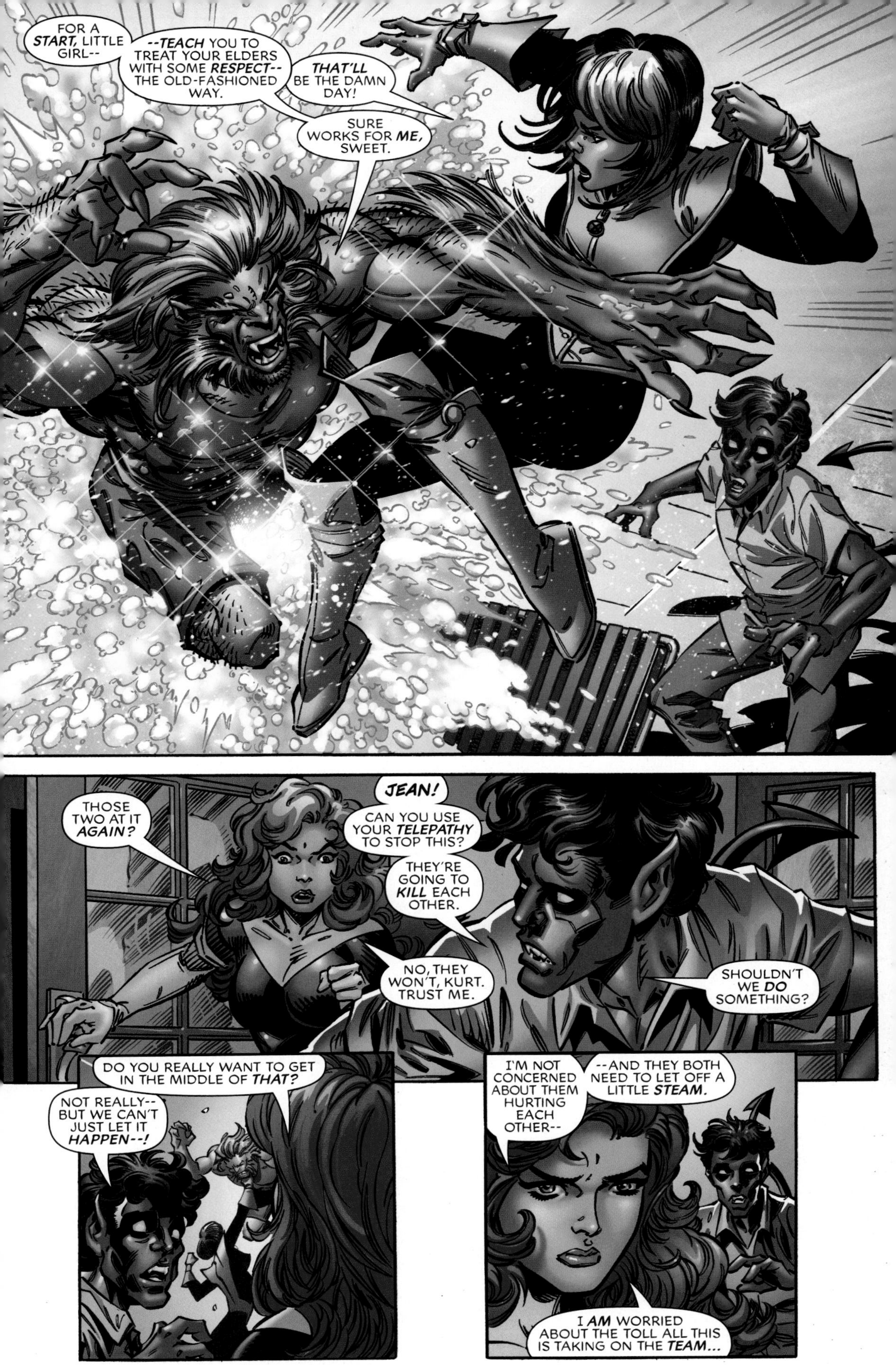
FOR A START, LITTLE GIRL--
--TEACH YOU TO TREAT YOUR ELDERS WITH SOME RESPECT-- THE OLD-FASHIONED WAY.
THAT'LL BE THE DAMN DAY!
SURE WORKS FOR ME, SWEET.
THOSE TWO AT IT AGAIN?
JEAN!
CAN YOU USE YOUR TELEPATHY TO STOP THIS?
THEY'RE GOING TO KILL EACH OTHER.
NO, THEY WON'T, KURT. TRUST ME.
SHOULDN'T WE DO SOMETHING?
DO YOU REALLY WANT TO GET IN THE MIDDLE OF THAT?
NOT REALLY-- BUT WE CAN'T JUST LET IT HAPPEN--!
I'M NOT CONCERNED ABOUT THEM HURTING EACH OTHER--
--AND THEY BOTH NEED TO LET OFF A LITTLE STEAM.
I AM WORRIED ABOUT THE TOLL ALL THIS IS TAKING ON THE TEAM...

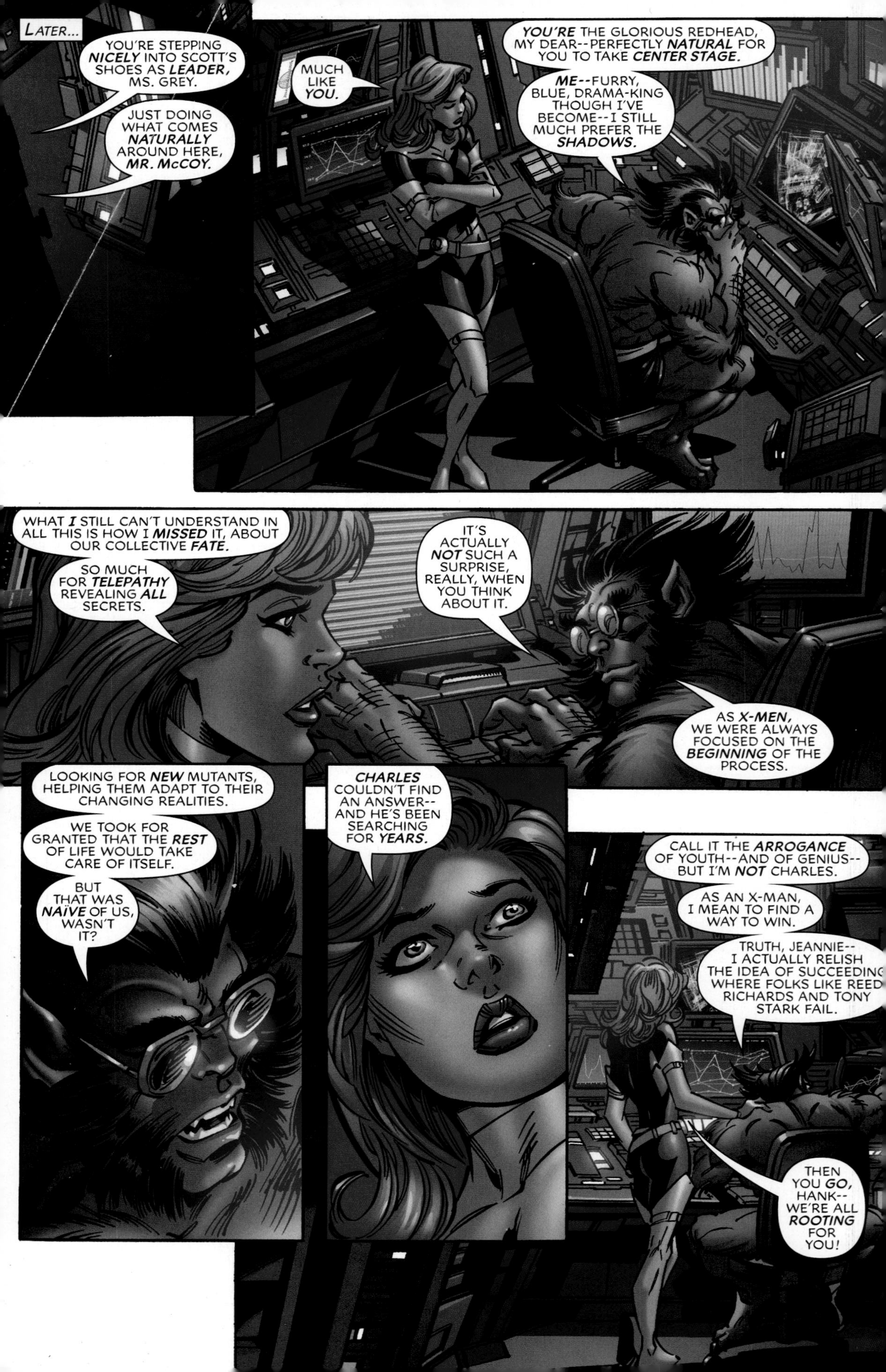
LATER...
YOU'RE STEPPING NICELY INTO SCOTT'S SHOES AS LEADER, MS. GREY.
JUST DOING WHAT COMES NATURALLY AROUND HERE, MR. McCOY.
MUCH LIKE YOU.
YOU'RE THE GLORIOUS REDHEAD, MY DEAR--PERFECTLY NATURAL FOR YOU TO TAKE CENTER STAGE.
ME--FURRY, BLUE, DRAMA-KING THOUGH I'VE BECOME--I STILL MUCH PREFER THE SHADOWS.
WHAT I STILL CAN'T UNDERSTAND IN ALL THIS IS HOW I MISSED IT, ABOUT OUR COLLECTIVE FATE.
SO MUCH FOR TELEPATHY REVEALING ALL SECRETS.
IT'S ACTUALLY NOT SUCH A SURPRISE, REALLY, WHEN YOU THINK ABOUT IT.
AS X-MEN, WE WERE ALWAYS FOCUSED ON THE BEGINNING OF THE PROCESS.
LOOKING FOR NEW MUTANTS, HELPING THEM ADAPT TO THEIR CHANGING REALITIES.
WE TOOK FOR GRANTED THAT THE REST OF LIFE WOULD TAKE CARE OF ITSELF.
BUT THAT WAS NAÏVE OF US, WASN'T IT?
CHARLES COULDN'T FIND AN ANSWER--AND HE'S BEEN SEARCHING FOR YEARS.
CALL IT THE ARROGANCE OF YOUTH--AND OF GENIUS--BUT I'M NOT CHARLES.
AS AN X-MAN, I MEAN TO FIND A WAY TO WIN.
TRUTH, JEANNIE--I ACTUALLY RELISH THE IDEA OF SUCCEEDING WHERE FOLKS LIKE REED RICHARDS AND TONY STARK FAIL.
THEN YOU GO, HANK--WE'RE ALL ROOTING FOR YOU!

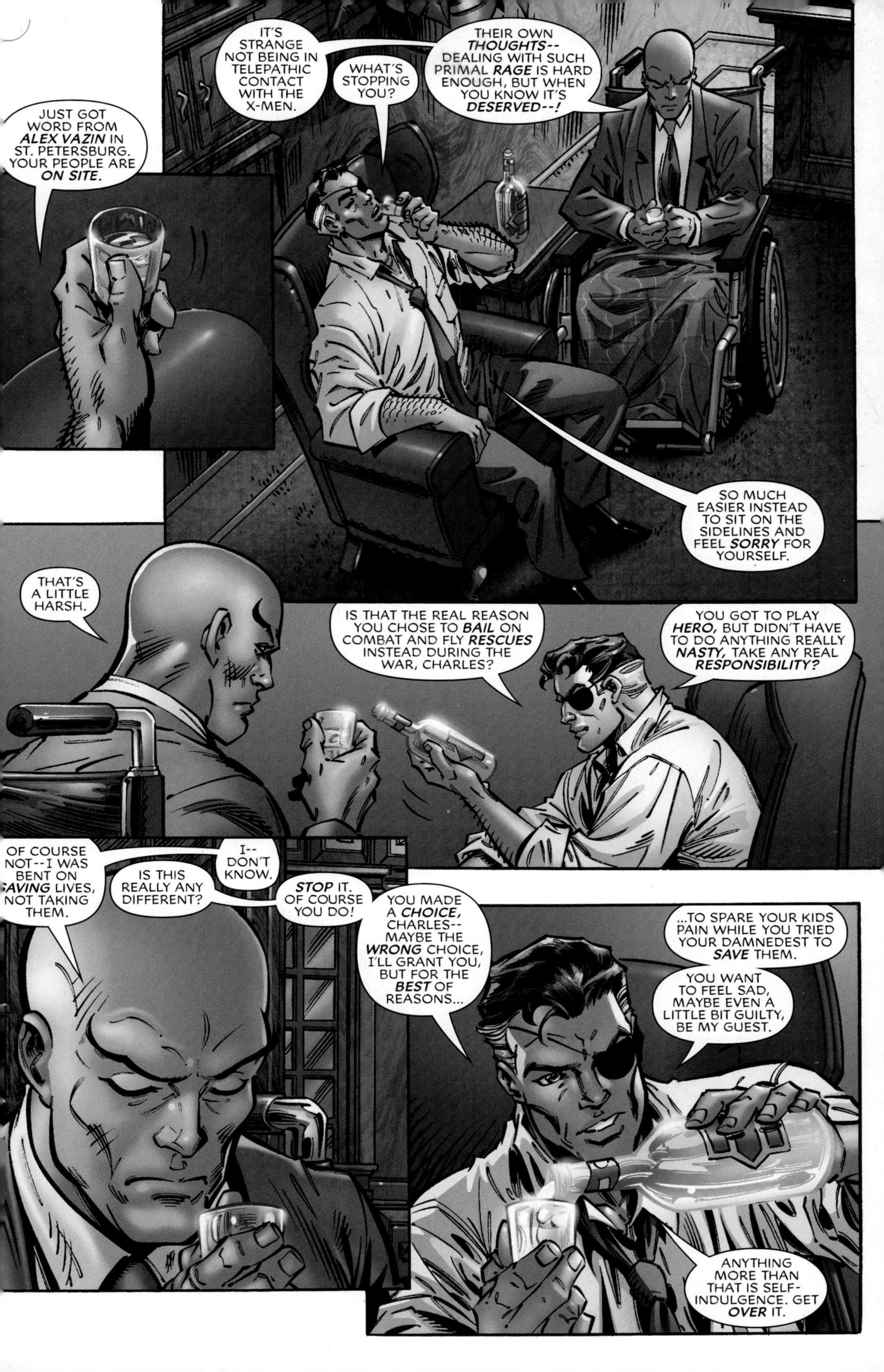
JUST GOT WORD FROM ALEX VAZIN IN ST. PETERSBURG. YOUR PEOPLE ARE ON SITE.
IT'S STRANGE NOT BEING IN TELEPATHIC CONTACT WITH THE X-MEN.
WHAT'S STOPPING YOU?
THEIR OWN THOUGHTS-- DEALING WITH SUCH PRIMAL RAGE IS HARD ENOUGH, BUT WHEN YOU KNOW IT'S DESERVED--!
SO MUCH EASIER INSTEAD TO SIT ON THE SIDELINES AND FEEL SORRY FOR YOURSELF.
THAT'S A LITTLE HARSH.
IS THAT THE REAL REASON YOU CHOSE TO BAIL ON COMBAT AND FLY RESCUES INSTEAD DURING THE WAR, CHARLES?
YOU GOT TO PLAY HERO, BUT DIDN'T HAVE TO DO ANYTHING REALLY NASTY, TAKE ANY REAL RESPONSIBILITY?
OF COURSE NOT--I WAS BENT ON SAVING LIVES, NOT TAKING THEM.
IS THIS REALLY ANY DIFFERENT?
I-- DON'T KNOW.
STOP IT. OF COURSE YOU DO!
YOU MADE A CHOICE, CHARLES-- MAYBE THE WRONG CHOICE, I'LL GRANT YOU, BUT FOR THE BEST OF REASONS...
...TO SPARE YOUR KIDS PAIN WHILE YOU TRIED YOUR DAMNEDEST TO SAVE THEM.
YOU WANT TO FEEL SAD, MAYBE EVEN A LITTLE BIT GUILTY, BE MY GUEST.
ANYTHING MORE THAN THAT IS SELF-INDULGENCE. GET OVER IT.

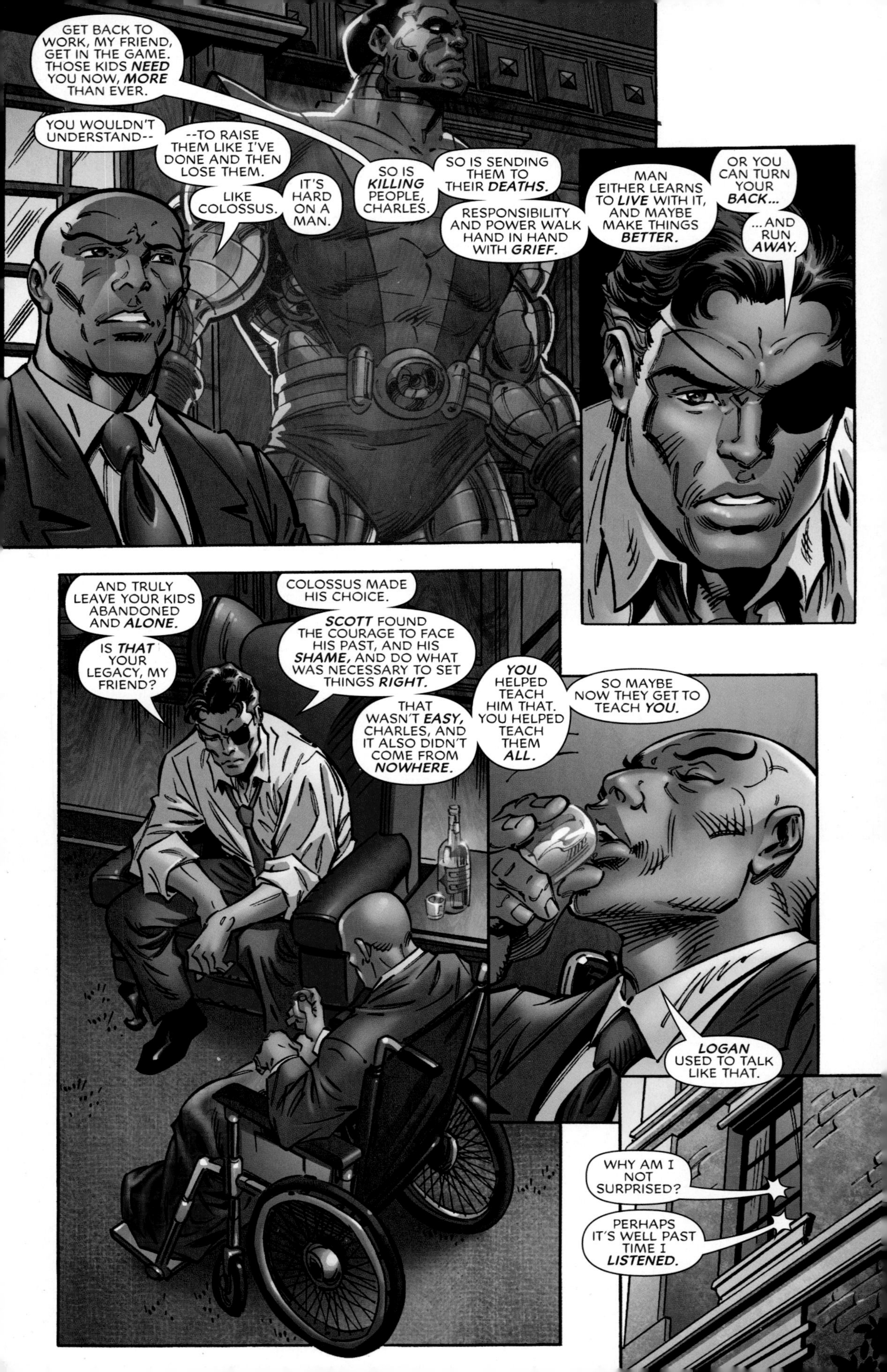
GET BACK TO WORK, MY FRIEND, GET IN THE GAME. THOSE KIDS NEED YOU NOW, MORE THAN EVER.
YOU WOULDN'T UNDERSTAND--
--TO RAISE THEM LIKE I'VE DONE AND THEN LOSE THEM.
LIKE COLOSSUS.
IT'S HARD ON A MAN.
SO IS KILLING PEOPLE, CHARLES.
SO IS SENDING THEM TO THEIR DEATHS.
RESPONSIBILITY AND POWER WALK HAND IN HAND WITH GRIEF.
MAN EITHER LEARNS TO LIVE WITH IT, AND MAYBE MAKE THINGS BETTER.
OR YOU CAN TURN YOUR BACK...
...AND RUN AWAY.
AND TRULY LEAVE YOUR KIDS ABANDONED AND ALONE.
IS THAT YOUR LEGACY, MY FRIEND?
COLOSSUS MADE HIS CHOICE.
SCOTT FOUND THE COURAGE TO FACE HIS PAST, AND HIS SHAME, AND DO WHAT WAS NECESSARY TO SET THINGS RIGHT.
THAT WASN'T EASY, CHARLES, AND IT ALSO DIDN'T COME FROM NOWHERE.
YOU HELPED TEACH HIM THAT. YOU HELPED TEACH THEM ALL.
SO MAYBE NOW THEY GET TO TEACH YOU.
LOGAN USED TO TALK LIKE THAT.
WHY AM I NOT SURPRISED?
PERHAPS IT'S WELL PAST TIME I LISTENED.

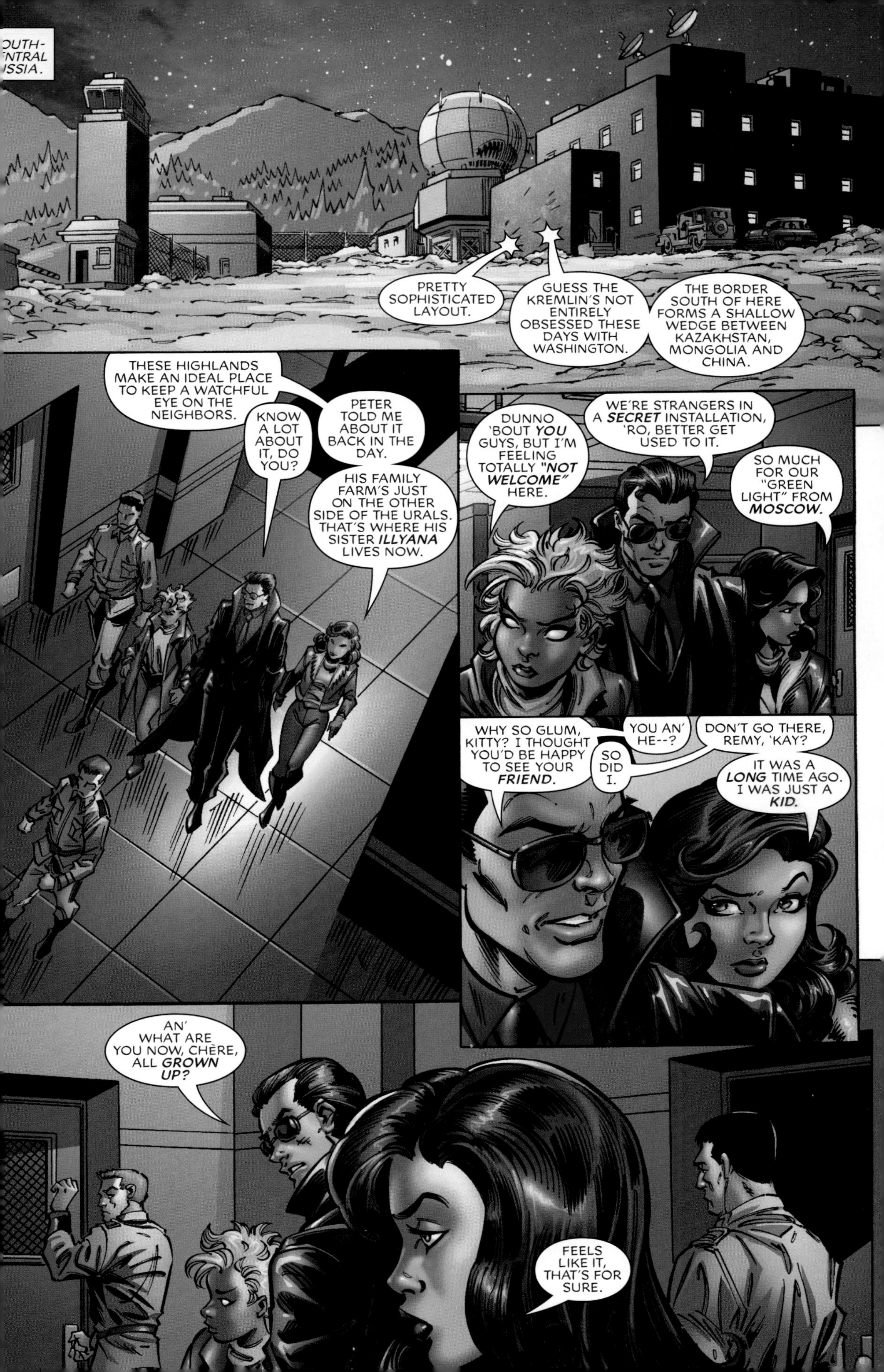

OUTH-
NTRAL
SSIA.
PRETTY SOPHISTICATED LAYOUT.
GUESS THE KREMLIN'S NOT ENTIRELY OBSESSED THESE DAYS WITH WASHINGTON.
THE BORDER SOUTH OF HERE FORMS A SHALLOW WEDGE BETWEEN KAZAKHSTAN, MONGOLIA AND CHINA.
THESE HIGHLANDS MAKE AN IDEAL PLACE TO KEEP A WATCHFUL EYE ON THE NEIGHBORS.
KNOW A LOT ABOUT IT, DO YOU?
PETER TOLD ME ABOUT IT BACK IN THE DAY.
HIS FAMILY FARM'S JUST ON THE OTHER SIDE OF THE URALS. THAT'S WHERE HIS SISTER ILLYANA LIVES NOW.
DUNNO 'BOUT YOU GUYS, BUT I'M FEELING TOTALLY "NOT WELCOME" HERE.
WE'RE STRANGERS IN A SECRET INSTALLATION, 'RO, BETTER GET USED TO IT.
SO MUCH FOR OUR "GREEN LIGHT" FROM MOSCOW.
WHY SO GLUM, KITTY? I THOUGHT YOU'D BE HAPPY TO SEE YOUR FRIEND.
SO DID I.
YOU AN' HE--?
DON'T GO THERE, REMY, 'KAY?
IT WAS A LONG TIME AGO. I WAS JUST A KID.
AN' WHAT ARE YOU NOW, CHÈRE, ALL GROWN UP?
FEELS LIKE IT, THAT'S FOR SURE.

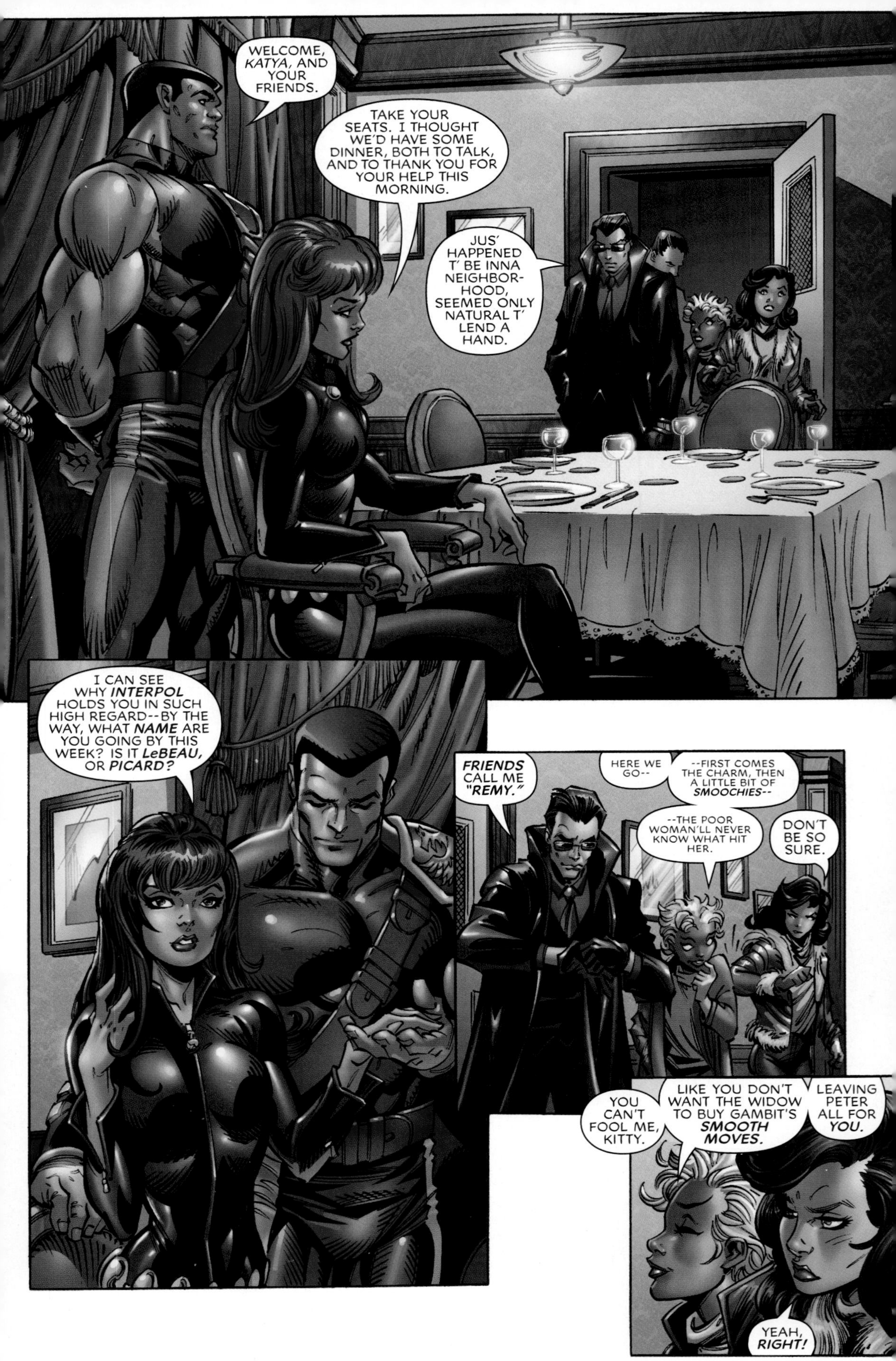
WELCOME, KATYA, AND YOUR FRIENDS.
TAKE YOUR SEATS. I THOUGHT WE'D HAVE SOME DINNER, BOTH TO TALK, AND TO THANK YOU FOR YOUR HELP THIS MORNING.
JUS' HAPPENED T' BE INNA NEIGHBOR-HOOD, SEEMED ONLY NATURAL T' LEND A HAND.
I CAN SEE WHY INTERPOL HOLDS YOU IN SUCH HIGH REGARD--BY THE WAY, WHAT NAME ARE YOU GOING BY THIS WEEK? IS IT LeBEAU, OR PICARD?
FRIENDS CALL ME "REMY."
HERE WE GO--
--FIRST COMES THE CHARM, THEN A LITTLE BIT OF SMOOCHIES--
--THE POOR WOMAN'LL NEVER KNOW WHAT HIT HER.
DON'T BE SO SURE.
YOU CAN'T FOOL ME, KITTY.
LIKE YOU DON'T WANT THE WIDOW TO BUY GAMBIT'S SMOOTH MOVES.
LEAVING PETER ALL FOR YOU.
YEAH, RIGHT!

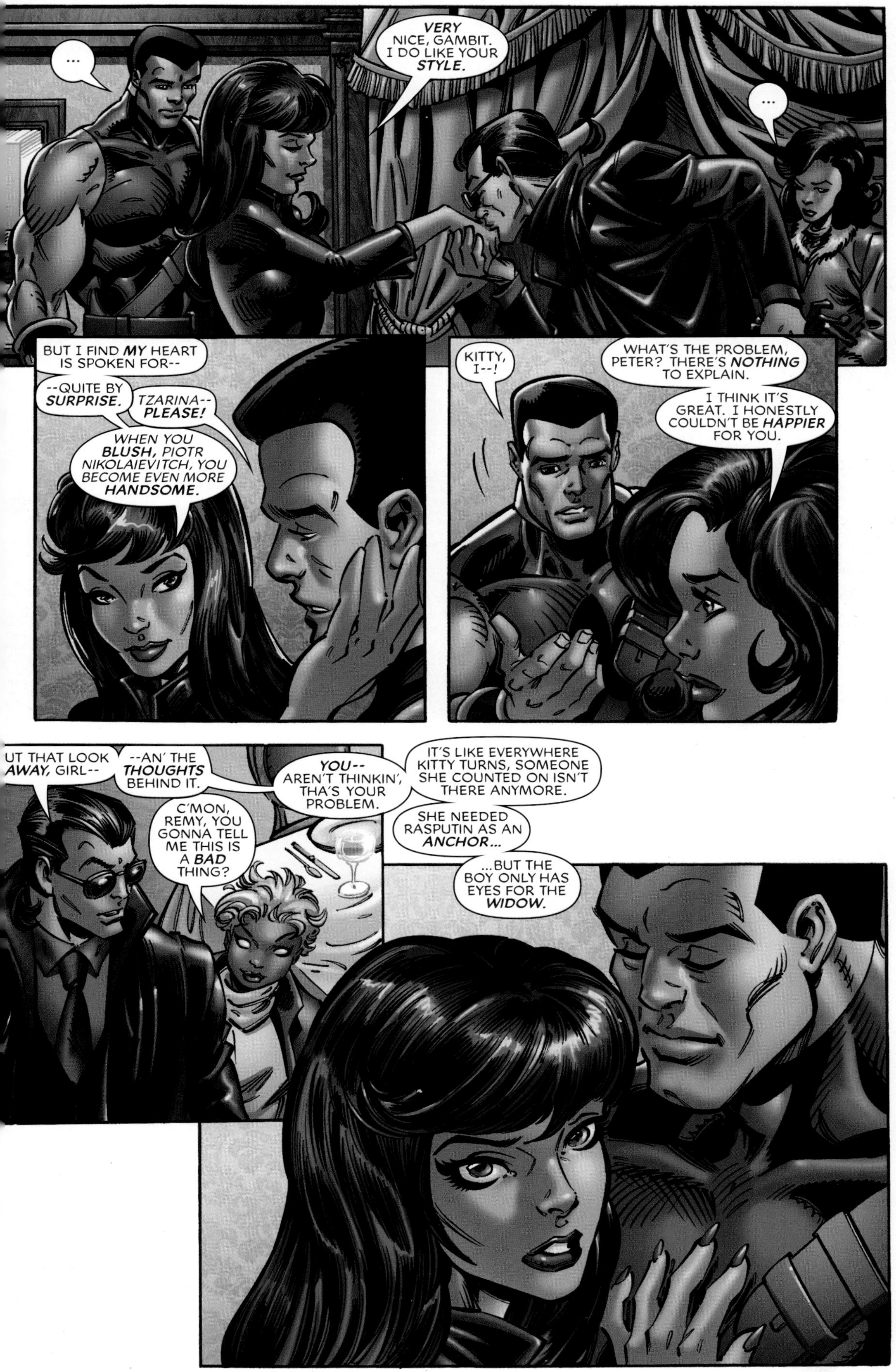
...
VERY NICE, GAMBIT. I DO LIKE YOUR STYLE.
...
BUT I FIND MY HEART IS SPOKEN FOR--
--QUITE BY SURPRISE.
TZARINA-- PLEASE!
WHEN YOU BLUSH, PIOTR NIKOLAIEVITCH, YOU BECOME EVEN MORE HANDSOME.
KITTY, I--!
WHAT'S THE PROBLEM, PETER? THERE'S NOTHING TO EXPLAIN.
I THINK IT'S GREAT. I HONESTLY COULDN'T BE HAPPIER FOR YOU.
UT THAT LOOK AWAY, GIRL--
--AN' THE THOUGHTS BEHIND IT.
C'MON, REMY, YOU GONNA TELL ME THIS IS A BAD THING?
YOU-- AREN'T THINKIN', THA'S YOUR PROBLEM.
IT'S LIKE EVERYWHERE KITTY TURNS, SOMEONE SHE COUNTED ON ISN'T THERE ANYMORE.
SHE NEEDED RASPUTIN AS AN ANCHOR...
...BUT THE BOY ONLY HAS EYES FOR THE WIDOW.

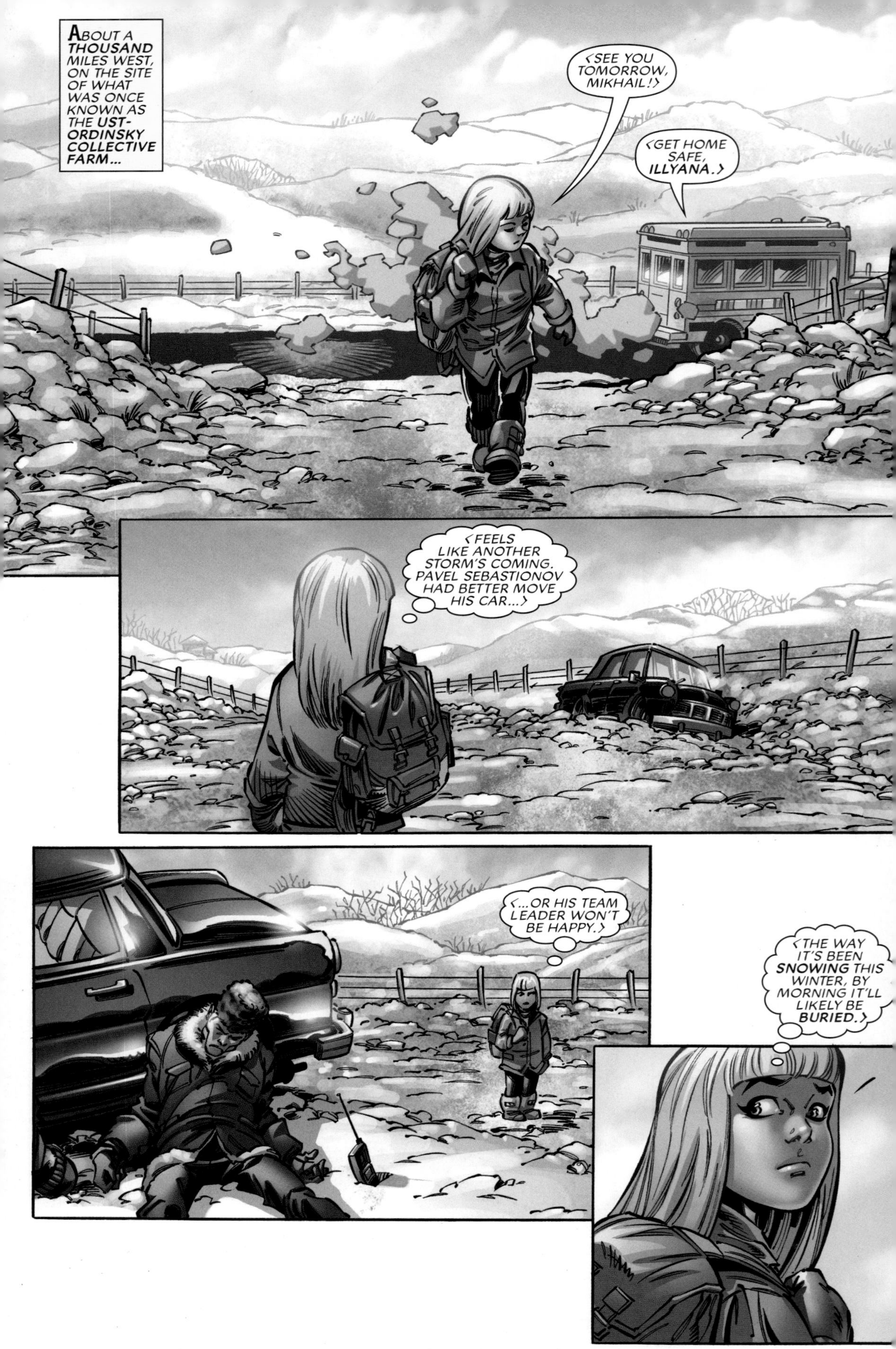
About a thousand miles west, on the site of what was once known as the Ust-Ordinsky Collective Farm...
<See you tomorrow, Mikhail!>
<Get home safe, Illyana.>
<Feels like another storm's coming. Pavel Sebastionov had better move his car...>
<...or his team leader won't be happy.>
<The way it's been snowing this winter, by morning it'll likely be buried.>

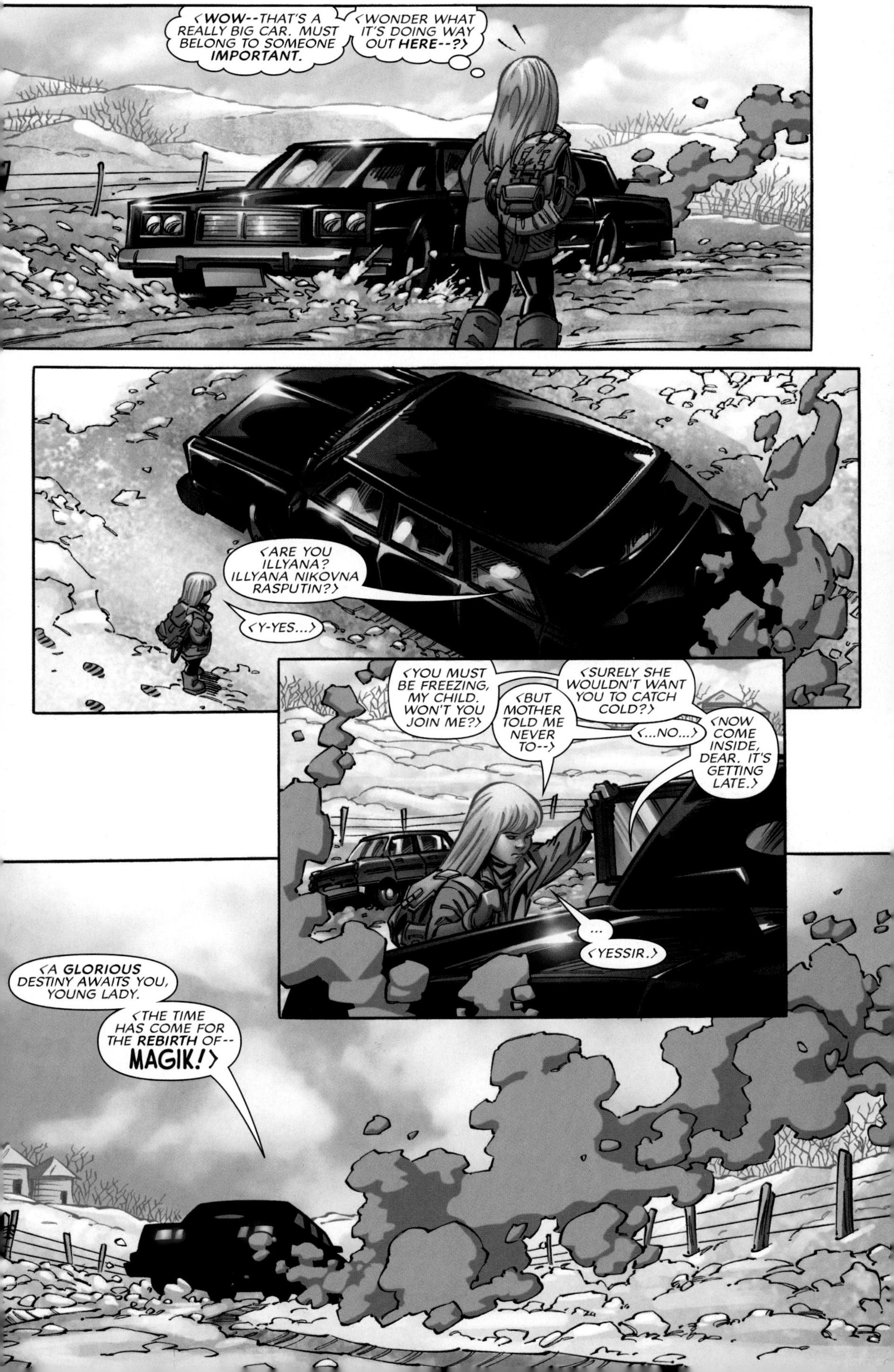

<WOW--THAT'S A REALLY BIG CAR. MUST BELONG TO SOMEONE IMPORTANT.
<WONDER WHAT IT'S DOING WAY OUT HERE--?>
<ARE YOU ILLYANA? ILLYANA NIKOVNA RASPUTIN?>
<Y-YES...>
<YOU MUST BE FREEZING, MY CHILD. WON'T YOU JOIN ME?>
<BUT MOTHER TOLD ME NEVER TO-->
<SURELY SHE WOULDN'T WANT YOU TO CATCH COLD?>
<...NO...>
<NOW COME INSIDE, DEAR. IT'S GETTING LATE.>
...
<YESSIR.>
<A GLORIOUS DESTINY AWAITS YOU, YOUNG LADY.
<THE TIME HAS COME FOR THE REBIRTH OF-- MAGIK!>

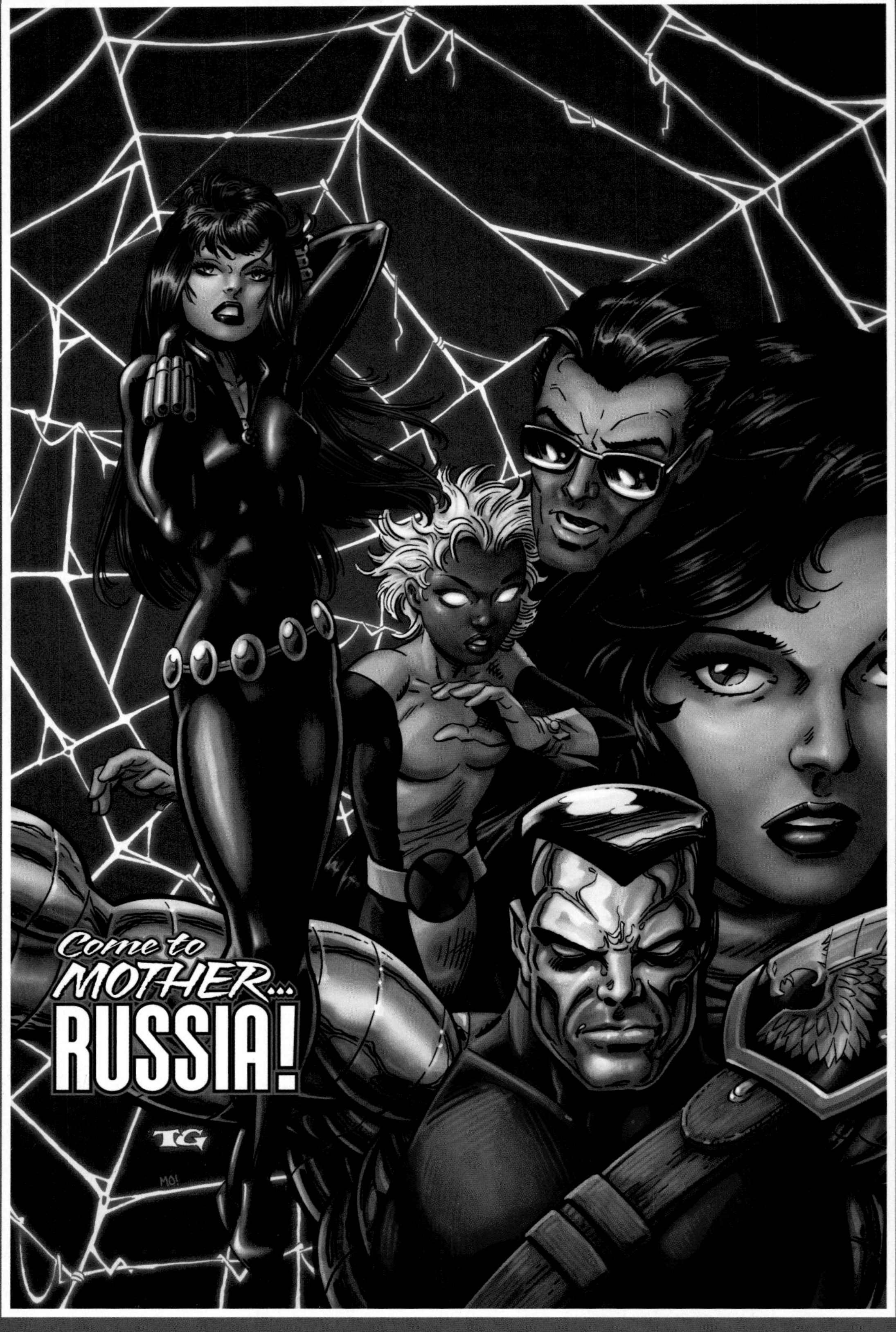
Come to MOTHER... RUSSIA!
TG
MO!

TWELVE

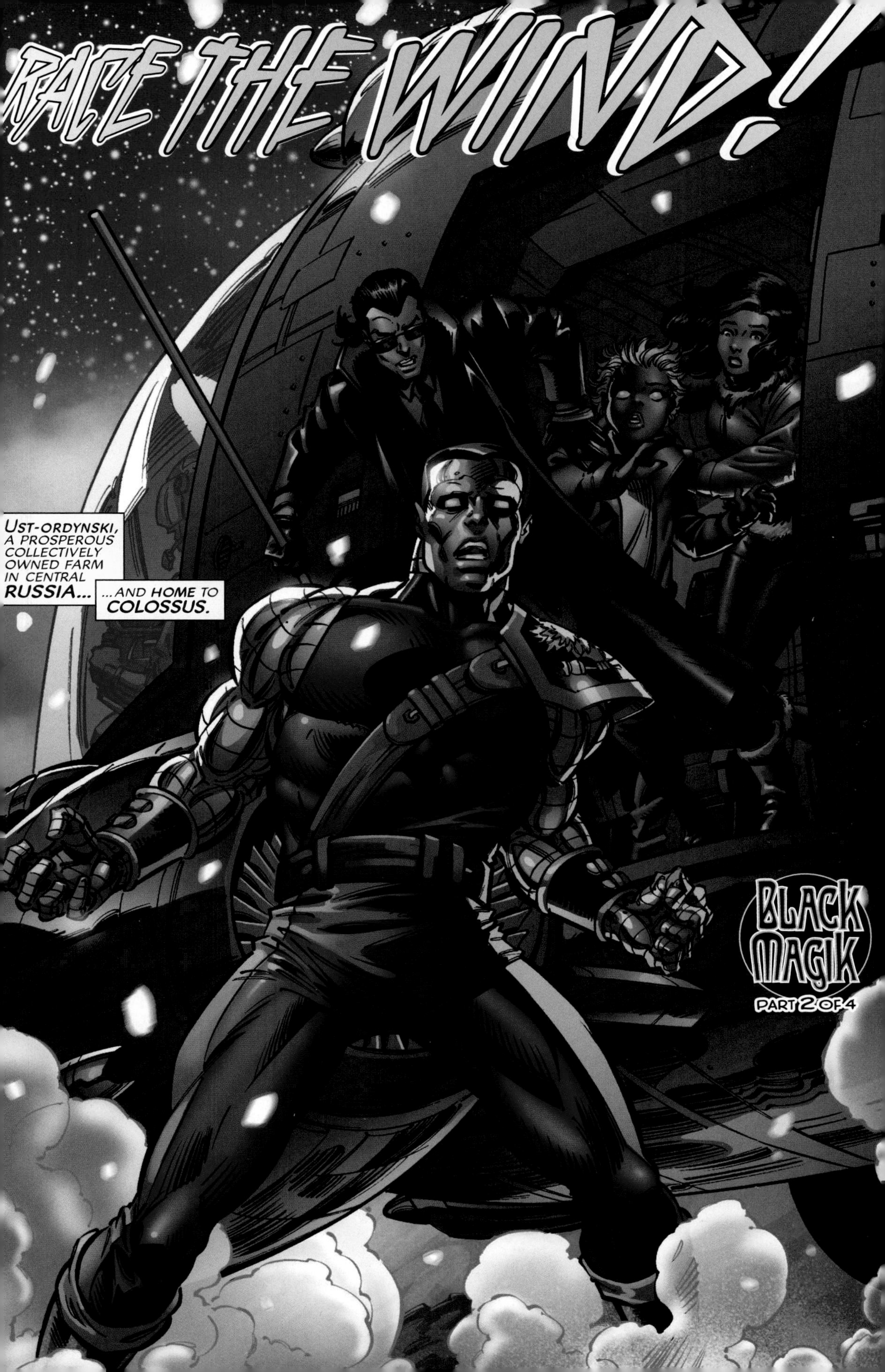
RAIZE THE WIND!
UST-ORDYNSKI, A PROSPEROUS COLLECTIVELY OWNED FARM IN CENTRAL RUSSIA...
...AND HOME TO COLOSSUS.
BLACK MAGIK
PART 2 OF 4

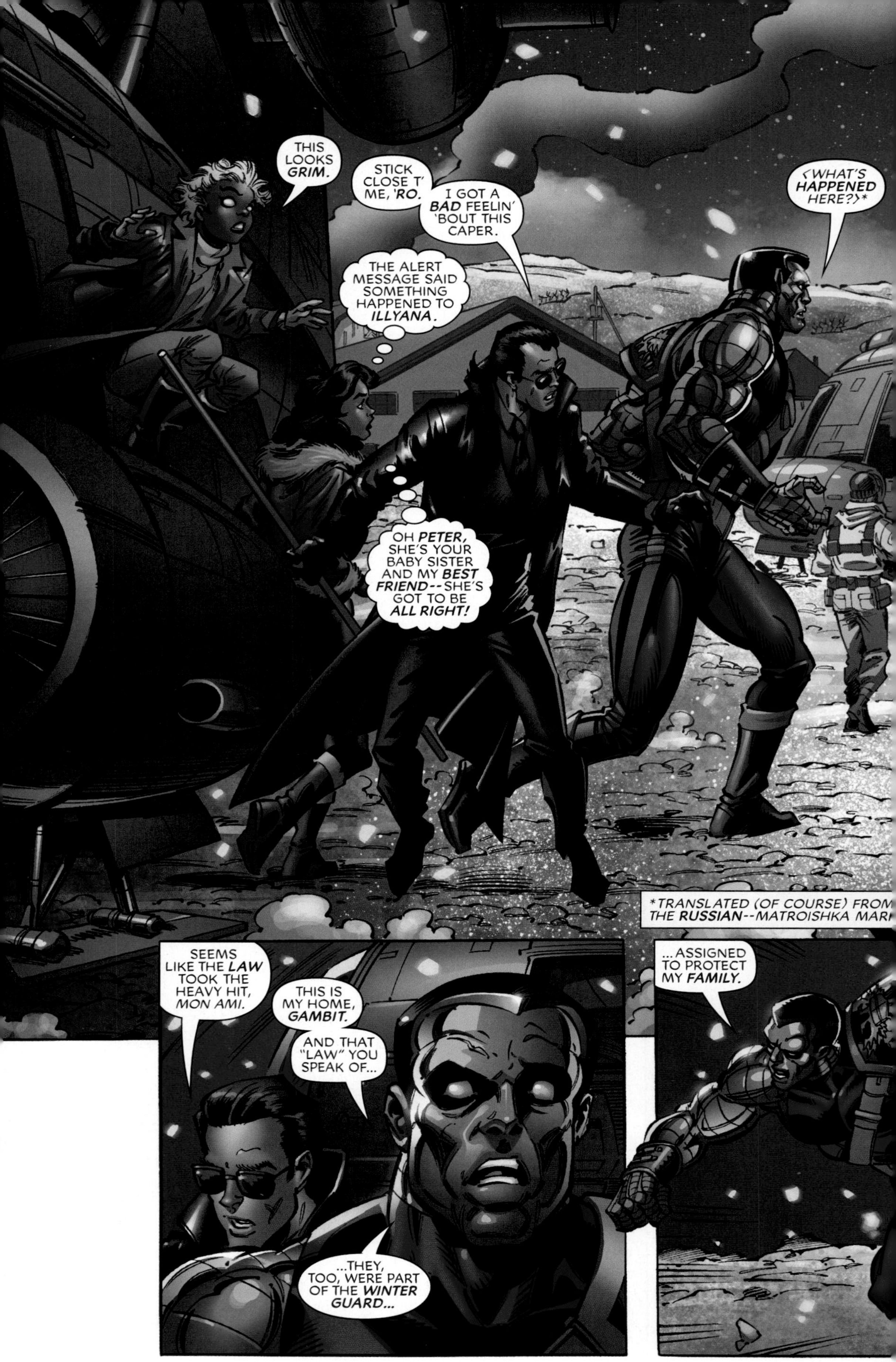
THIS LOOKS GRIM.
STICK CLOSE T' ME, 'RO.
I GOT A BAD FEELIN' 'BOUT THIS CAPER.
THE ALERT MESSAGE SAID SOMETHING HAPPENED TO ILLYANA.
OH PETER, SHE'S YOUR BABY SISTER AND MY BEST FRIEND--SHE'S GOT TO BE ALL RIGHT!
‹WHAT'S HAPPENED HERE?›*
*TRANSLATED (OF COURSE) FROM THE RUSSIAN--MATROISHKA MAR
SEEMS LIKE THE LAW TOOK THE HEAVY HIT, MON AMI.
THIS IS MY HOME, GAMBIT.
AND THAT "LAW" YOU SPEAK OF...
...THEY, TOO, WERE PART OF THE WINTER GUARD...
...ASSIGNED TO PROTECT MY FAMILY.

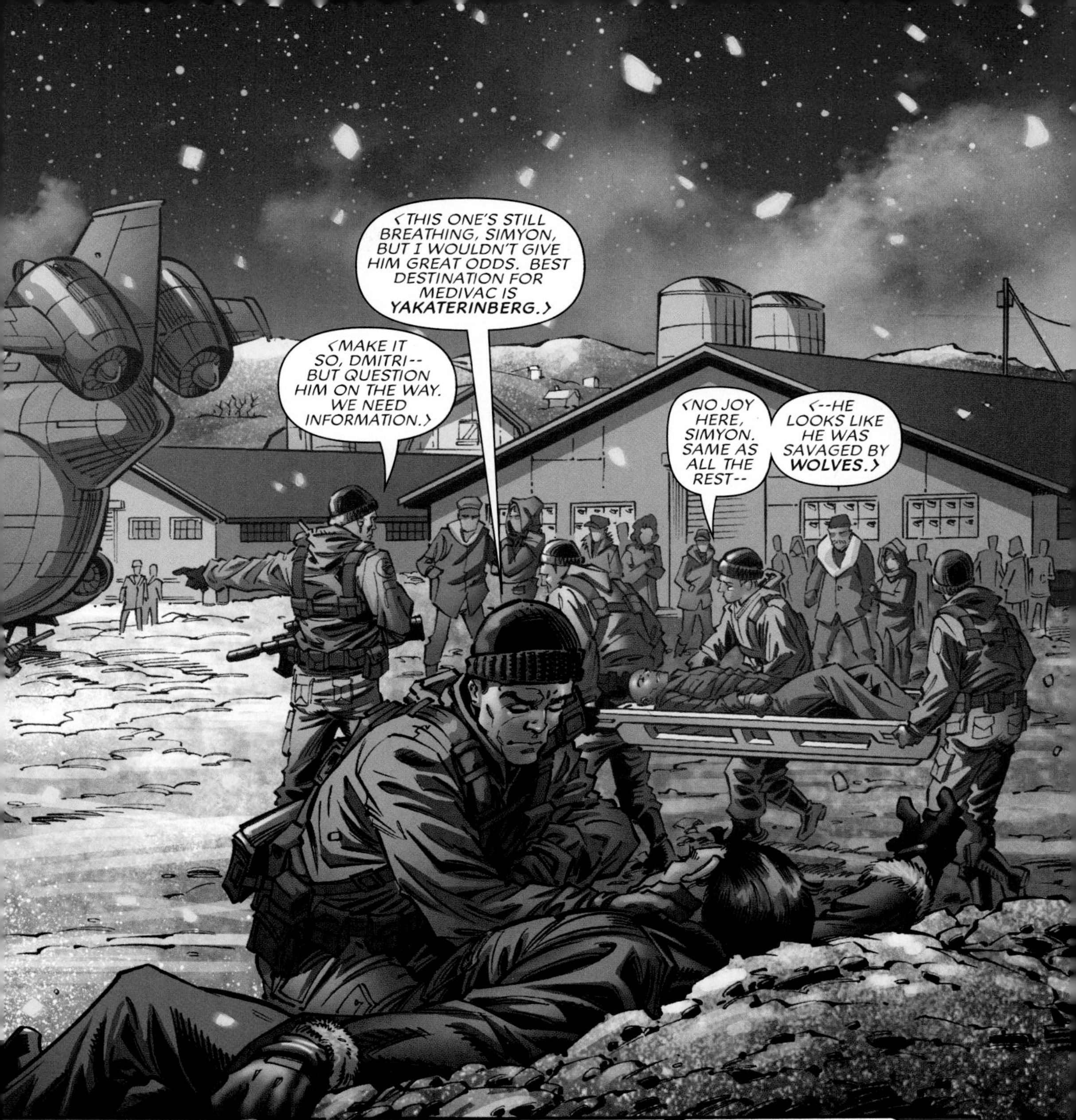
‹THIS ONE'S STILL BREATHING, SIMYON, BUT I WOULDN'T GIVE HIM GREAT ODDS. BEST DESTINATION FOR MEDIVAC IS YAKATERINBERG.›
‹MAKE IT SO, DMITRI-- BUT QUESTION HIM ON THE WAY. WE NEED INFORMATION.›
‹NO JOY HERE, SIMYON. SAME AS ALL THE REST--
‹--HE LOOKS LIKE HE WAS SAVAGED BY WOLVES.›

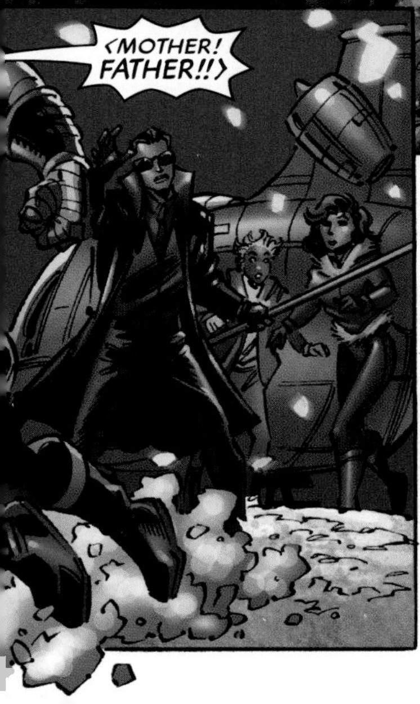
‹MOTHER! FATHER!!›

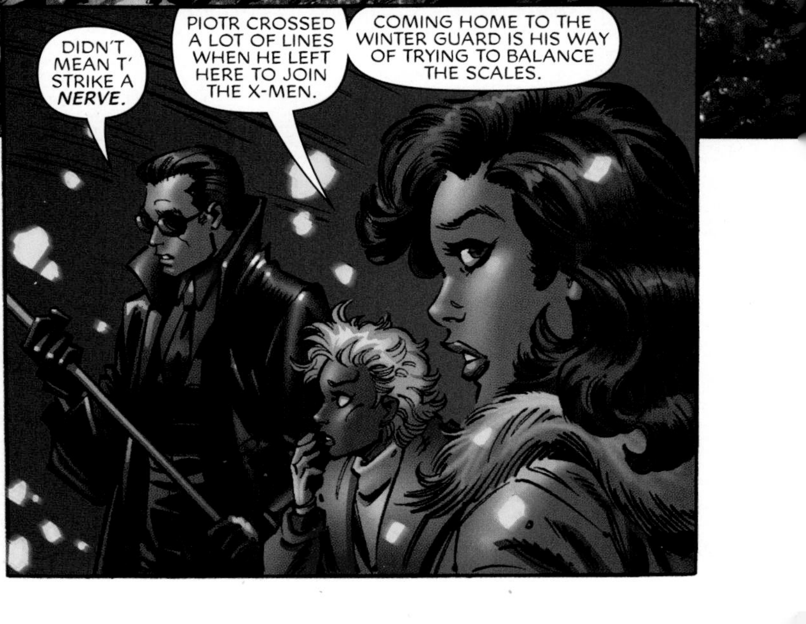
DIDN'T MEAN T' STRIKE A NERVE.
PIOTR CROSSED A LOT OF LINES WHEN HE LEFT HERE TO JOIN THE X-MEN.
COMING HOME TO THE WINTER GUARD IS HIS WAY OF TRYING TO BALANCE THE SCALES.

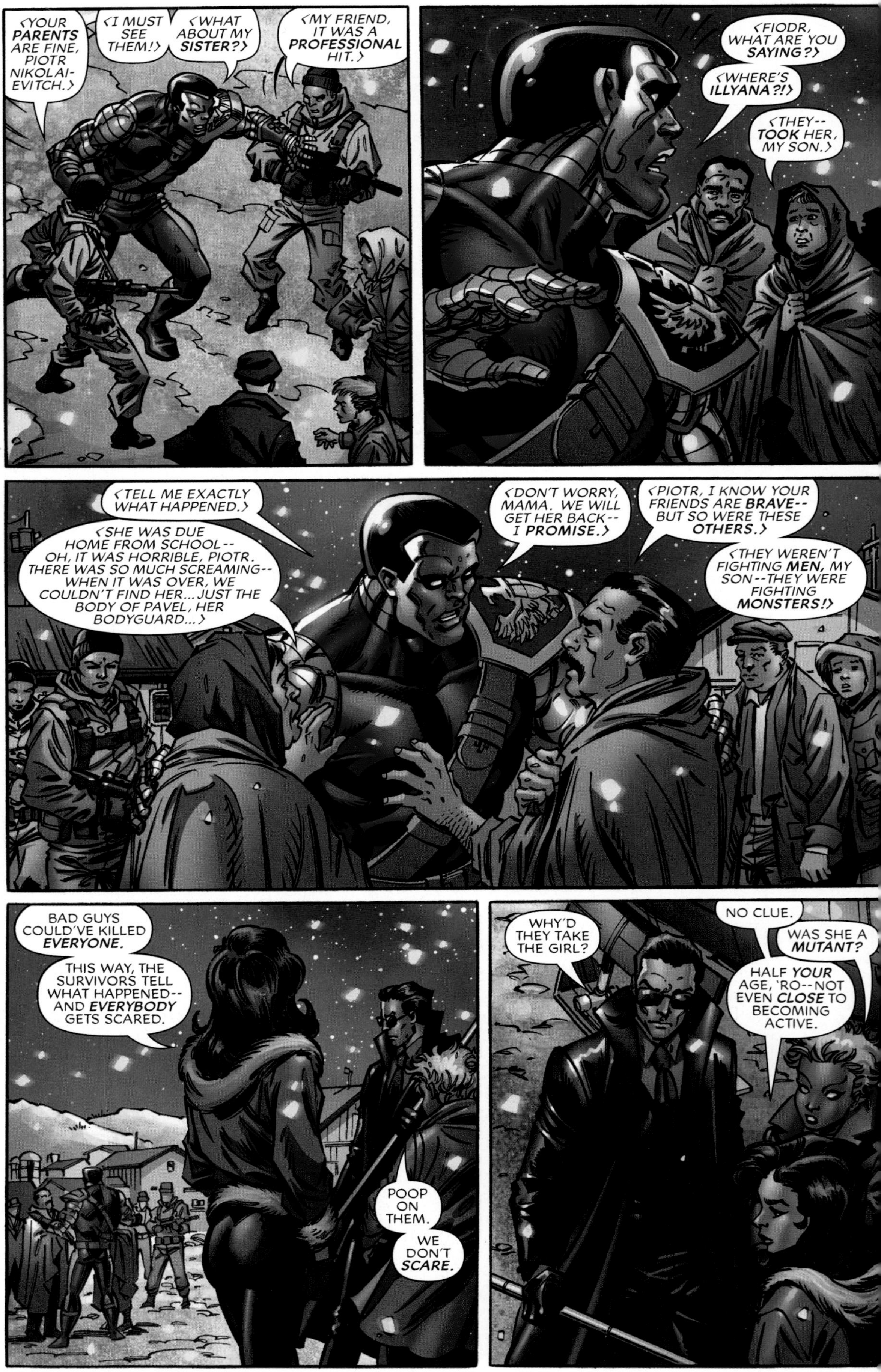

<YOUR PARENTS ARE FINE, PIOTR NIKOLAI-EVITCH.>
<I MUST SEE THEM!>
<WHAT ABOUT MY SISTER?>
<MY FRIEND, IT WAS A PROFESSIONAL HIT.>
<FIODR, WHAT ARE YOU SAYING?>
<WHERE'S ILLYANA?!>
<THEY--TOOK HER, MY SON.>
<TELL ME EXACTLY WHAT HAPPENED.>
<SHE WAS DUE HOME FROM SCHOOL--OH, IT WAS HORRIBLE, PIOTR. THERE WAS SO MUCH SCREAMING--WHEN IT WAS OVER, WE COULDN'T FIND HER... JUST THE BODY OF PAVEL, HER BODYGUARD...>
<DON'T WORRY, MAMA. WE WILL GET HER BACK--I PROMISE.>
<PIOTR, I KNOW YOUR FRIENDS ARE BRAVE--BUT SO WERE THESE OTHERS.>
<THEY WEREN'T FIGHTING MEN, MY SON--THEY WERE FIGHTING MONSTERS!>
BAD GUYS COULD'VE KILLED EVERYONE.
THIS WAY, THE SURVIVORS TELL WHAT HAPPENED--AND EVERYBODY GETS SCARED.
POOP ON THEM.
WE DON'T SCARE.
WHY'D THEY TAKE THE GIRL?
NO CLUE.
WAS SHE A MUTANT?
HALF YOUR AGE, 'RO--NOT EVEN CLOSE TO BECOMING ACTIVE.

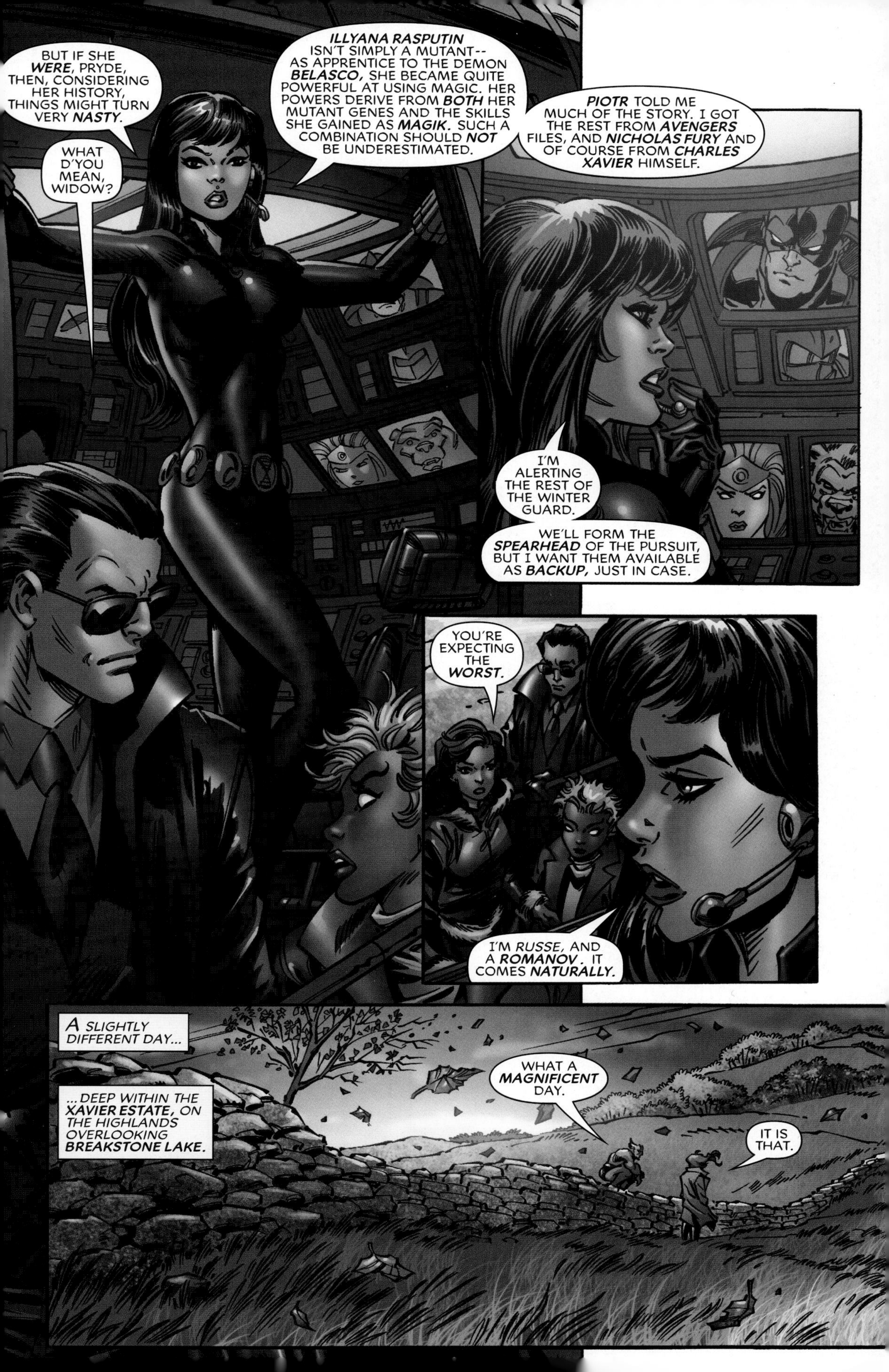
BUT IF SHE WERE, PRYDE, THEN, CONSIDERING HER HISTORY, THINGS MIGHT TURN VERY NASTY.
WHAT D'YOU MEAN, WIDOW?
ILLYANA RASPUTIN ISN'T SIMPLY A MUTANT-- AS APPRENTICE TO THE DEMON BELASCO, SHE BECAME QUITE POWERFUL AT USING MAGIC. HER POWERS DERIVE FROM BOTH HER MUTANT GENES AND THE SKILLS SHE GAINED AS MAGIK. SUCH A COMBINATION SHOULD NOT BE UNDERESTIMATED.
PIOTR TOLD ME MUCH OF THE STORY. I GOT THE REST FROM AVENGERS FILES, AND NICHOLAS FURY AND OF COURSE FROM CHARLES XAVIER HIMSELF.
I'M ALERTING THE REST OF THE WINTER GUARD.
WE'LL FORM THE SPEARHEAD OF THE PURSUIT, BUT I WANT THEM AVAILABLE AS BACKUP, JUST IN CASE.
YOU'RE EXPECTING THE WORST.
I'M RUSSE, AND A ROMANOV. IT COMES NATURALLY.
A SLIGHTLY DIFFERENT DAY...
...DEEP WITHIN THE XAVIER ESTATE, ON THE HIGHLANDS OVERLOOKING BREAKSTONE LAKE.
WHAT A MAGNIFICENT DAY.
IT IS THAT.

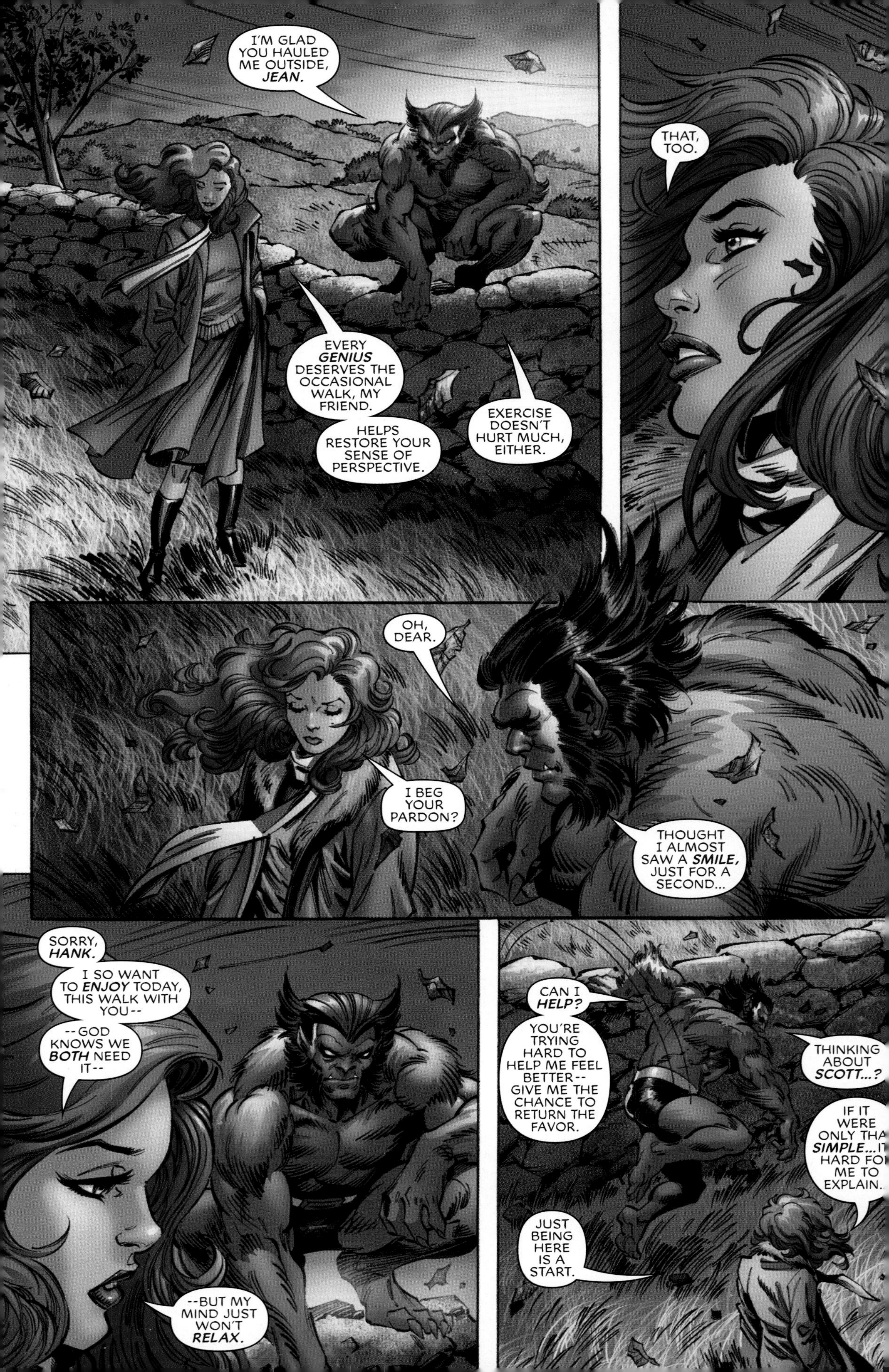
I'M GLAD YOU HAULED ME OUTSIDE, JEAN.
EVERY GENIUS DESERVES THE OCCASIONAL WALK, MY FRIEND.
HELPS RESTORE YOUR SENSE OF PERSPECTIVE.
EXERCISE DOESN'T HURT MUCH, EITHER.
THAT, TOO.
OH, DEAR.
I BEG YOUR PARDON?
THOUGHT I ALMOST SAW A SMILE, JUST FOR A SECOND...
SORRY, HANK.
I SO WANT TO ENJOY TODAY, THIS WALK WITH YOU--
--GOD KNOWS WE BOTH NEED IT--
--BUT MY MIND JUST WON'T RELAX.
CAN I HELP?
YOU'RE TRYING HARD TO HELP ME FEEL BETTER--GIVE ME THE CHANCE TO RETURN THE FAVOR.
THINKING ABOUT SCOTT...?
IF IT WERE ONLY THA SIMPLE...IT HARD FO ME TO EXPLAIN.
JUST BEING HERE IS A START.

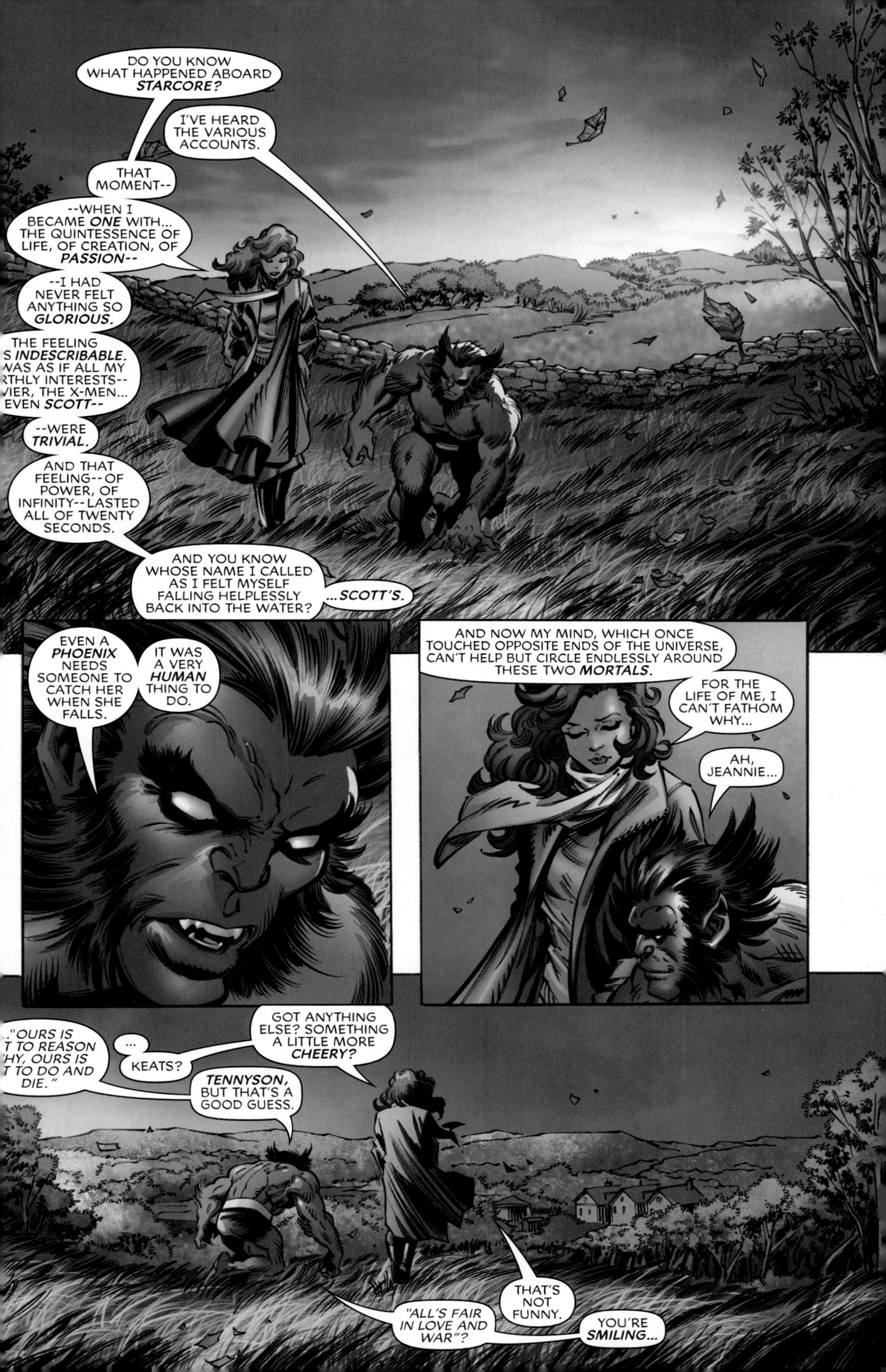
DO YOU KNOW WHAT HAPPENED ABOARD STARCORE?
I'VE HEARD THE VARIOUS ACCOUNTS.
THAT MOMENT--
--WHEN I BECAME ONE WITH... THE QUINTESSENCE OF LIFE, OF CREATION, OF PASSION--
--I HAD NEVER FELT ANYTHING SO GLORIOUS.
THE FEELING S INDESCRIBABLE. WAS AS IF ALL MY RTHLY INTERESTS-- VIER, THE X-MEN... EVEN SCOTT--
--WERE TRIVIAL.
AND THAT FEELING--OF POWER, OF INFINITY--LASTED ALL OF TWENTY SECONDS.
AND YOU KNOW WHOSE NAME I CALLED AS I FELT MYSELF FALLING HELPLESSLY BACK INTO THE WATER?
...SCOTT'S.
EVEN A PHOENIX NEEDS SOMEONE TO CATCH HER WHEN SHE FALLS.
IT WAS A VERY HUMAN THING TO DO.
AND NOW MY MIND, WHICH ONCE TOUCHED OPPOSITE ENDS OF THE UNIVERSE, CAN'T HELP BUT CIRCLE ENDLESSLY AROUND THESE TWO MORTALS.
FOR THE LIFE OF ME, I CAN'T FATHOM WHY...
AH, JEANNIE...
..."OURS IS T TO REASON HY, OURS IS T TO DO AND DIE."
... KEATS?
GOT ANYTHING ELSE? SOMETHING A LITTLE MORE CHEERY?
TENNYSON, BUT THAT'S A GOOD GUESS.
"ALL'S FAIR IN LOVE AND WAR"?
THAT'S NOT FUNNY.
YOU'RE SMILING...

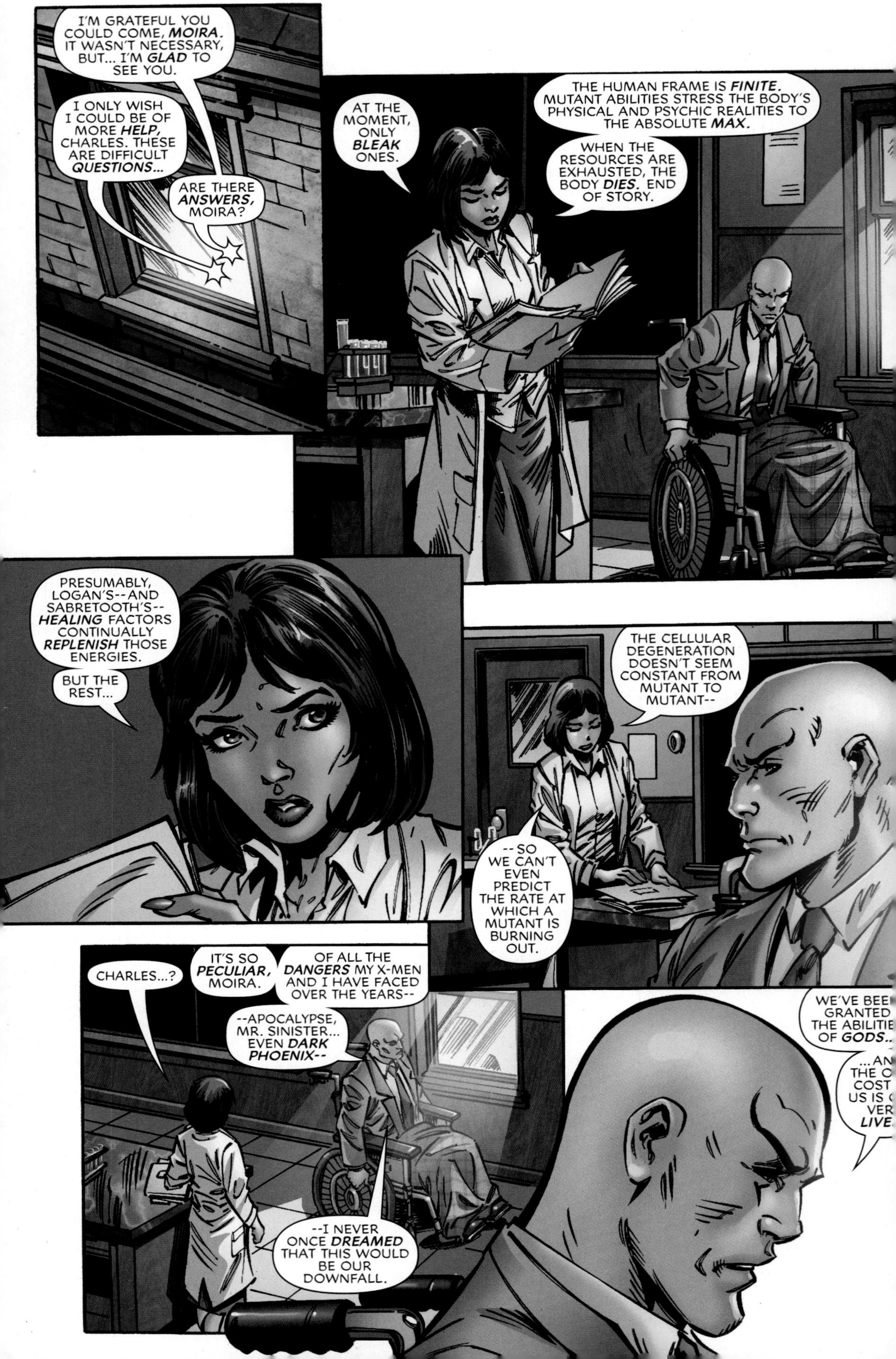
I'M GRATEFUL YOU COULD COME, MOIRA. IT WASN'T NECESSARY, BUT... I'M GLAD TO SEE YOU.
I ONLY WISH I COULD BE OF MORE HELP, CHARLES. THESE ARE DIFFICULT QUESTIONS...
ARE THERE ANSWERS, MOIRA?
AT THE MOMENT, ONLY BLEAK ONES.
THE HUMAN FRAME IS FINITE. MUTANT ABILITIES STRESS THE BODY'S PHYSICAL AND PSYCHIC REALITIES TO THE ABSOLUTE MAX.
WHEN THE RESOURCES ARE EXHAUSTED, THE BODY DIES. END OF STORY.
PRESUMABLY, LOGAN'S--AND SABRETOOTH'S--HEALING FACTORS CONTINUALLY REPLENISH THOSE ENERGIES.
BUT THE REST...
THE CELLULAR DEGENERATION DOESN'T SEEM CONSTANT FROM MUTANT TO MUTANT--
--SO WE CAN'T EVEN PREDICT THE RATE AT WHICH A MUTANT IS BURNING OUT.
CHARLES...?
IT'S SO PECULIAR, MOIRA.
OF ALL THE DANGERS MY X-MEN AND I HAVE FACED OVER THE YEARS--
--APOCALYPSE, MR. SINISTER... EVEN DARK PHOENIX--
--I NEVER ONCE DREAMED THAT THIS WOULD BE OUR DOWNFALL.

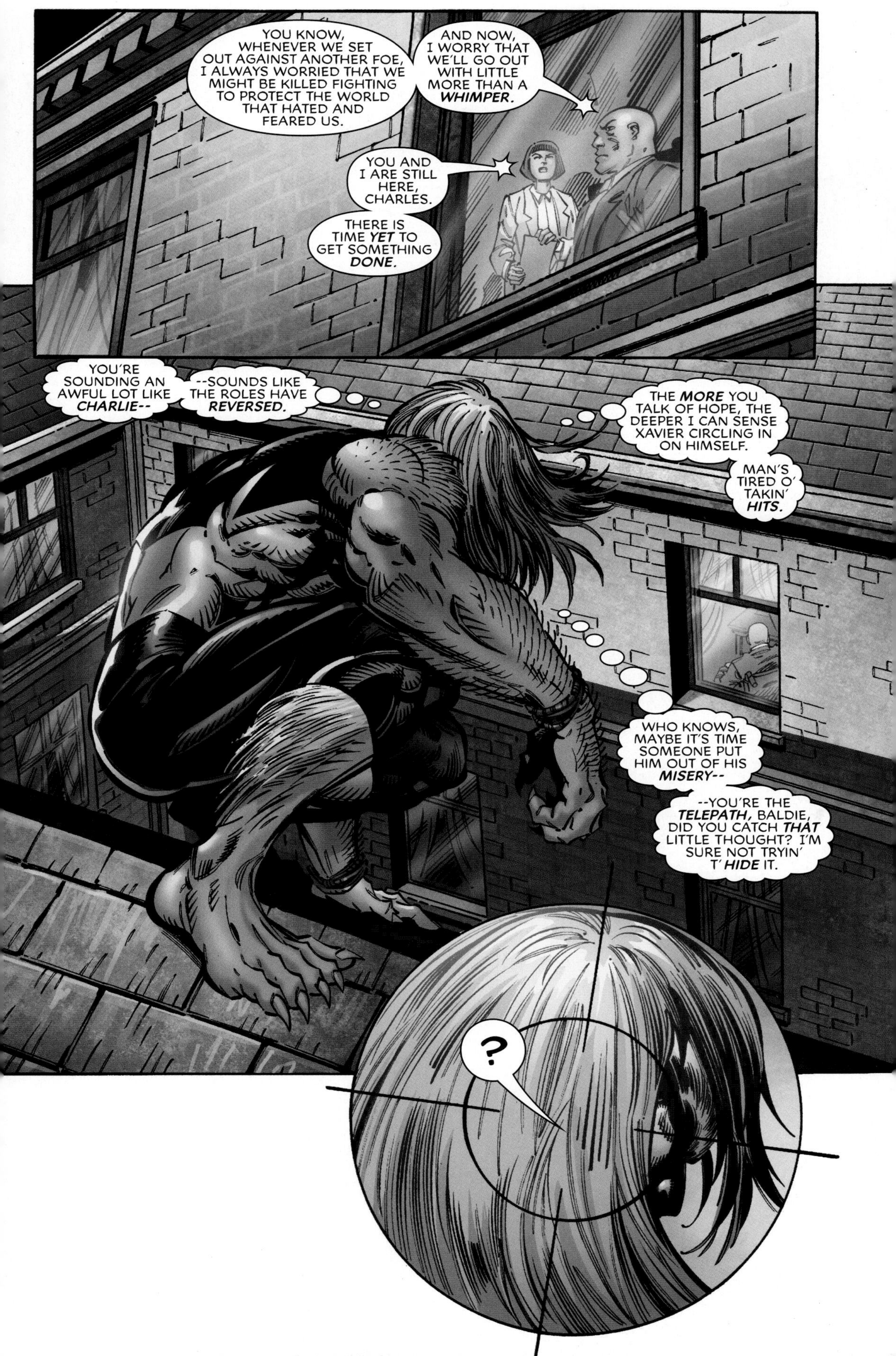

YOU KNOW, WHENEVER WE SET OUT AGAINST ANOTHER FOE, I ALWAYS WORRIED THAT WE MIGHT BE KILLED FIGHTING TO PROTECT THE WORLD THAT HATED AND FEARED US.
AND NOW, I WORRY THAT WE'LL GO OUT WITH LITTLE MORE THAN A *WHIMPER*.
YOU AND I ARE STILL HERE, CHARLES.
THERE IS TIME *YET* TO GET SOMETHING *DONE*.
YOU'RE SOUNDING AN AWFUL LOT LIKE *CHARLIE*--
--SOUNDS LIKE THE ROLES HAVE *REVERSED*.
THE *MORE* YOU TALK OF HOPE, THE DEEPER I CAN SENSE XAVIER CIRCLING IN ON HIMSELF.
MAN'S TIRED O' TAKIN' *HITS*.
WHO KNOWS, MAYBE IT'S TIME SOMEONE PUT HIM OUT OF HIS *MISERY*--
--YOU'RE THE *TELEPATH*, BALDIE, DID YOU CATCH *THAT* LITTLE THOUGHT? I'M SURE NOT TRYIN' T' *HIDE* IT.
?

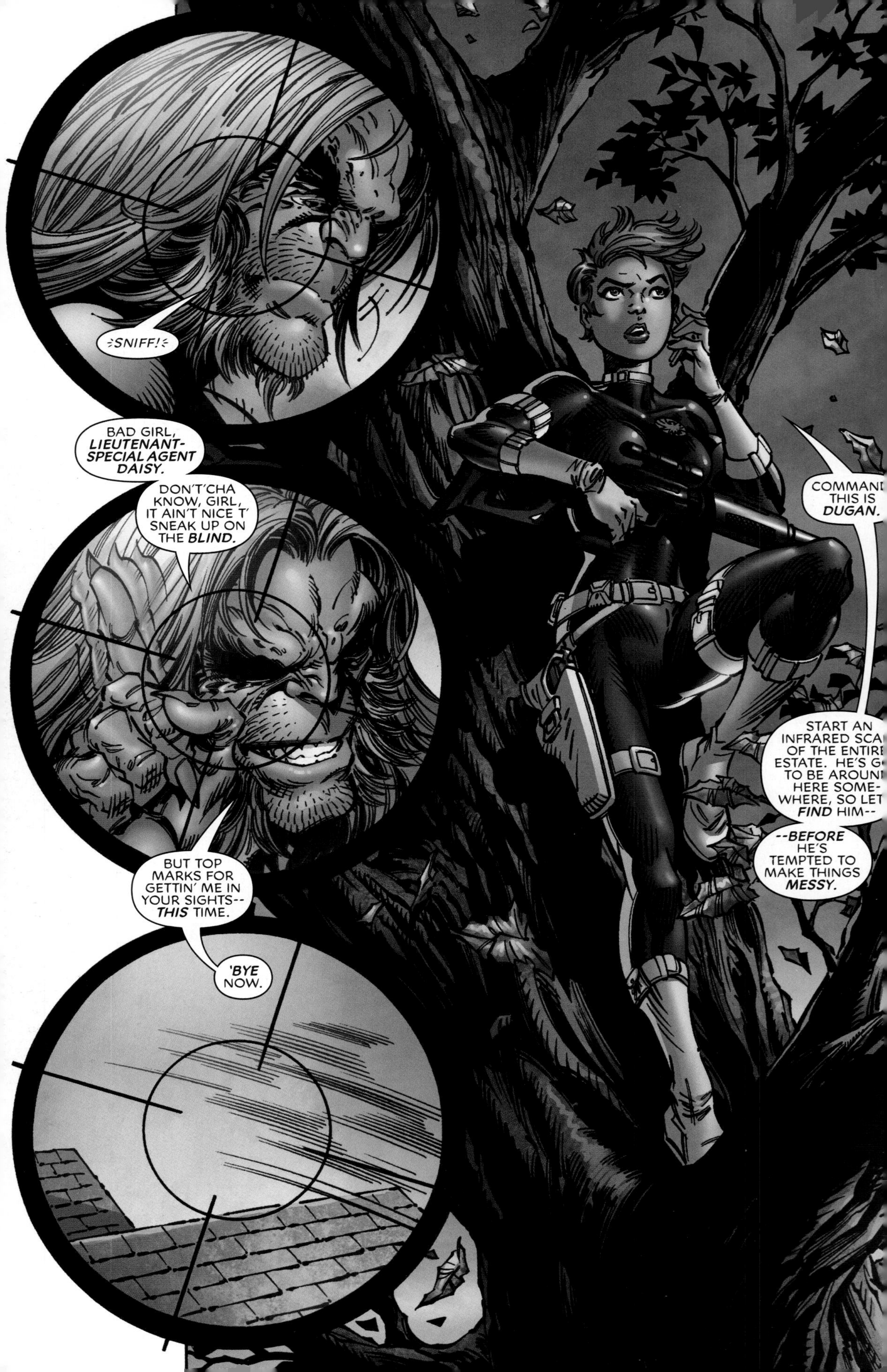
SNIFF!
BAD GIRL, LIEUTENANT-SPECIAL AGENT DAISY.
DON'T'CHA KNOW, GIRL, IT AIN'T NICE T' SNEAK UP ON THE BLIND.
BUT TOP MARKS FOR GETTIN' ME IN YOUR SIGHTS-- THIS TIME.
'BYE NOW.
COMMAND THIS IS DUGAN.
START AN INFRARED SCA OF THE ENTIRE ESTATE. HE'S G TO BE AROUN HERE SOME-WHERE, SO LET FIND HIM--
--BEFORE HE'S TEMPTED TO MAKE THINGS MESSY.

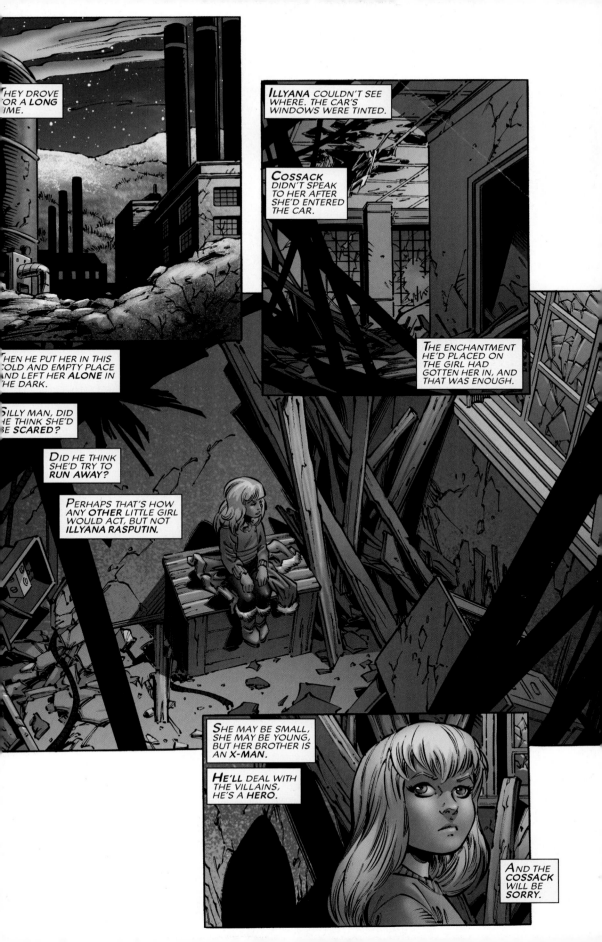

THEY DROVE FOR A **LONG** TIME.

ILLYANA COULDN'T SEE WHERE. THE CAR'S WINDOWS WERE TINTED.

COSSACK DIDN'T SPEAK TO HER AFTER SHE'D ENTERED THE CAR.

THE ENCHANTMENT HE'D PLACED ON THE GIRL HAD GOTTEN HER IN, AND THAT WAS ENOUGH.

THEN HE PUT HER IN THIS COLD AND EMPTY PLACE AND LEFT HER **ALONE** IN THE DARK.

SILLY MAN, DID HE THINK SHE'D BE **SCARED?**

DID HE THINK SHE'D TRY TO **RUN AWAY?**

PERHAPS THAT'S HOW ANY **OTHER** LITTLE GIRL WOULD ACT, BUT NOT ILLYANA RASPUTIN.

SHE MAY BE SMALL, SHE MAY BE YOUNG, BUT HER BROTHER IS AN **X-MAN.**

HE'LL DEAL WITH THE VILLAINS, HE'S A **HERO.**

AND THE **COSSACK** WILL BE **SORRY.**

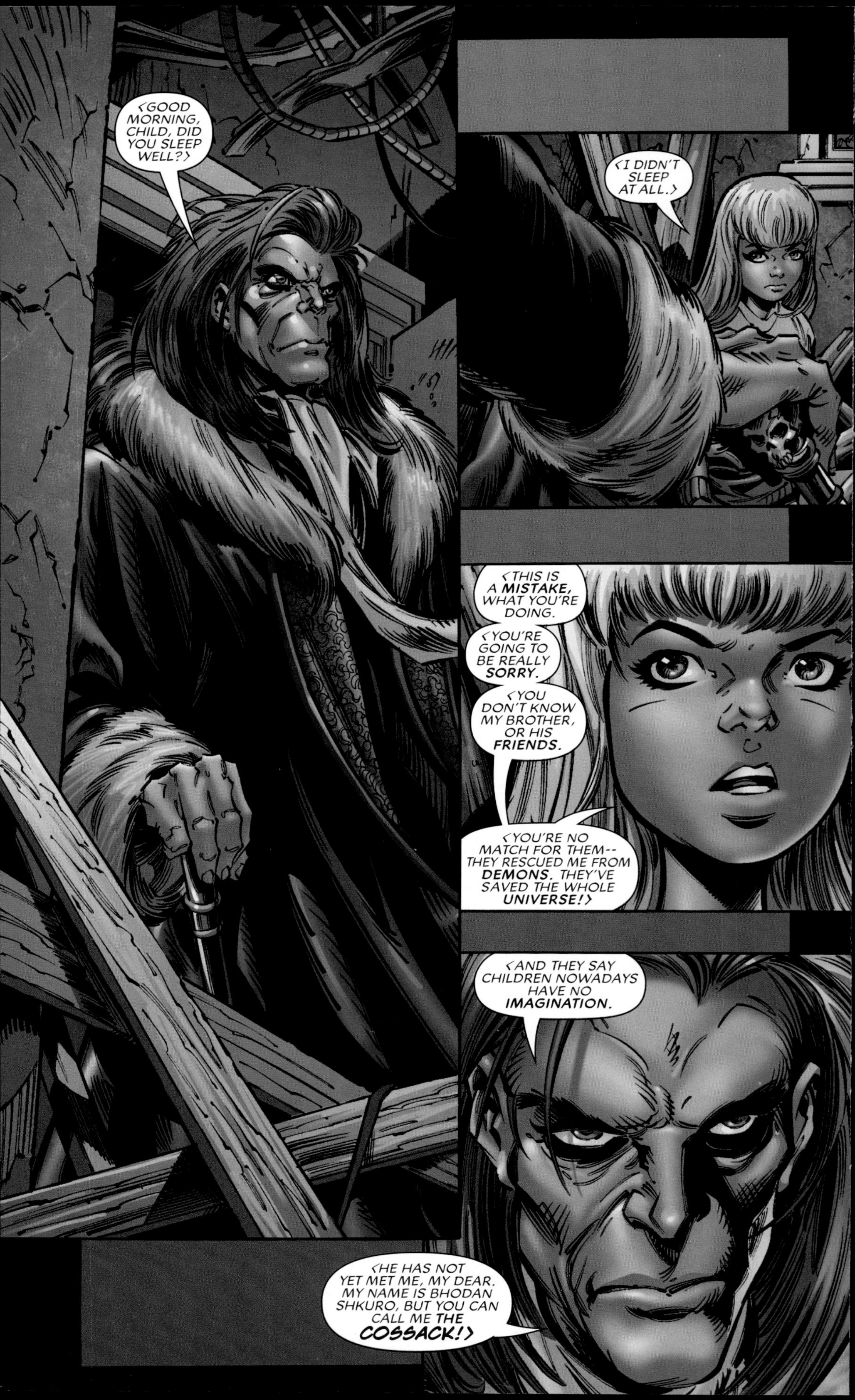
<GOOD MORNING, CHILD, DID YOU SLEEP WELL?>
<I DIDN'T SLEEP AT ALL.>
<THIS IS A **MISTAKE**, WHAT YOU'RE DOING.
<YOU'RE GOING TO BE REALLY **SORRY**.
<YOU DON'T KNOW MY BROTHER, OR HIS **FRIENDS**.
<YOU'RE NO MATCH FOR THEM-- THEY RESCUED ME FROM **DEMONS**. THEY'VE SAVED THE WHOLE **UNIVERSE**!>
<AND THEY SAY CHILDREN NOWADAYS HAVE NO **IMAGINATION**.
<HE HAS NOT YET MET ME, MY DEAR. MY NAME IS BHODAN SHKURO, BUT YOU CAN CALL ME **THE COSSACK**!>

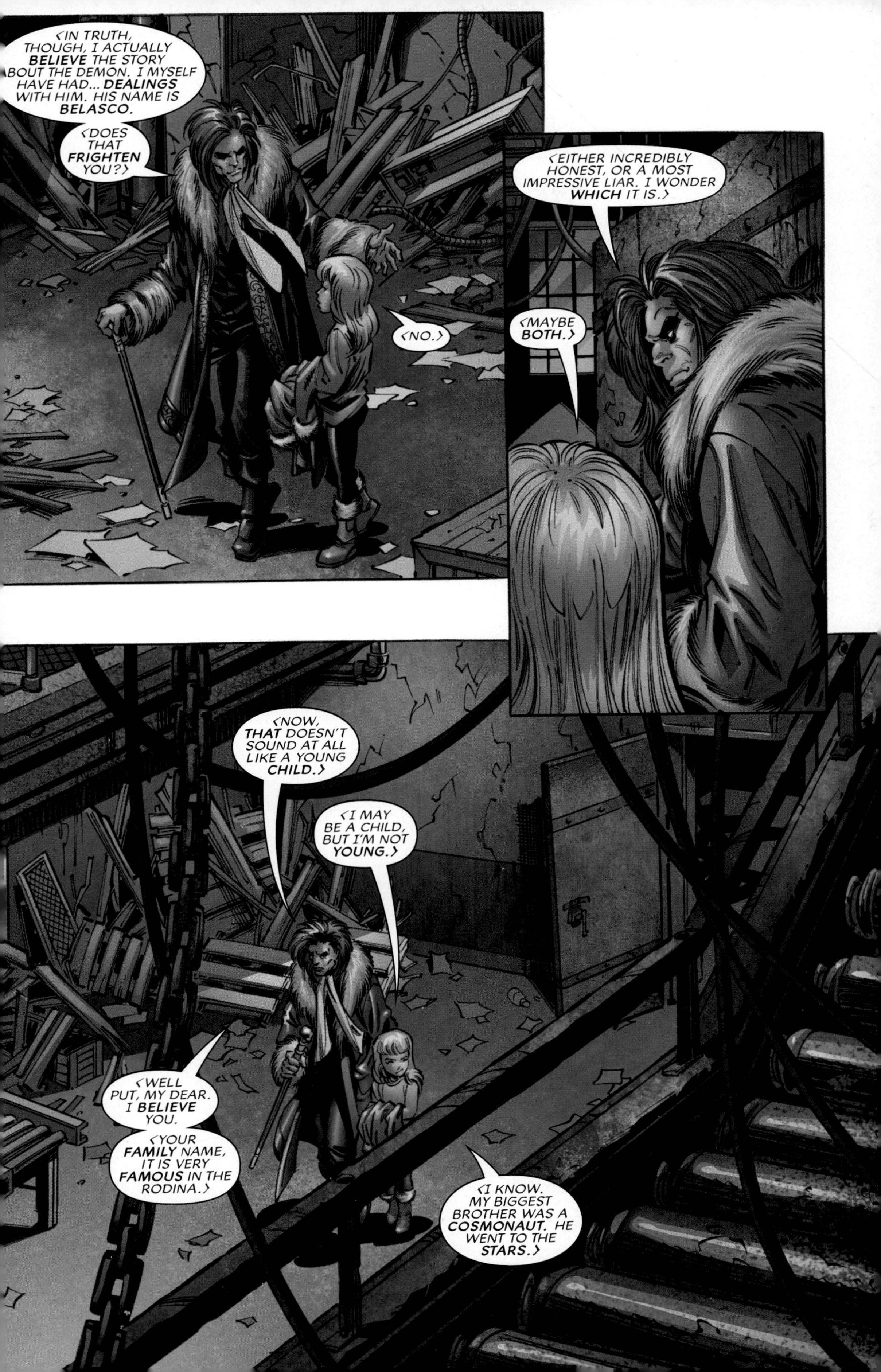
‹IN TRUTH, THOUGH, I ACTUALLY BELIEVE THE STORY BOUT THE DEMON. I MYSELF HAVE HAD... DEALINGS WITH HIM. HIS NAME IS BELASCO.
‹DOES THAT FRIGHTEN YOU?›
‹NO.›
‹EITHER INCREDIBLY HONEST, OR A MOST IMPRESSIVE LIAR. I WONDER WHICH IT IS.›
‹MAYBE BOTH.›
‹NOW, THAT DOESN'T SOUND AT ALL LIKE A YOUNG CHILD.›
‹I MAY BE A CHILD, BUT I'M NOT YOUNG.›
‹WELL PUT, MY DEAR. I BELIEVE YOU.
‹YOUR FAMILY NAME, IT IS VERY FAMOUS IN THE RODINA.›
‹I KNOW. MY BIGGEST BROTHER WAS A COSMONAUT. HE WENT TO THE STARS.›

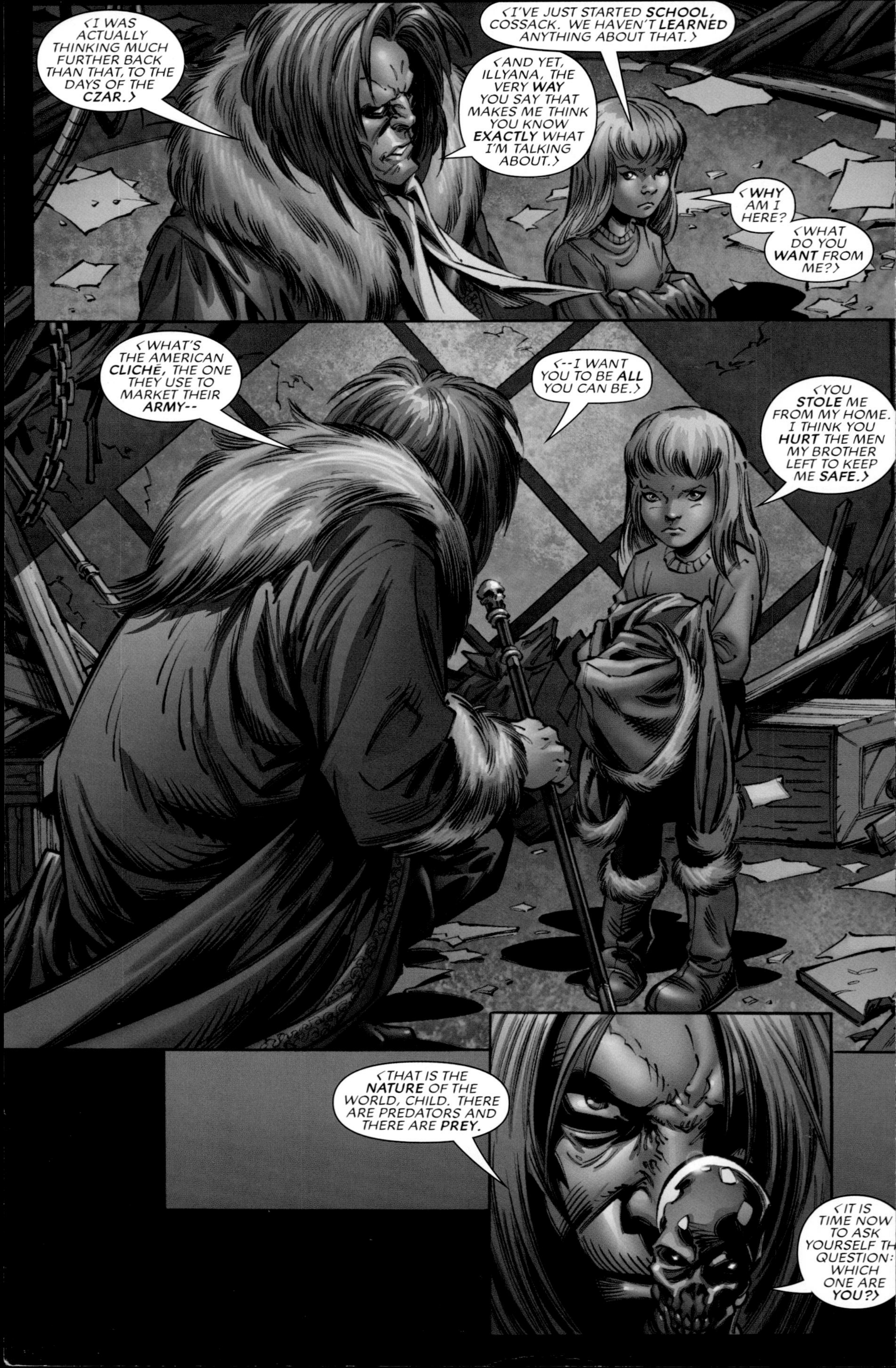
<I WAS ACTUALLY THINKING MUCH FURTHER BACK THAN THAT, TO THE DAYS OF THE **CZAR.**>
<I'VE JUST STARTED **SCHOOL**, COSSACK. WE HAVEN'T **LEARNED** ANYTHING ABOUT THAT.>
<AND YET, ILLYANA, THE VERY **WAY** YOU SAY THAT MAKES ME THINK YOU KNOW **EXACTLY** WHAT I'M TALKING ABOUT.>
<**WHY** AM I HERE?
<WHAT DO YOU **WANT** FROM ME?>
<WHAT'S THE AMERICAN **CLICHÉ**, THE ONE THEY USE TO MARKET THEIR **ARMY**--
<--I WANT YOU TO BE **ALL** YOU CAN BE.>
<YOU **STOLE** ME FROM MY HOME. I THINK YOU **HURT** THE MEN MY BROTHER LEFT TO KEEP ME **SAFE.**>
<THAT IS THE **NATURE** OF THE WORLD, CHILD. THERE ARE PREDATORS AND THERE ARE **PREY**.
<IT IS TIME NOW TO ASK YOURSELF TH QUESTION: WHICH ONE ARE **YOU?**>

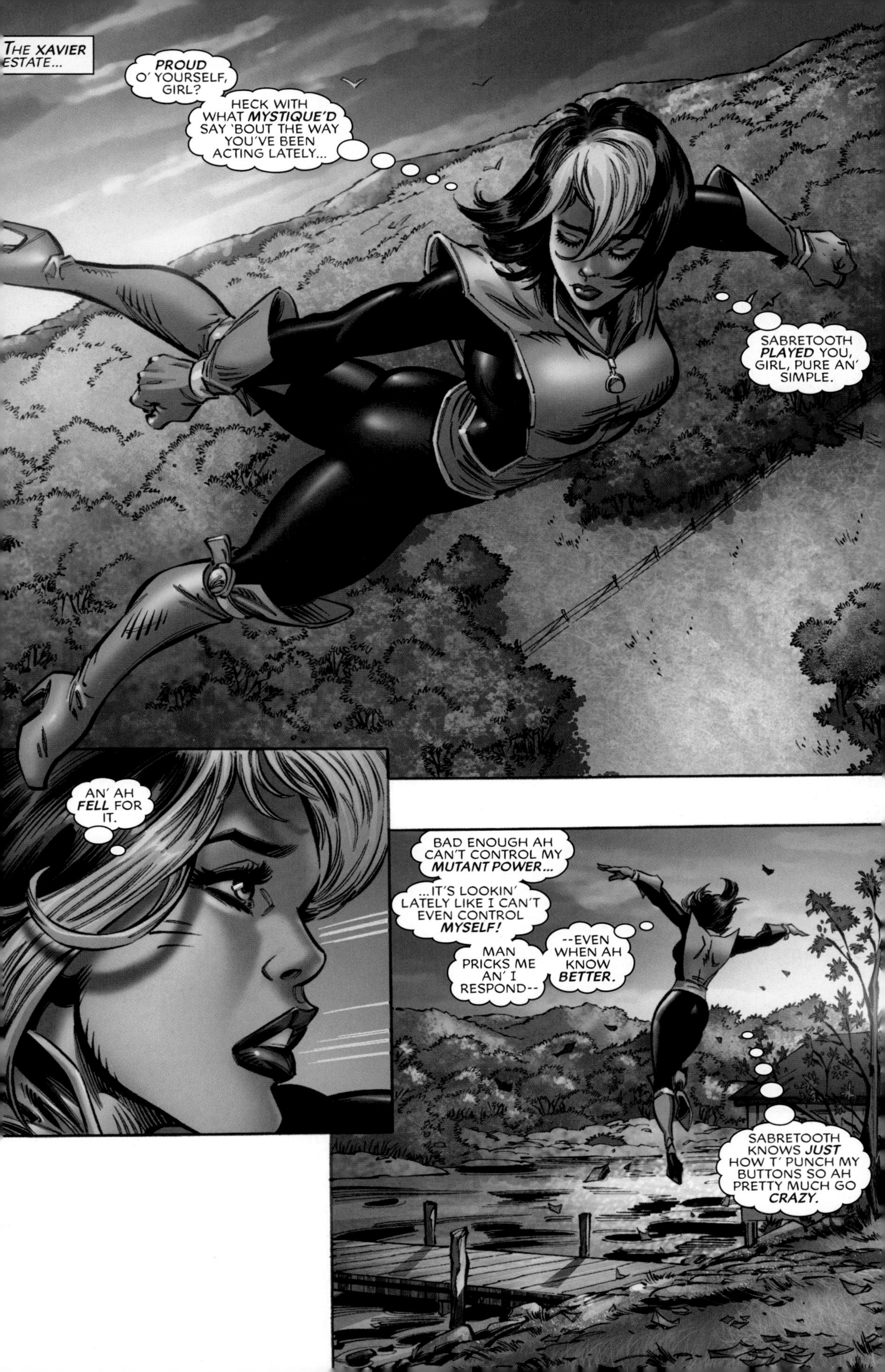
THE XAVIER ESTATE...
PROUD O' YOURSELF, GIRL?
HECK WITH WHAT MYSTIQUE'D SAY 'BOUT THE WAY YOU'VE BEEN ACTING LATELY...
SABRETOOTH PLAYED YOU, GIRL, PURE AN' SIMPLE.
AN' AH FELL FOR IT.
BAD ENOUGH AH CAN'T CONTROL MY MUTANT POWER...
...IT'S LOOKIN' LATELY LIKE I CAN'T EVEN CONTROL MYSELF!
MAN PRICKS ME AN' I RESPOND--
--EVEN WHEN AH KNOW BETTER.
SABRETOOTH KNOWS JUST HOW T' PUNCH MY BUTTONS SO AH PRETTY MUCH GO CRAZY.

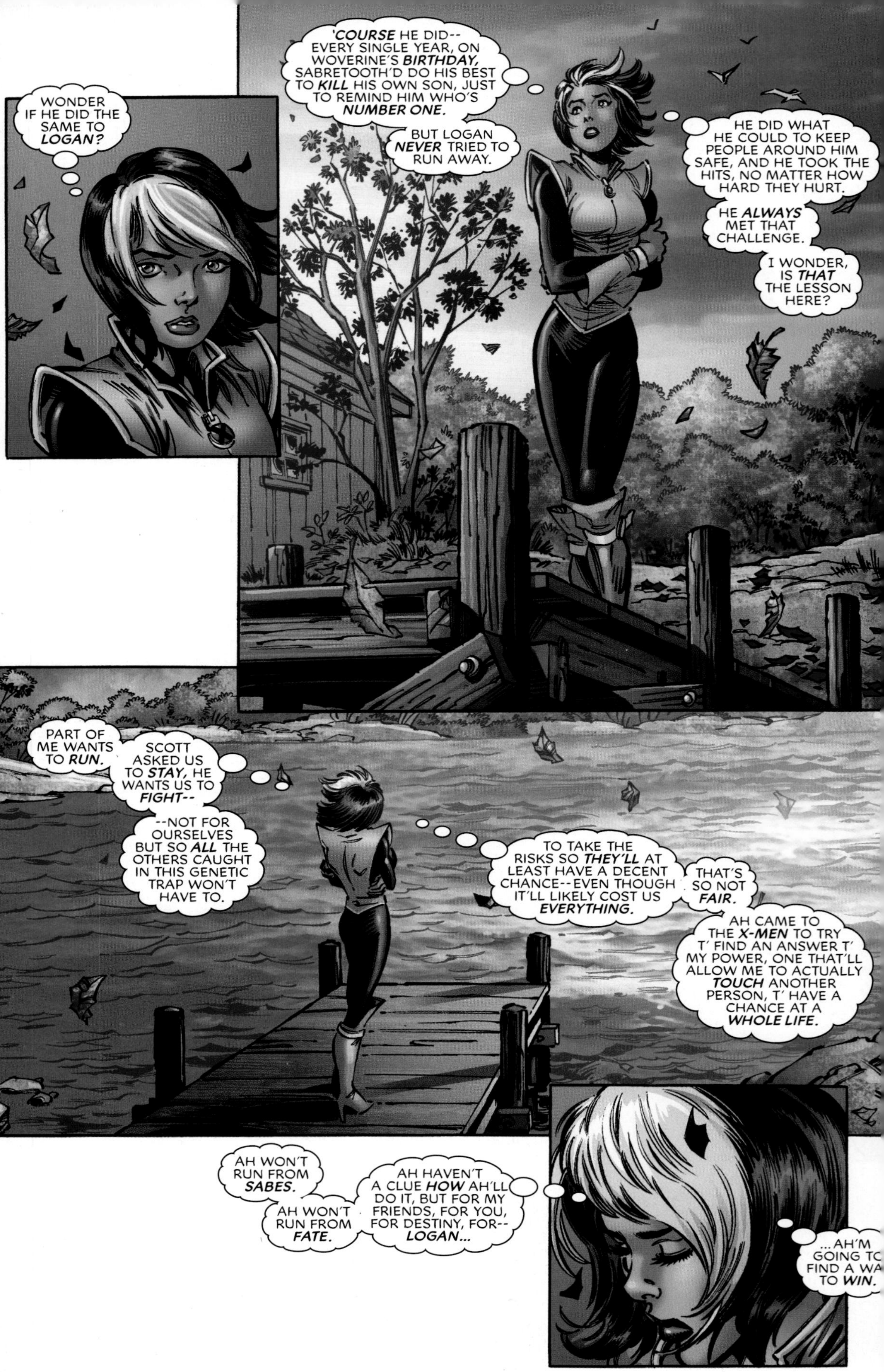
WONDER IF HE DID THE SAME TO LOGAN?
'COURSE HE DID-- EVERY SINGLE YEAR, ON WOVERINE'S BIRTHDAY, SABRETOOTH'D DO HIS BEST TO KILL HIS OWN SON, JUST TO REMIND HIM WHO'S NUMBER ONE.
BUT LOGAN NEVER TRIED TO RUN AWAY.
HE DID WHAT HE COULD TO KEEP PEOPLE AROUND HIM SAFE, AND HE TOOK THE HITS, NO MATTER HOW HARD THEY HURT.
HE ALWAYS MET THAT CHALLENGE.
I WONDER, IS THAT THE LESSON HERE?
PART OF ME WANTS TO RUN.
SCOTT ASKED US TO STAY, HE WANTS US TO FIGHT--
--NOT FOR OURSELVES BUT SO ALL THE OTHERS CAUGHT IN THIS GENETIC TRAP WON'T HAVE TO.
TO TAKE THE RISKS SO THEY'LL AT LEAST HAVE A DECENT CHANCE--EVEN THOUGH IT'LL LIKELY COST US EVERYTHING.
THAT'S SO NOT FAIR.
AH CAME TO THE X-MEN TO TRY T' FIND AN ANSWER T' MY POWER, ONE THAT'LL ALLOW ME TO ACTUALLY TOUCH ANOTHER PERSON, T' HAVE A CHANCE AT A WHOLE LIFE.
AH WON'T RUN FROM SABES.
AH WON'T RUN FROM FATE.
AH HAVEN'T A CLUE HOW AH'LL DO IT, BUT FOR MY FRIENDS, FOR YOU, FOR DESTINY, FOR-- LOGAN...
...AH'M GOING TO FIND A WA TO WIN.

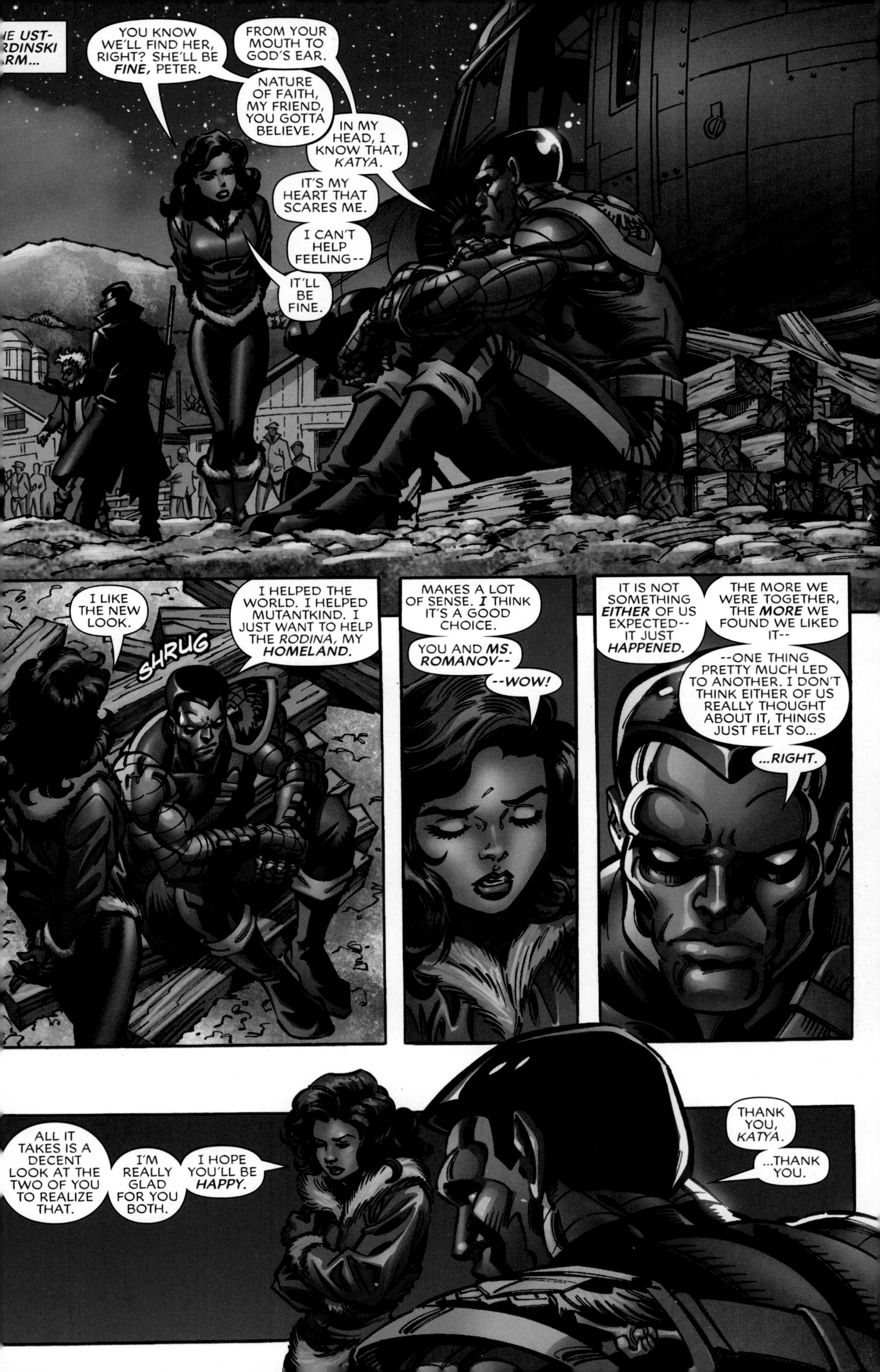

...THE UST-
...RDINSKI
...ARM...
YOU KNOW WE'LL FIND HER, RIGHT? SHE'LL BE FINE, PETER.
FROM YOUR MOUTH TO GOD'S EAR.
NATURE OF FAITH, MY FRIEND, YOU GOTTA BELIEVE.
IN MY HEAD, I KNOW THAT, KATYA.
IT'S MY HEART THAT SCARES ME.
I CAN'T HELP FEELING--
IT'LL BE FINE.
I LIKE THE NEW LOOK.
SHRUG
I HELPED THE WORLD. I HELPED MUTANTKIND. I JUST WANT TO HELP THE RODINA, MY HOMELAND.
MAKES A LOT OF SENSE. I THINK IT'S A GOOD CHOICE.
YOU AND MS. ROMANOV--
--WOW!
IT IS NOT SOMETHING EITHER OF US EXPECTED-- IT JUST HAPPENED.
THE MORE WE WERE TOGETHER, THE MORE WE FOUND WE LIKED IT--
--ONE THING PRETTY MUCH LED TO ANOTHER. I DON'T THINK EITHER OF US REALLY THOUGHT ABOUT IT, THINGS JUST FELT SO...
...RIGHT.
ALL IT TAKES IS A DECENT LOOK AT THE TWO OF YOU TO REALIZE THAT.
I'M REALLY GLAD FOR YOU BOTH.
I HOPE YOU'LL BE HAPPY.
THANK YOU, KATYA.
...THANK YOU.

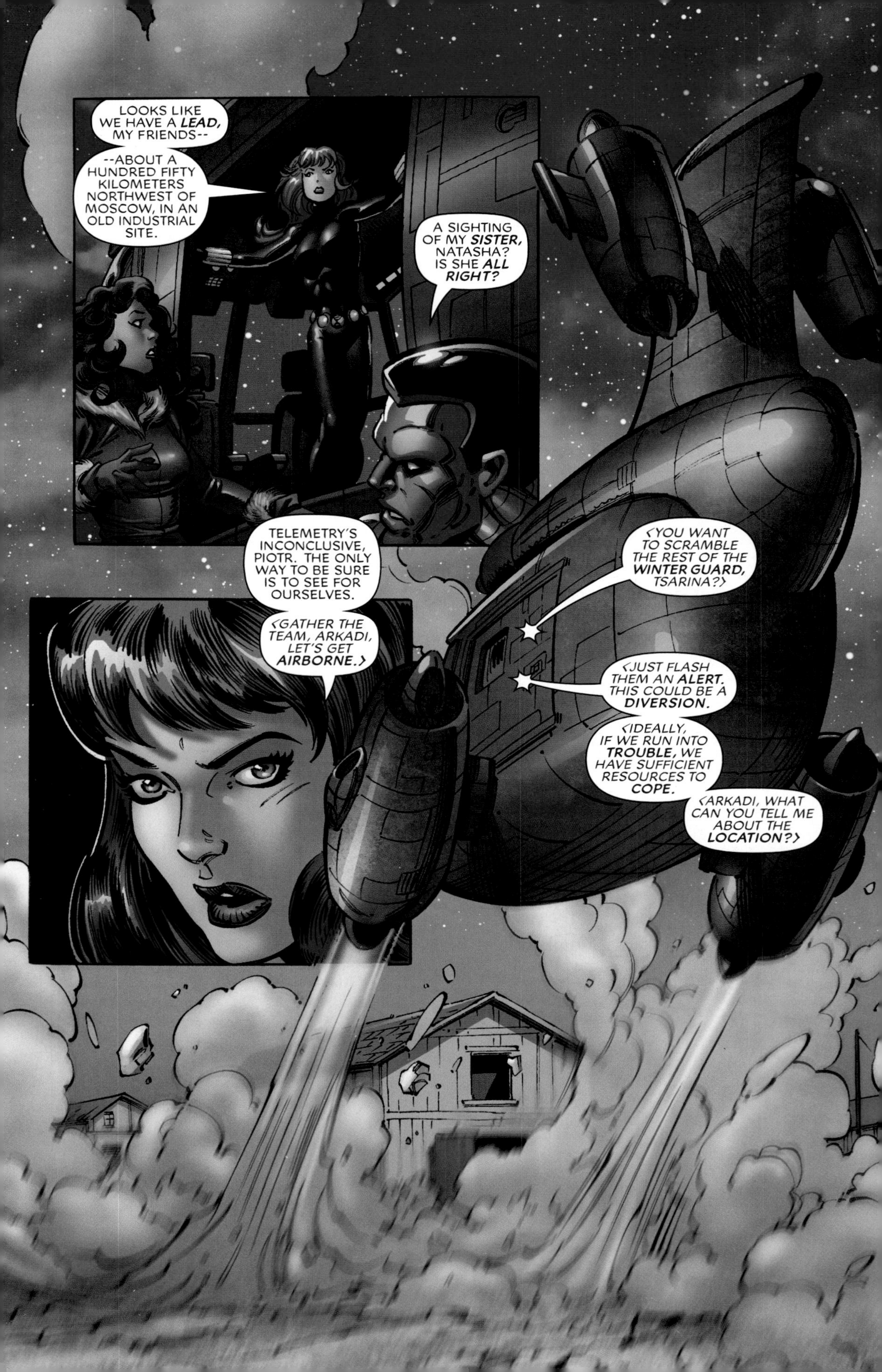

LOOKS LIKE WE HAVE A LEAD, MY FRIENDS--
--ABOUT A HUNDRED FIFTY KILOMETERS NORTHWEST OF MOSCOW, IN AN OLD INDUSTRIAL SITE.
A SIGHTING OF MY SISTER, NATASHA? IS SHE ALL RIGHT?
TELEMETRY'S INCONCLUSIVE, PIOTR. THE ONLY WAY TO BE SURE IS TO SEE FOR OURSELVES.
<GATHER THE TEAM, ARKADI, LET'S GET AIRBORNE.>
<YOU WANT TO SCRAMBLE THE REST OF THE WINTER GUARD, TSARINA?>
<JUST FLASH THEM AN ALERT. THIS COULD BE A DIVERSION.
<IDEALLY, IF WE RUN INTO TROUBLE, WE HAVE SUFFICIENT RESOURCES TO COPE.
<ARKADI, WHAT CAN YOU TELL ME ABOUT THE LOCATION?>

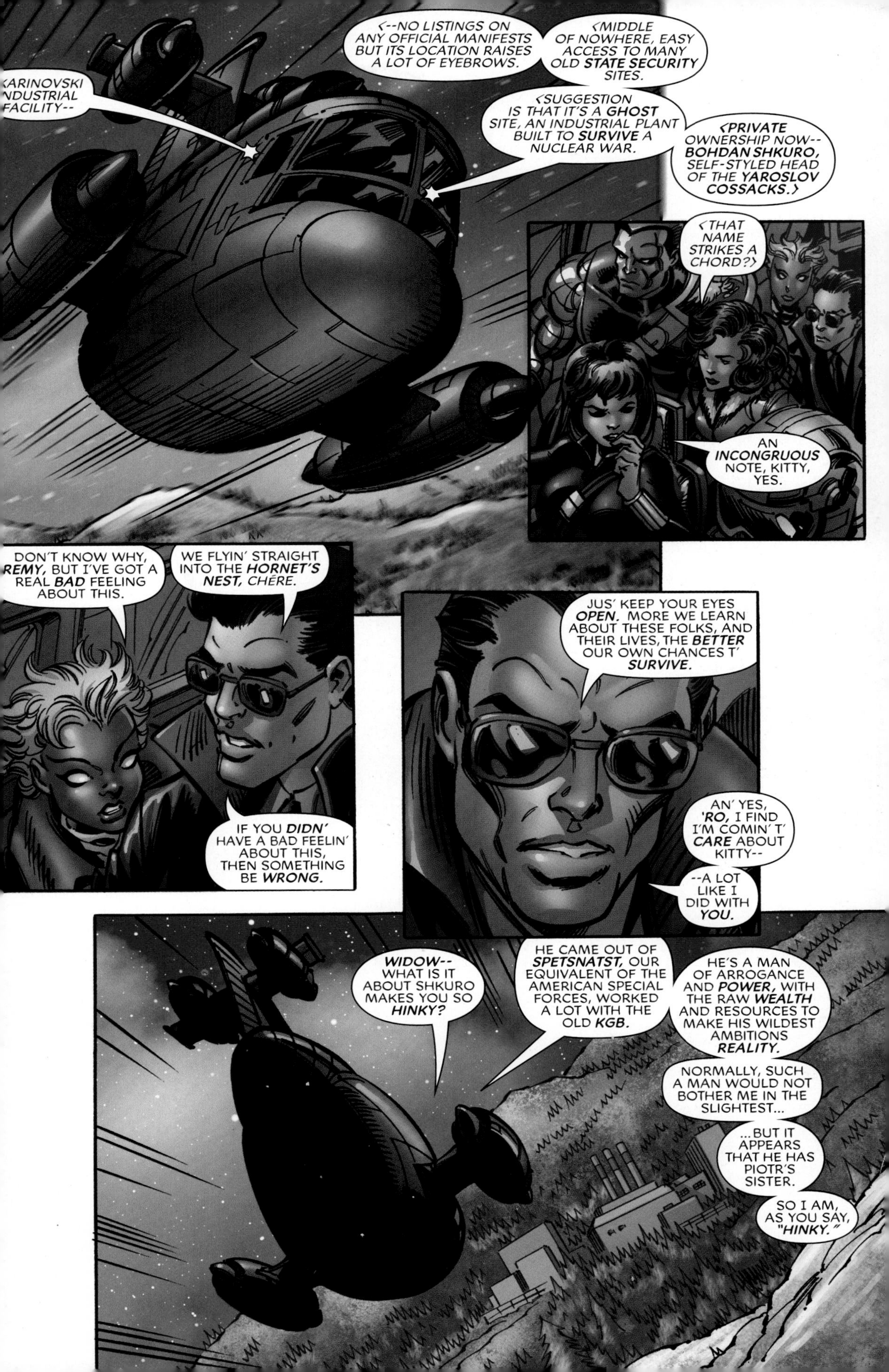
KARINOVSKI INDUSTRIAL FACILITY--
<--NO LISTINGS ON ANY OFFICIAL MANIFESTS BUT ITS LOCATION RAISES A LOT OF EYEBROWS.
<MIDDLE OF NOWHERE, EASY ACCESS TO MANY OLD STATE SECURITY SITES.
<SUGGESTION IS THAT IT'S A GHOST SITE, AN INDUSTRIAL PLANT BUILT TO SURVIVE A NUCLEAR WAR.
<PRIVATE OWNERSHIP NOW-- BOHDAN SHKURO, SELF-STYLED HEAD OF THE YAROSLOV COSSACKS.>
<THAT NAME STRIKES A CHORD?>
AN INCONGRUOUS NOTE, KITTY, YES.
DON'T KNOW WHY, REMY, BUT I'VE GOT A REAL BAD FEELING ABOUT THIS.
WE FLYIN' STRAIGHT INTO THE HORNET'S NEST, CHÉRE.
IF YOU DIDN' HAVE A BAD FEELIN' ABOUT THIS, THEN SOMETHING BE WRONG.
JUS' KEEP YOUR EYES OPEN. MORE WE LEARN ABOUT THESE FOLKS, AND THEIR LIVES, THE BETTER OUR OWN CHANCES T' SURVIVE.
AN' YES, 'RO, I FIND I'M COMIN' T' CARE ABOUT KITTY--
--A LOT LIKE I DID WITH YOU.
WIDOW-- WHAT IS IT ABOUT SHKURO MAKES YOU SO HINKY?
HE CAME OUT OF SPETSNATST, OUR EQUIVALENT OF THE AMERICAN SPECIAL FORCES, WORKED A LOT WITH THE OLD KGB.
HE'S A MAN OF ARROGANCE AND POWER, WITH THE RAW WEALTH AND RESOURCES TO MAKE HIS WILDEST AMBITIONS REALITY.
NORMALLY, SUCH A MAN WOULD NOT BOTHER ME IN THE SLIGHTEST...
...BUT IT APPEARS THAT HE HAS PIOTR'S SISTER.
SO I AM, AS YOU SAY, "HINKY."

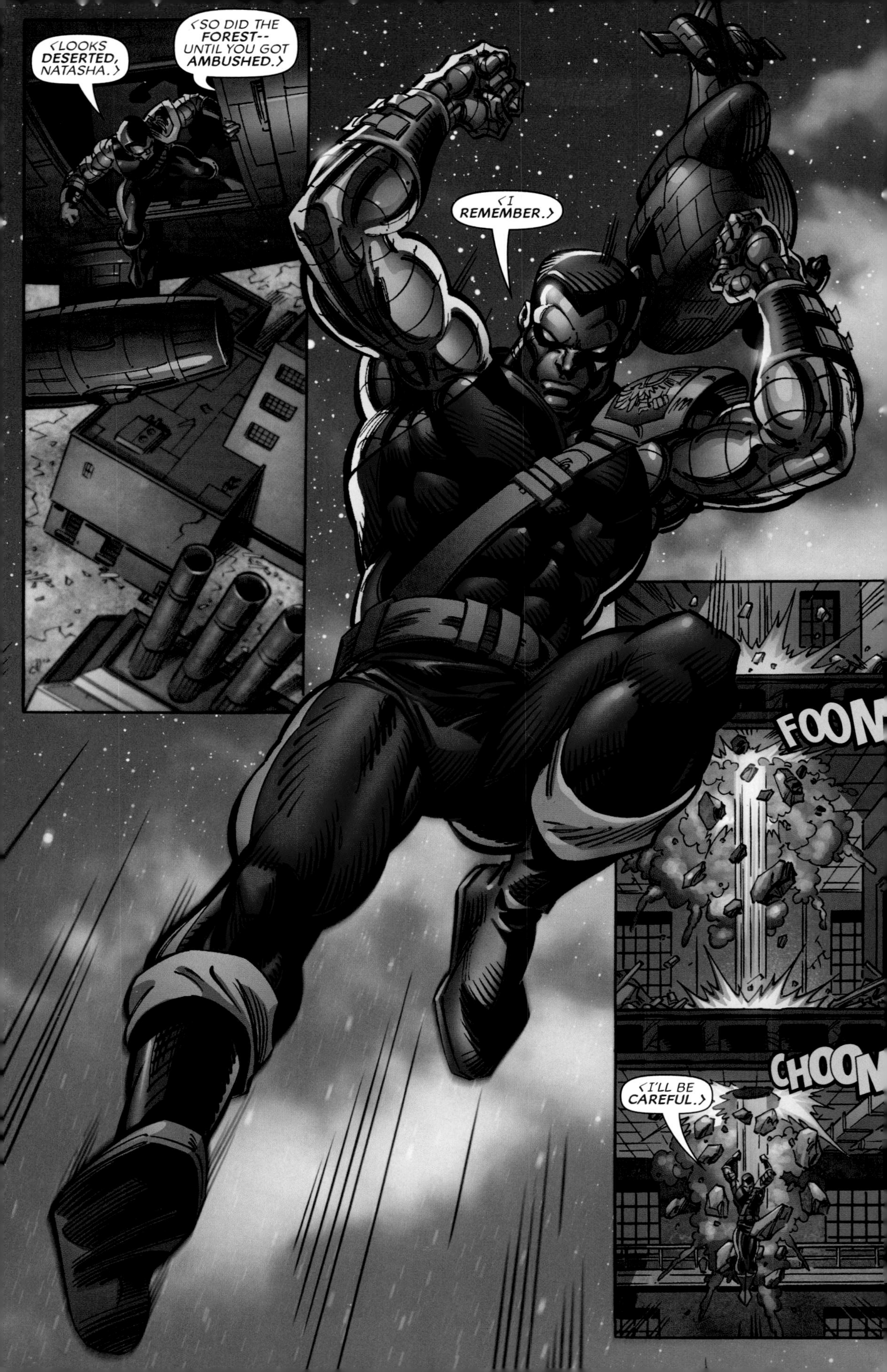

<LOOKS DESERTED, NATASHA.>
<SO DID THE FOREST-- UNTIL YOU GOT AMBUSHED.>
<I REMEMBER.>
FOOM
CHOOM
<I'LL BE CAREFUL.>

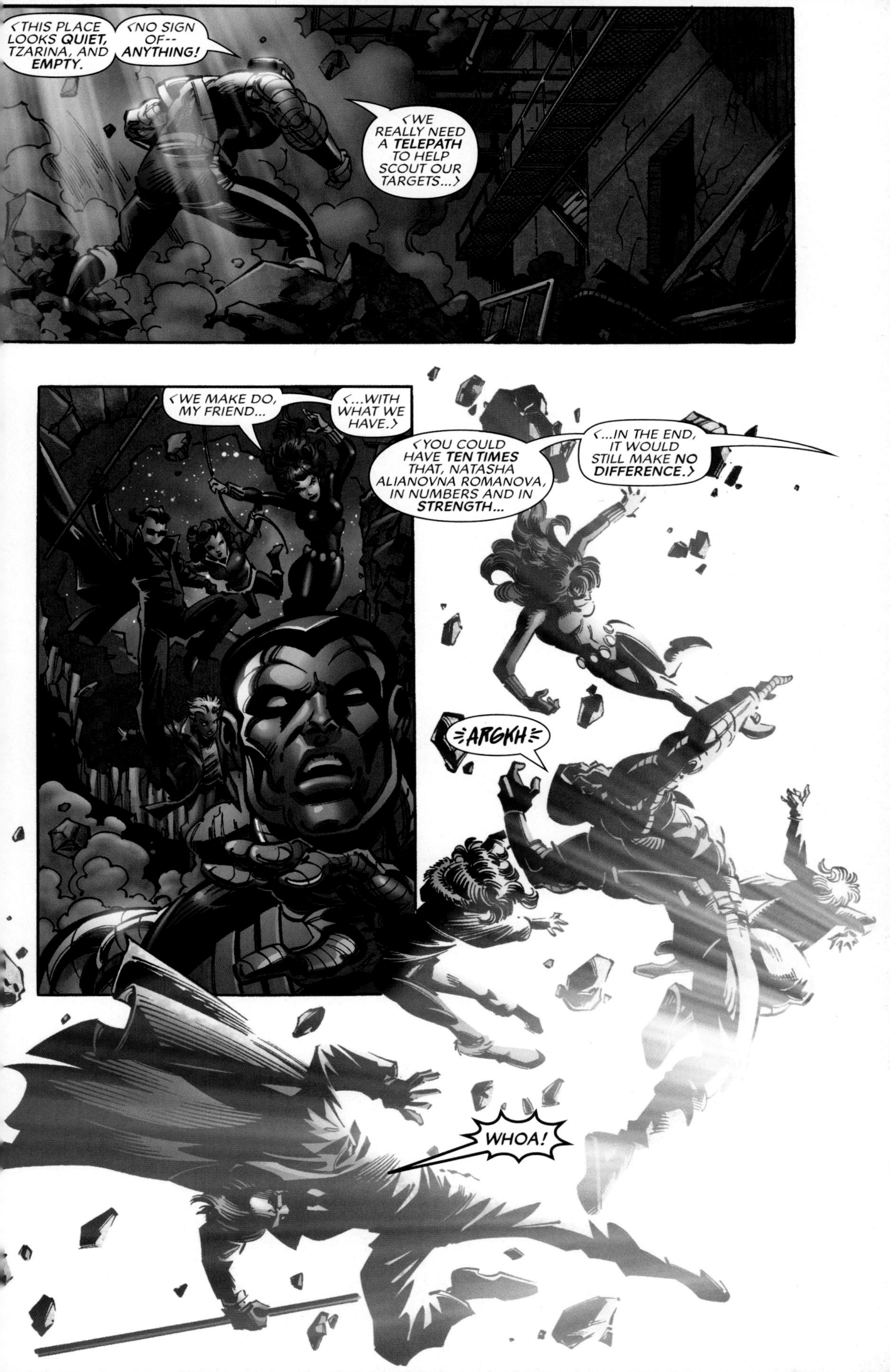

<THIS PLACE LOOKS QUIET, TZARINA, AND EMPTY.
<NO SIGN OF-- ANYTHING!
<WE REALLY NEED A TELEPATH TO HELP SCOUT OUR TARGETS...>
<WE MAKE DO, MY FRIEND...
<...WITH WHAT WE HAVE.>
<YOU COULD HAVE TEN TIMES THAT, NATASHA ALIANOVNA ROMANOVA, IN NUMBERS AND IN STRENGTH...
<...IN THE END, IT WOULD STILL MAKE NO DIFFERENCE.>
ARGKH
WHOA!

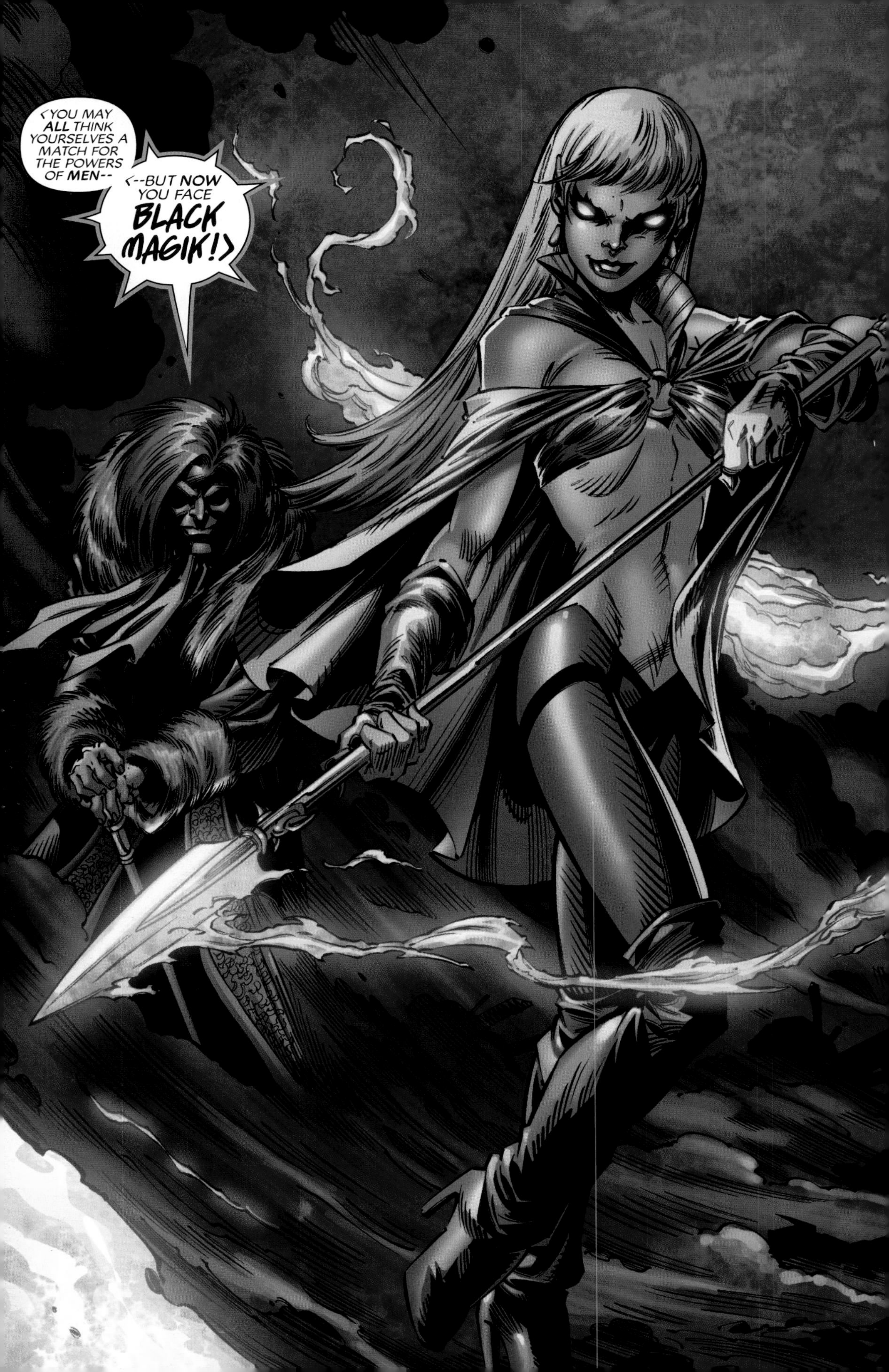
<YOU MAY ALL THINK YOURSELVES A MATCH FOR THE POWERS OF MEN--
<--BUT NOW YOU FACE BLACK MAGIK!>

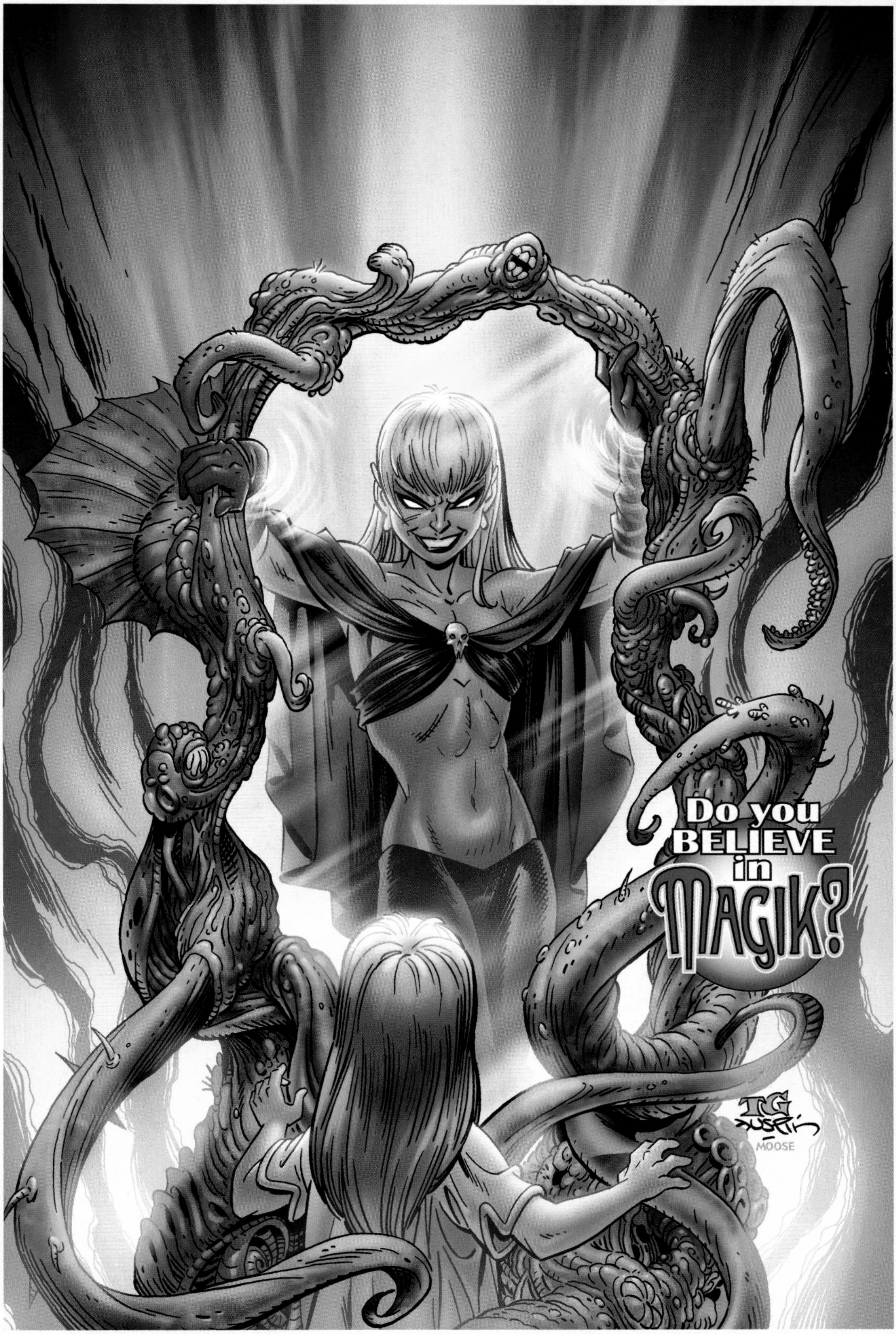
Do you BELIEVE in MAGIK?
TG
MOOSE

THIRTEEN

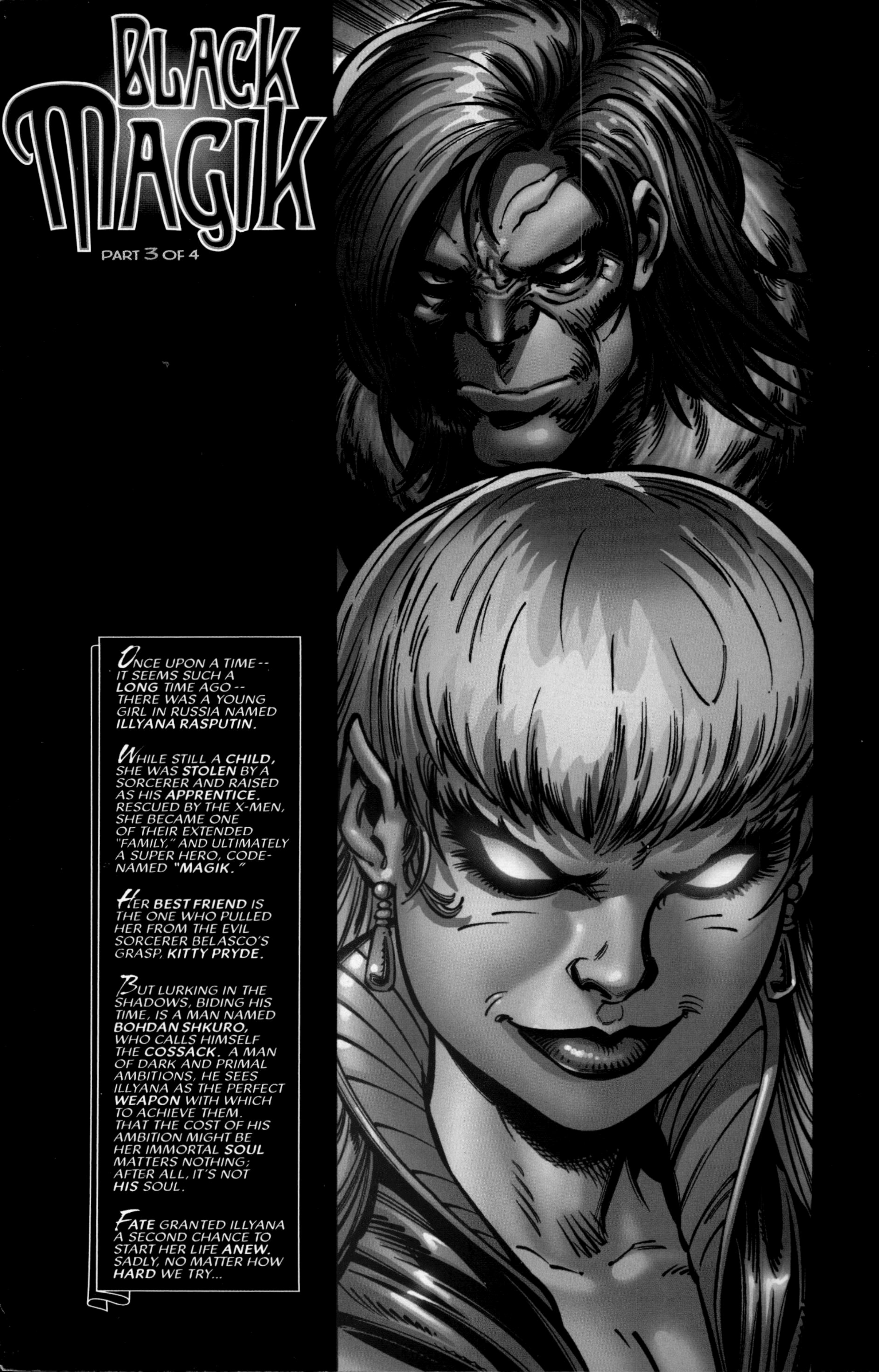
BLACK MAGIK
PART 3 OF 4
ONCE UPON A TIME -- IT SEEMS SUCH A LONG TIME AGO -- THERE WAS A YOUNG GIRL IN RUSSIA NAMED ILLYANA RASPUTIN.
WHILE STILL A CHILD, SHE WAS STOLEN BY A SORCERER AND RAISED AS HIS APPRENTICE. RESCUED BY THE X-MEN, SHE BECAME ONE OF THEIR EXTENDED "FAMILY," AND ULTIMATELY A SUPER HERO, CODE-NAMED "MAGIK."
HER BEST FRIEND IS THE ONE WHO PULLED HER FROM THE EVIL SORCERER BELASCO'S GRASP, KITTY PRYDE.
BUT LURKING IN THE SHADOWS, BIDING HIS TIME, IS A MAN NAMED BOHDAN SHKURO, WHO CALLS HIMSELF THE COSSACK. A MAN OF DARK AND PRIMAL AMBITIONS, HE SEES ILLYANA AS THE PERFECT WEAPON WITH WHICH TO ACHIEVE THEM. THAT THE COST OF HIS AMBITION MIGHT BE HER IMMORTAL SOUL MATTERS NOTHING; AFTER ALL, IT'S NOT HIS SOUL.
FATE GRANTED ILLYANA A SECOND CHANCE TO START HER LIFE ANEW. SADLY, NO MATTER HOW HARD WE TRY...

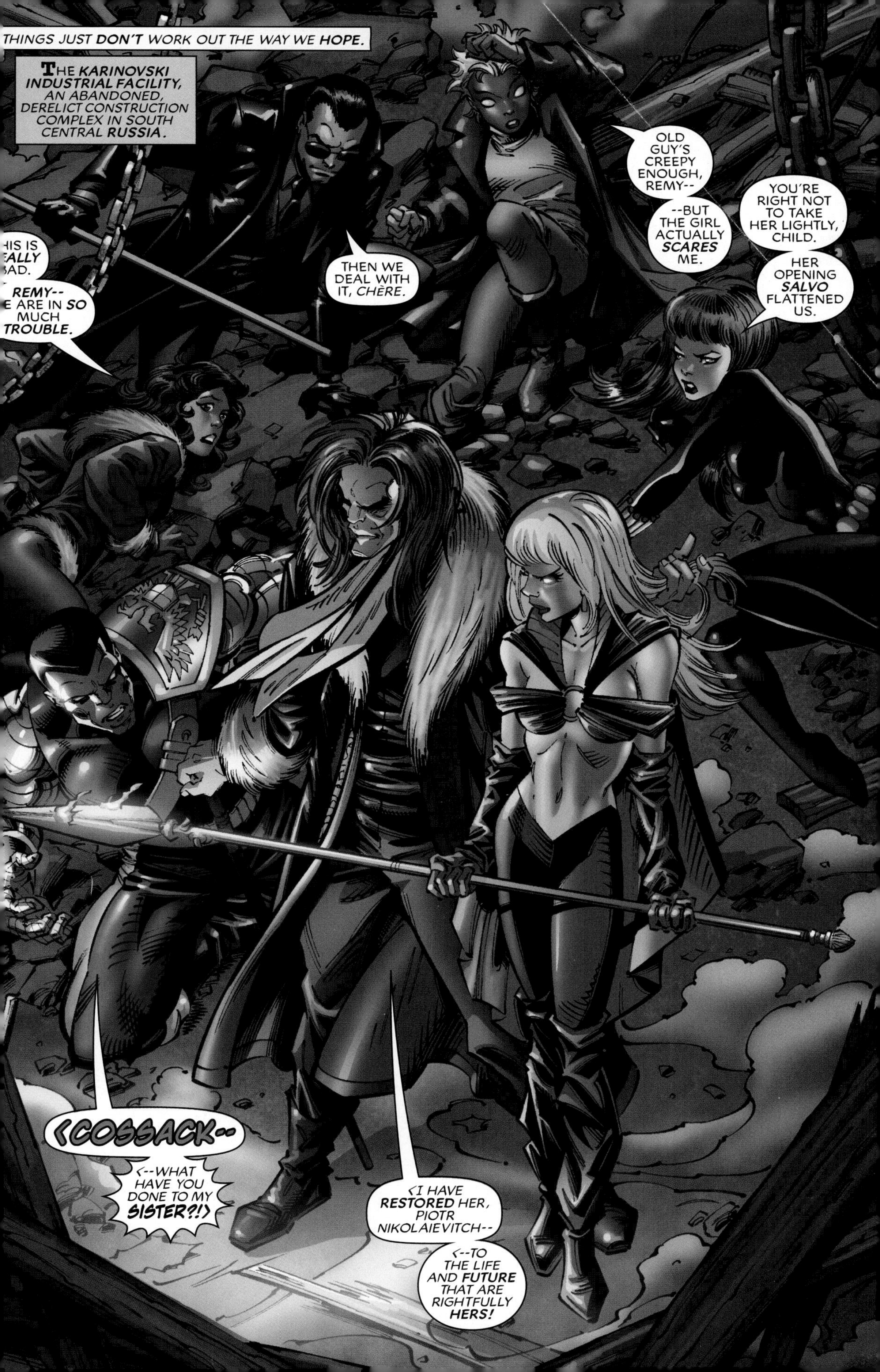
THINGS JUST DON'T WORK OUT THE WAY WE HOPE.
THE KARINOVSKI INDUSTRIAL FACILITY, AN ABANDONED, DERELICT CONSTRUCTION COMPLEX IN SOUTH CENTRAL RUSSIA.
OLD GUY'S CREEPY ENOUGH, REMY--
--BUT THE GIRL ACTUALLY SCARES ME.
YOU'RE RIGHT NOT TO TAKE HER LIGHTLY, CHILD.
HER OPENING SALVO FLATTENED US.
HIS IS EALLY AD.
REMY-- E ARE IN SO MUCH TROUBLE.
THEN WE DEAL WITH IT, CHÈRE.
<COSSACK--
<--WHAT HAVE YOU DONE TO MY SISTER?!>
<I HAVE RESTORED HER, PIOTR NIKOLAIEVITCH--
<--TO THE LIFE AND FUTURE THAT ARE RIGHTFULLY HERS!

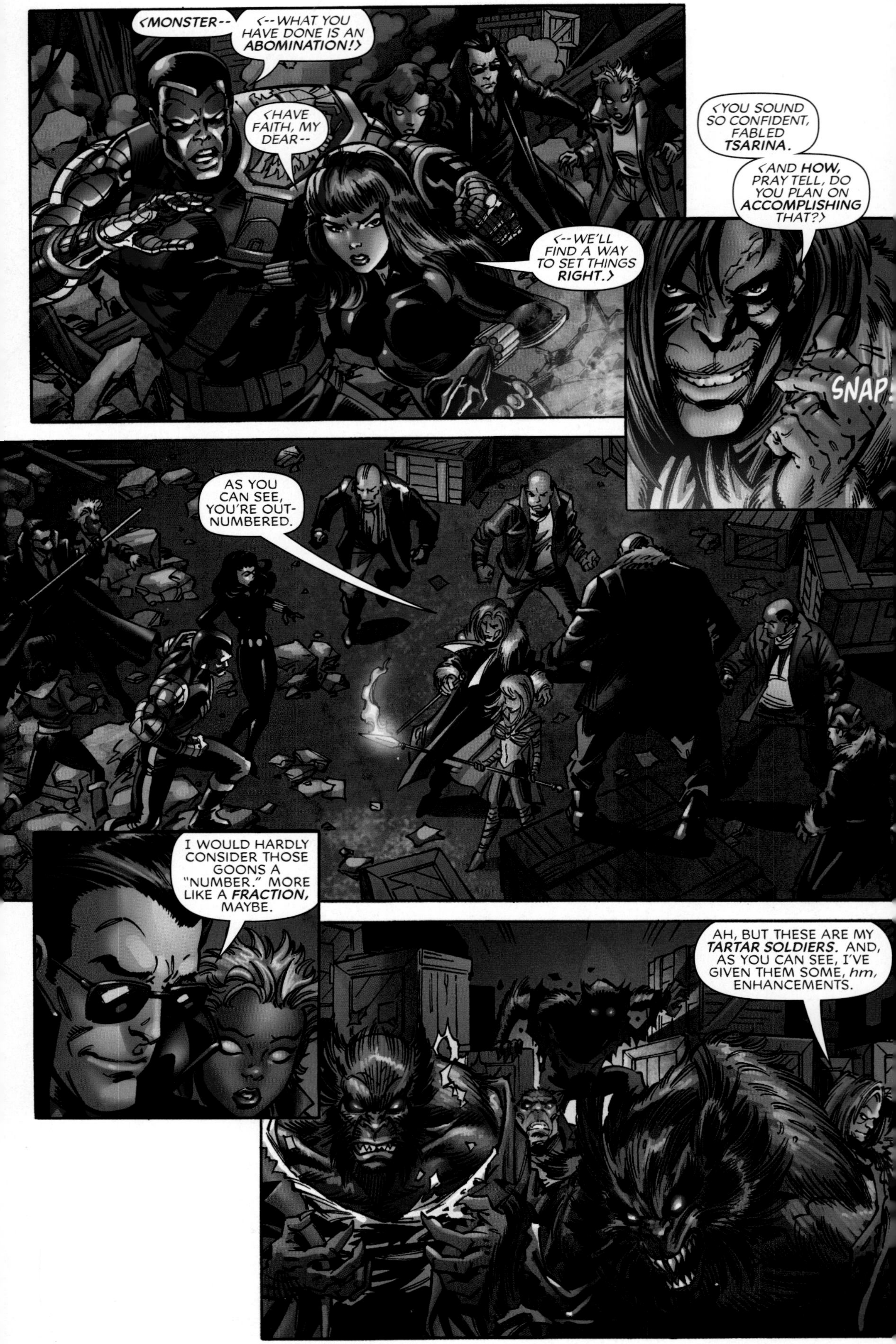

<MONSTER--
<--WHAT YOU HAVE DONE IS AN ABOMINATION!>
<HAVE FAITH, MY DEAR--
<--WE'LL FIND A WAY TO SET THINGS RIGHT.>
<YOU SOUND SO CONFIDENT, FABLED TSARINA.
<AND HOW, PRAY TELL, DO YOU PLAN ON ACCOMPLISHING THAT?>
SNAP!
AS YOU CAN SEE, YOU'RE OUT-NUMBERED.
I WOULD HARDLY CONSIDER THOSE GOONS A "NUMBER." MORE LIKE A FRACTION, MAYBE.
AH, BUT THESE ARE MY TARTAR SOLDIERS. AND, AS YOU CAN SEE, I'VE GIVEN THEM SOME, hm, ENHANCEMENTS.

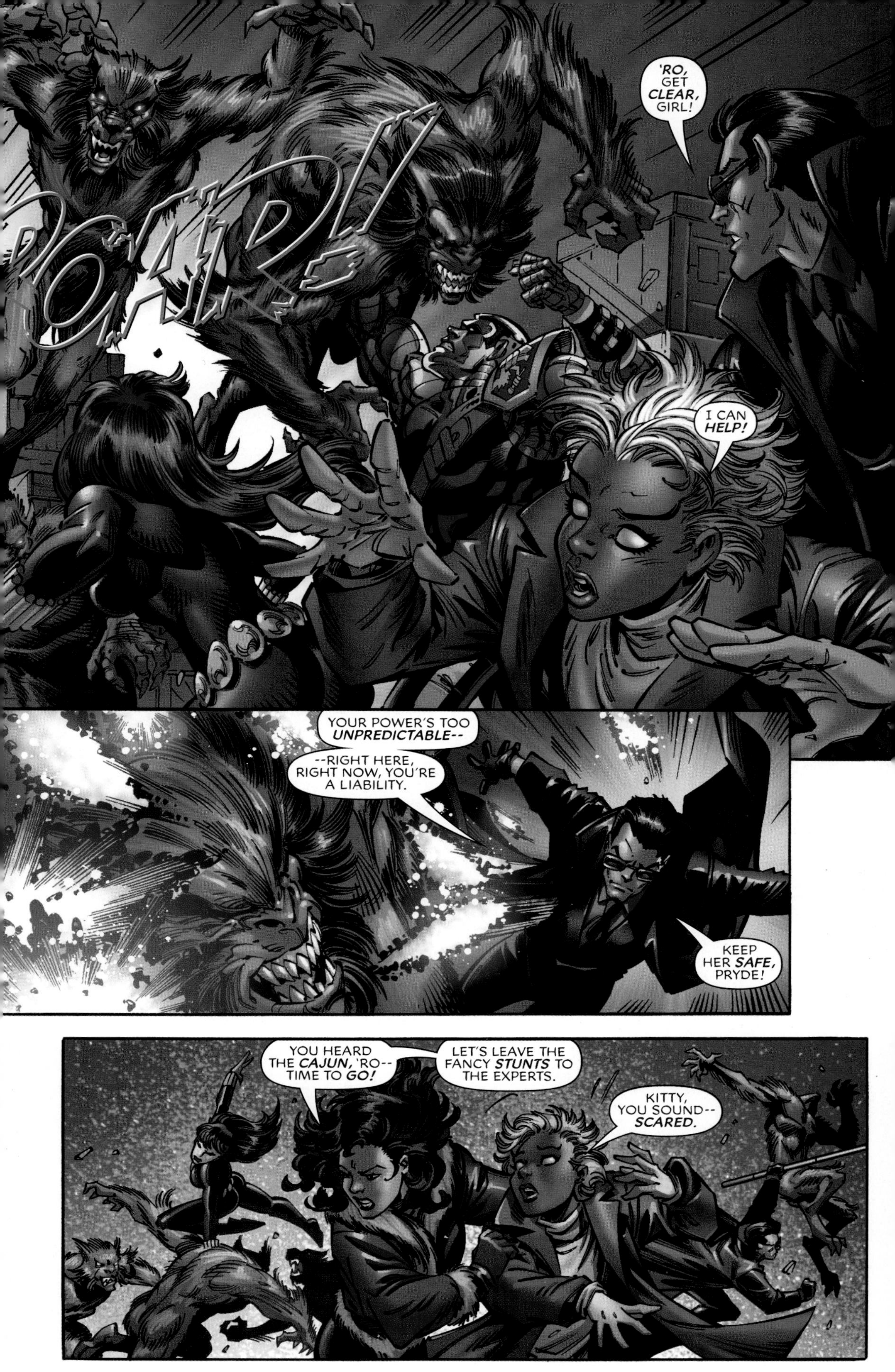
'RO, GET CLEAR, GIRL!
I CAN HELP!
YOUR POWER'S TOO UNPREDICTABLE--
--RIGHT HERE, RIGHT NOW, YOU'RE A LIABILITY.
KEEP HER SAFE, PRYDE!
YOU HEARD THE CAJUN, 'RO-- TIME TO GO!
LET'S LEAVE THE FANCY STUNTS TO THE EXPERTS.
KITTY, YOU SOUND-- SCARED.

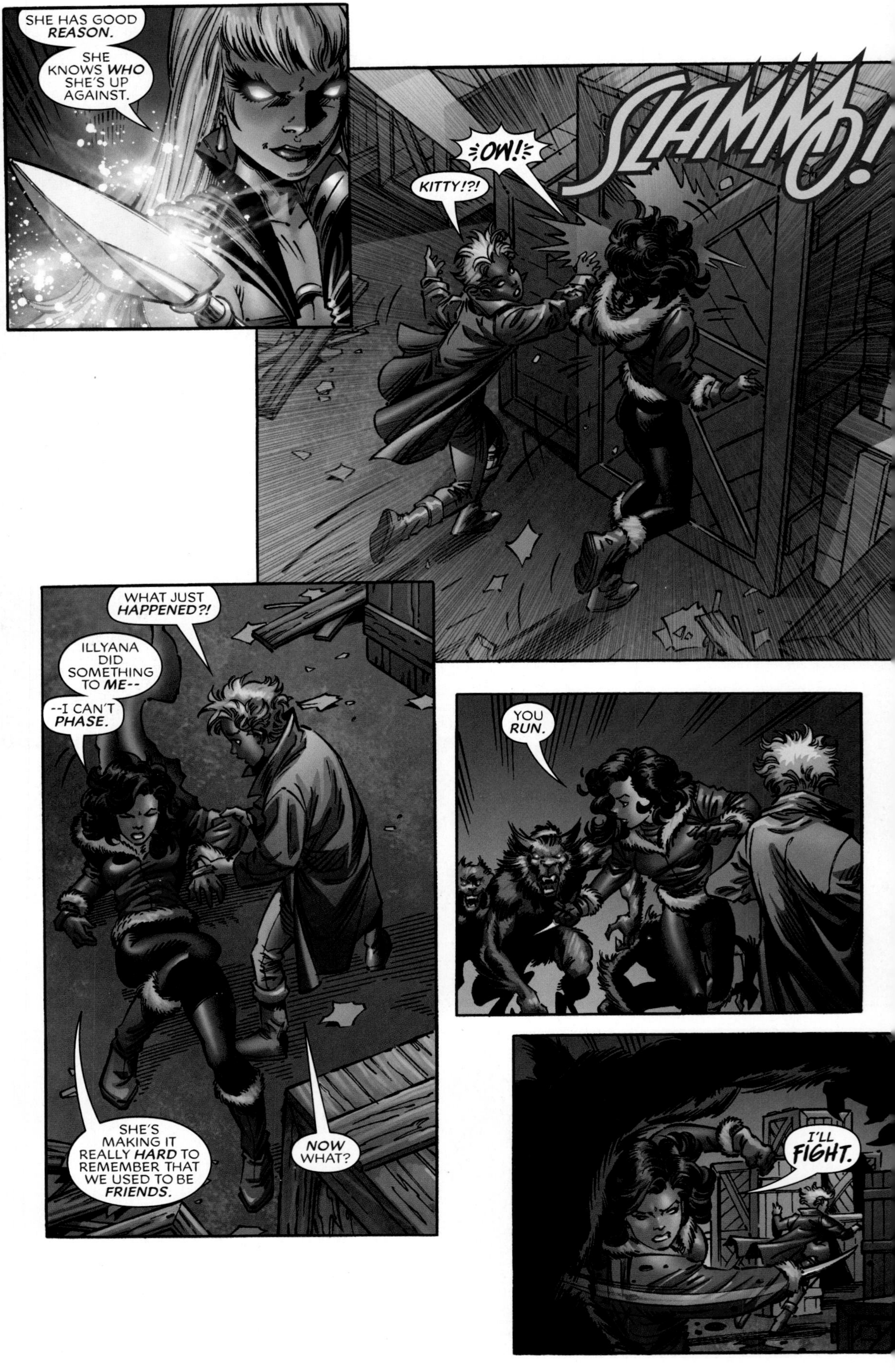
SHE HAS GOOD REASON.
SHE KNOWS WHO SHE'S UP AGAINST.
SLAMM!
OW!
KITTY!?!
WHAT JUST HAPPENED?!
ILLYANA DID SOMETHING TO ME--
--I CAN'T PHASE.
SHE'S MAKING IT REALLY HARD TO REMEMBER THAT WE USED TO BE FRIENDS.
NOW WHAT?
YOU RUN.
I'LL FIGHT.

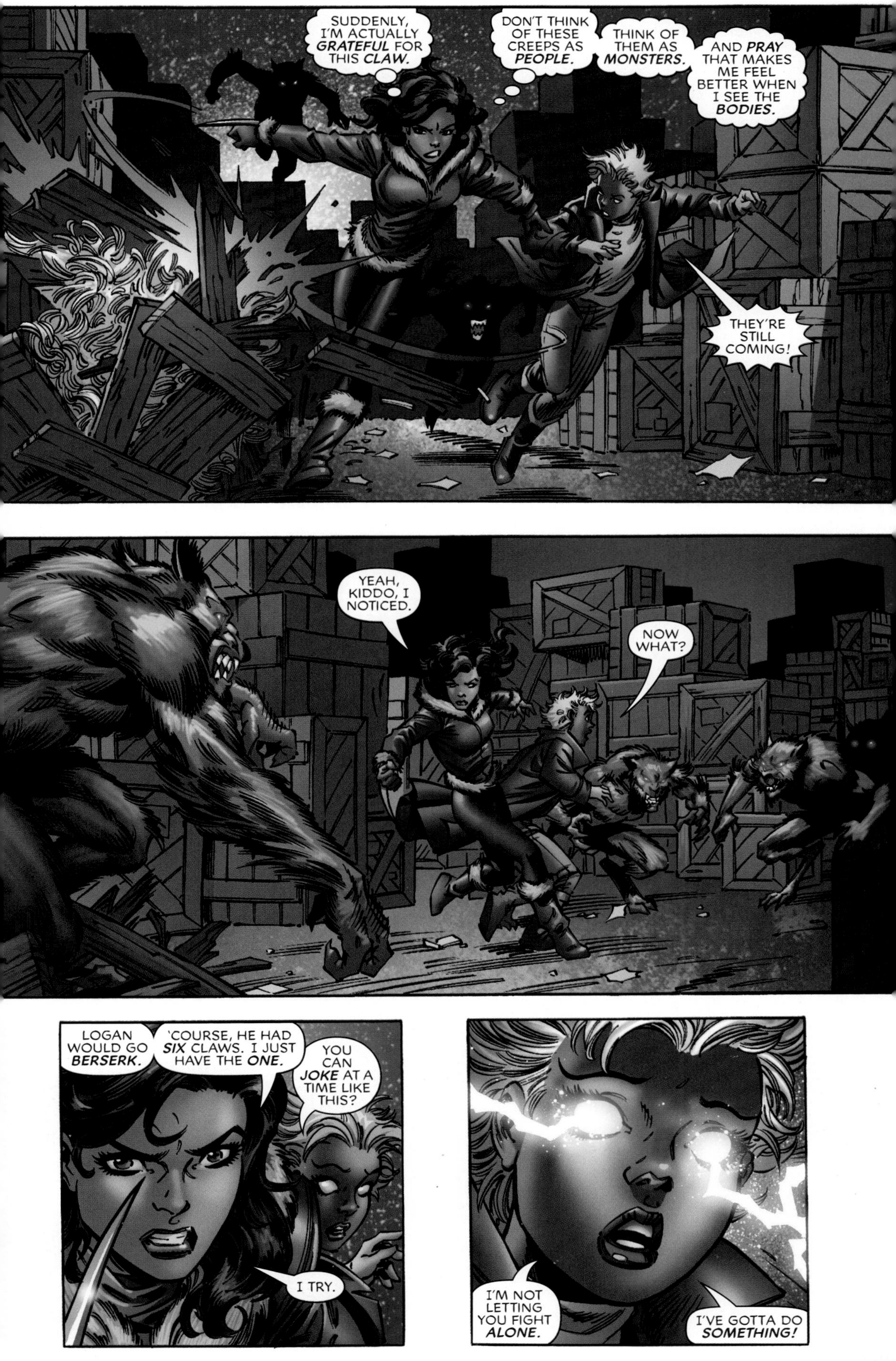
SUDDENLY, I'M ACTUALLY GRATEFUL FOR THIS CLAW.
DON'T THINK OF THESE CREEPS AS PEOPLE.
THINK OF THEM AS MONSTERS.
AND PRAY THAT MAKES ME FEEL BETTER WHEN I SEE THE BODIES.
THEY'RE STILL COMING!
YEAH, KIDDO, I NOTICED.
NOW WHAT?
LOGAN WOULD GO BERSERK.
'COURSE, HE HAD SIX CLAWS. I JUST HAVE THE ONE.
YOU CAN JOKE AT A TIME LIKE THIS?
I TRY.
I'M NOT LETTING YOU FIGHT ALONE.
I'VE GOTTA DO SOMETHING!

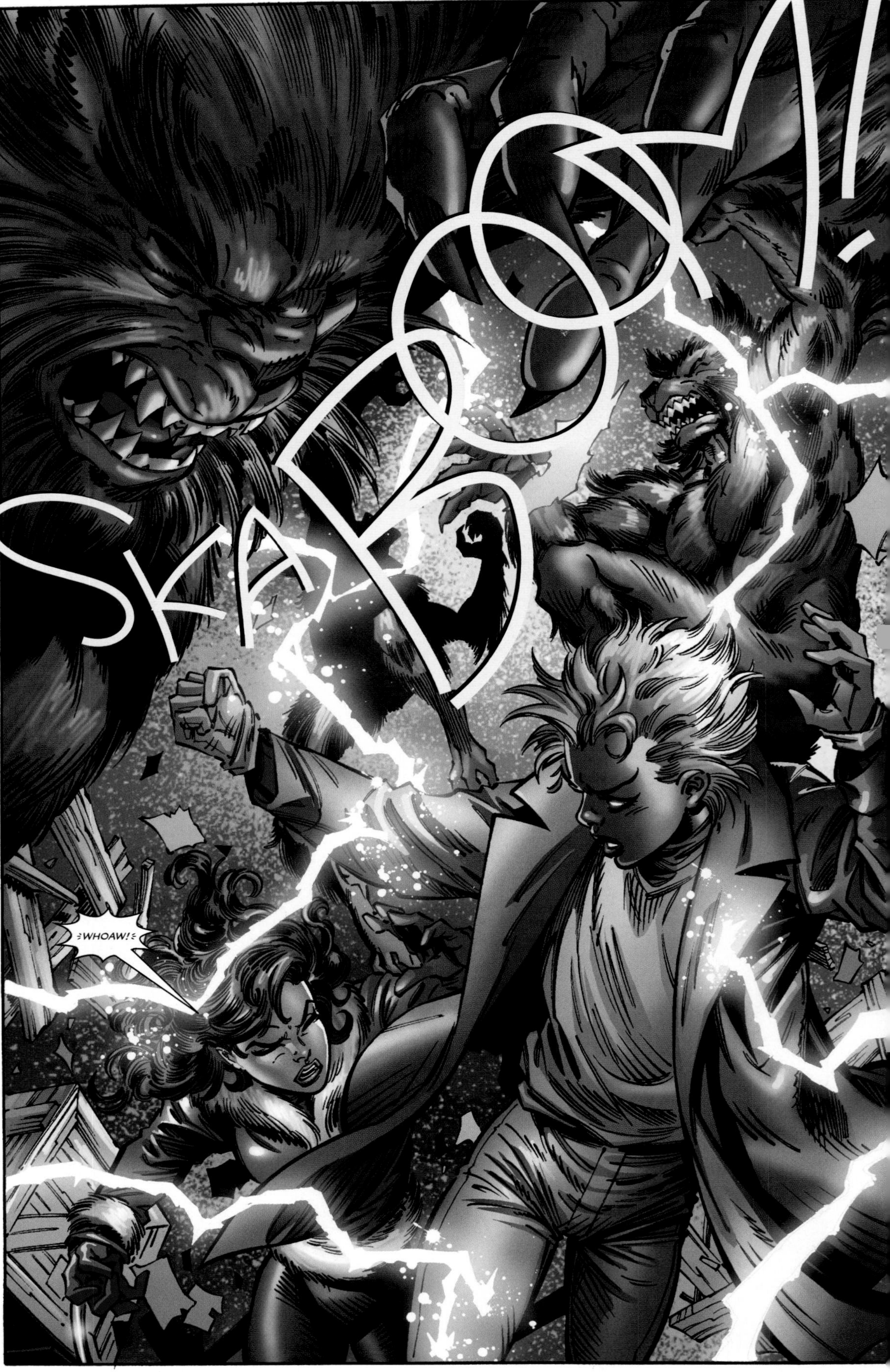
SKABOOOM!!
WHOAW!

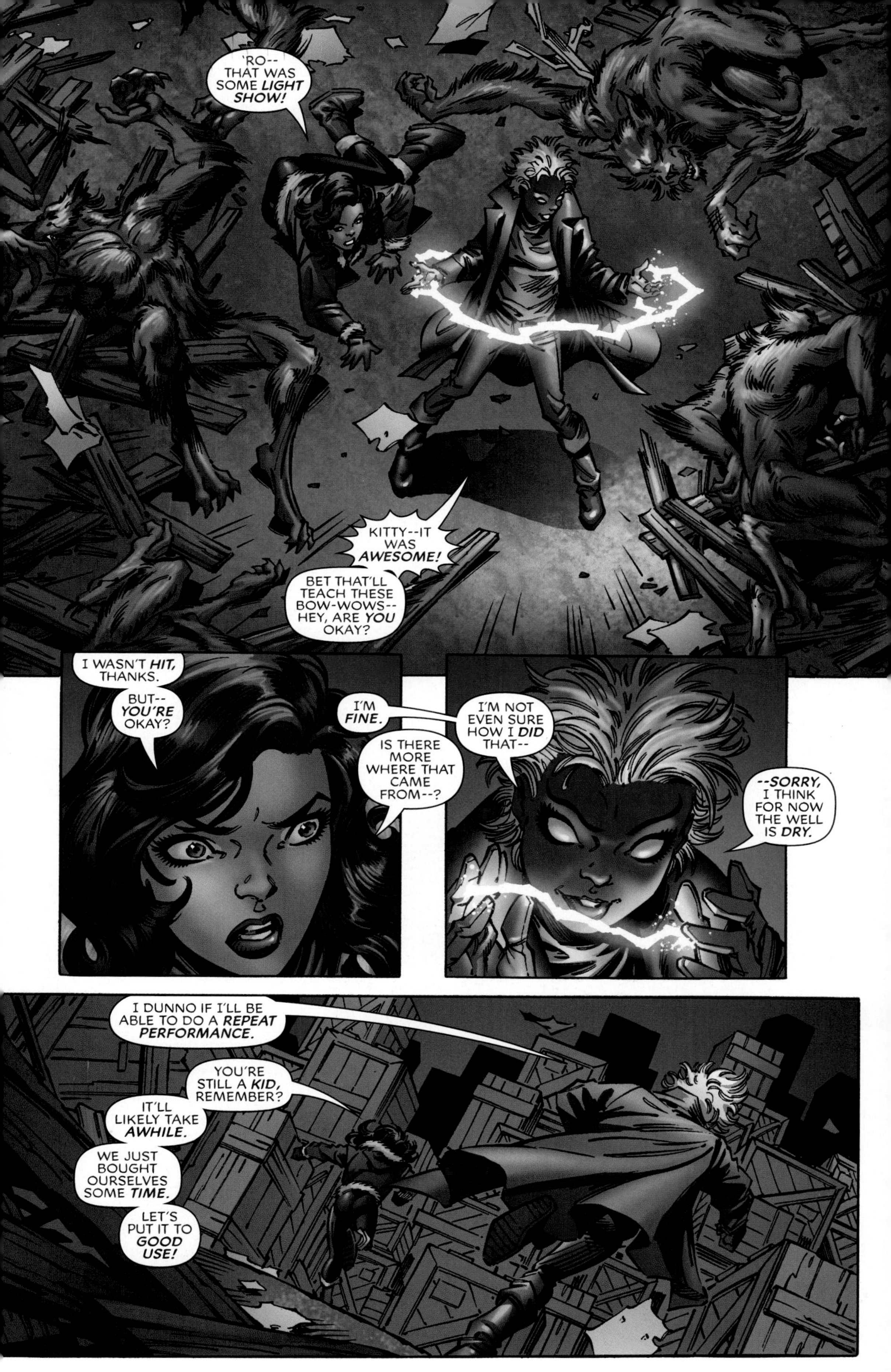
'RO-- THAT WAS SOME *LIGHT SHOW!*
KITTY--IT WAS *AWESOME!*
BET THAT'LL TEACH THESE BOW-WOWS-- HEY, ARE *YOU* OKAY?
I WASN'T *HIT,* THANKS.
BUT-- *YOU'RE* OKAY?
I'M *FINE*.
I'M NOT EVEN SURE HOW I *DID* THAT--
IS THERE MORE WHERE THAT CAME FROM--?
--SORRY, I THINK FOR NOW THE WELL IS *DRY.*
I DUNNO IF I'LL BE ABLE TO DO A *REPEAT PERFORMANCE.*
YOU'RE STILL A *KID,* REMEMBER?
IT'LL LIKELY TAKE *AWHILE.*
WE JUST BOUGHT OURSELVES SOME *TIME.*
LET'S PUT IT TO *GOOD USE!*

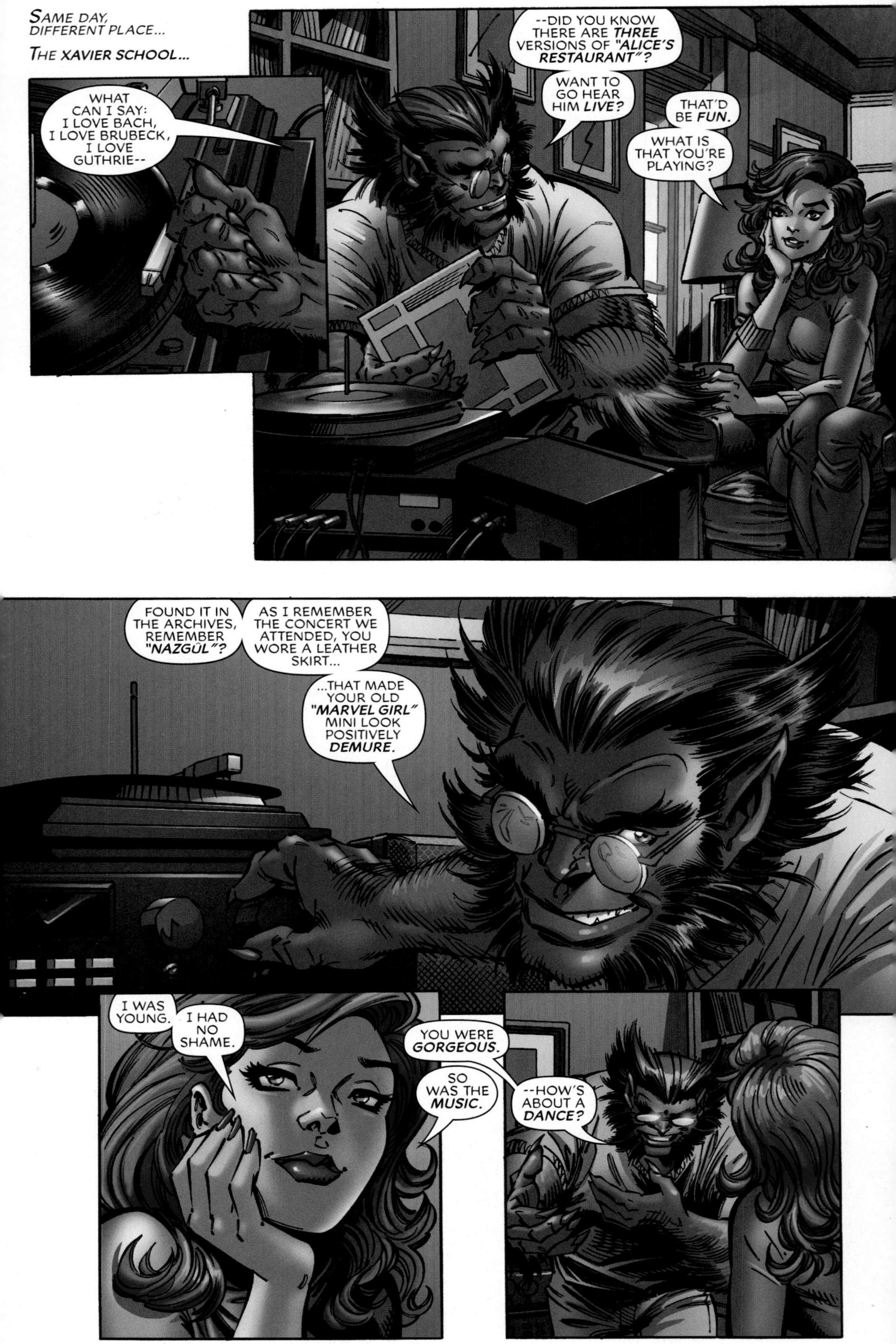
SAME DAY, DIFFERENT PLACE...
THE XAVIER SCHOOL...
WHAT CAN I SAY: I LOVE BACH, I LOVE BRUBECK, I LOVE GUTHRIE--
--DID YOU KNOW THERE ARE THREE VERSIONS OF "ALICE'S RESTAURANT"?
WANT TO GO HEAR HIM LIVE?
THAT'D BE FUN.
WHAT IS THAT YOU'RE PLAYING?
FOUND IT IN THE ARCHIVES, REMEMBER "NAZGÛL"?
AS I REMEMBER THE CONCERT WE ATTENDED, YOU WORE A LEATHER SKIRT...
...THAT MADE YOUR OLD "MARVEL GIRL" MINI LOOK POSITIVELY DEMURE.
I WAS YOUNG.
I HAD NO SHAME.
YOU WERE GORGEOUS.
SO WAS THE MUSIC.
--HOW'S ABOUT A DANCE?

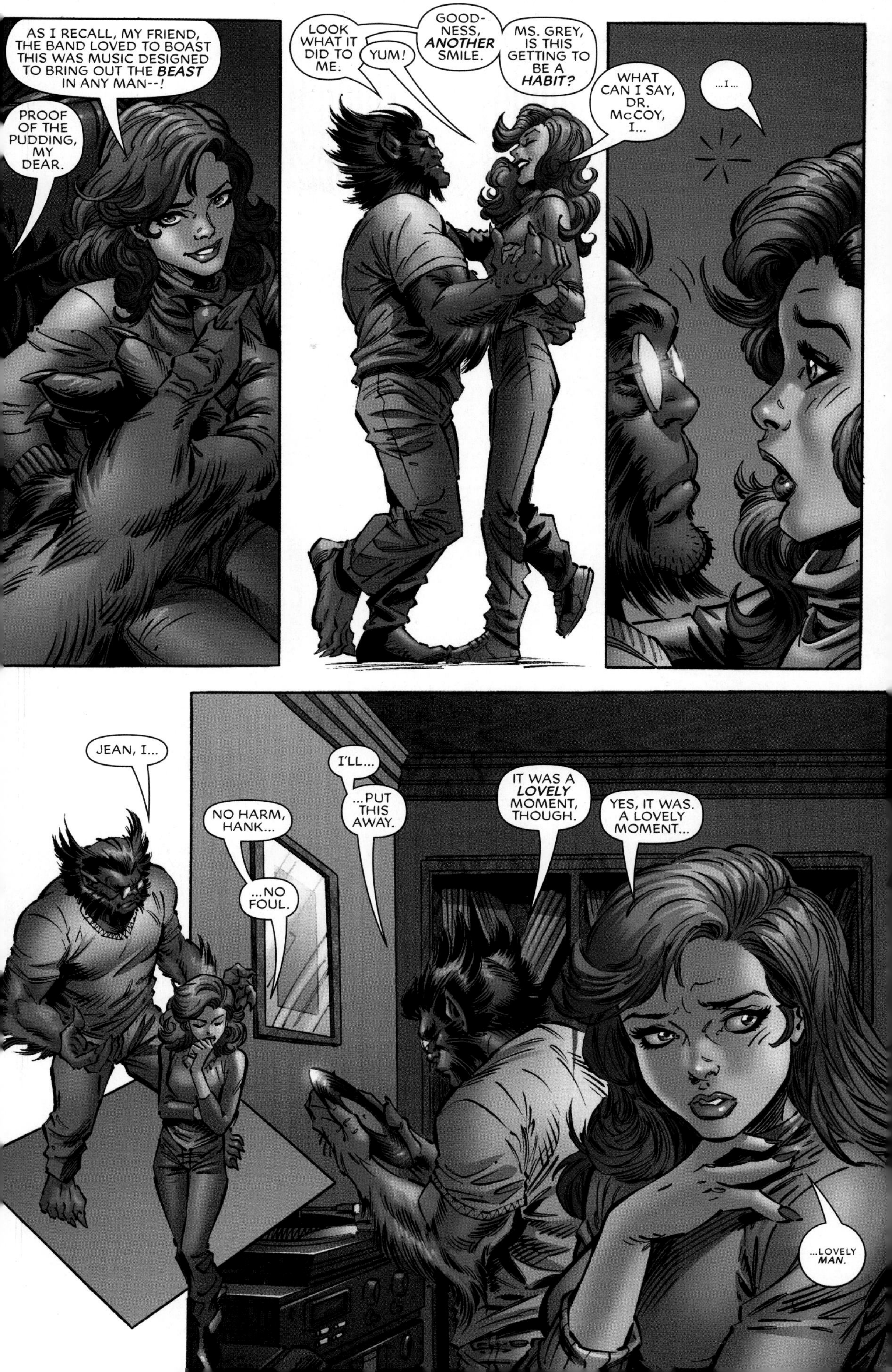
AS I RECALL, MY FRIEND, THE BAND LOVED TO BOAST THIS WAS MUSIC DESIGNED TO BRING OUT THE *BEAST* IN ANY MAN--!
PROOF OF THE PUDDING, MY DEAR.
LOOK WHAT IT DID TO ME.
GOODNESS, *ANOTHER* SMILE.
YUM!
MS. GREY, IS THIS GETTING TO BE A *HABIT?*
WHAT CAN I SAY, DR. McCOY, I...
...I...
JEAN, I...
NO HARM, HANK...
...NO FOUL.
I'LL...
...PUT THIS AWAY.
IT WAS A *LOVELY* MOMENT, THOUGH.
YES, IT WAS. A LOVELY MOMENT...
...LOVELY *MAN.*

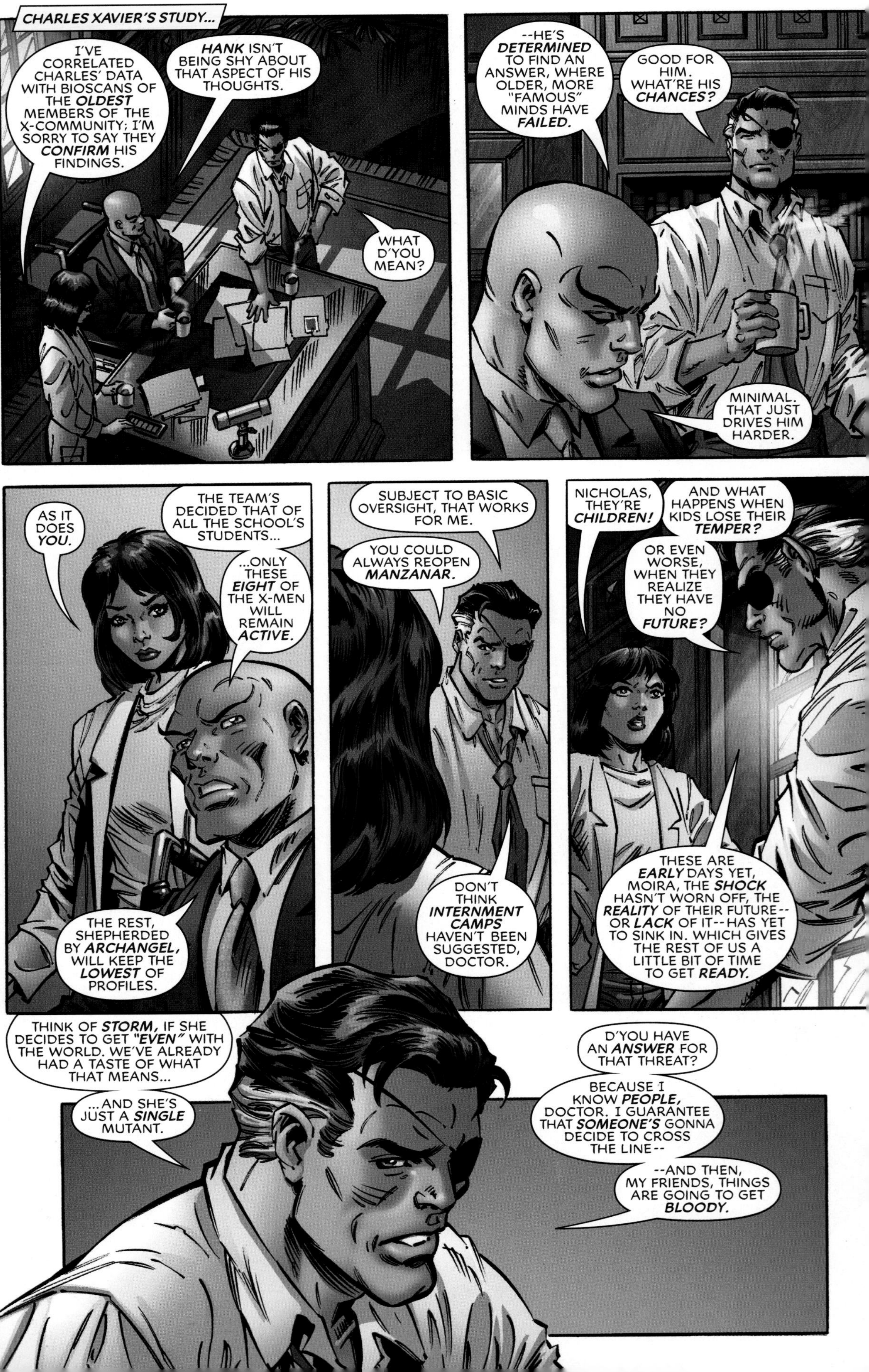
CHARLES XAVIER'S STUDY...
I'VE CORRELATED CHARLES' DATA WITH BIOSCANS OF THE OLDEST MEMBERS OF THE X-COMMUNITY; I'M SORRY TO SAY THEY CONFIRM HIS FINDINGS.
HANK ISN'T BEING SHY ABOUT THAT ASPECT OF HIS THOUGHTS.
WHAT D'YOU MEAN?
--HE'S DETERMINED TO FIND AN ANSWER, WHERE OLDER, MORE "FAMOUS" MINDS HAVE FAILED.
GOOD FOR HIM. WHAT'RE HIS CHANCES?
MINIMAL. THAT JUST DRIVES HIM HARDER.
AS IT DOES YOU.
THE TEAM'S DECIDED THAT OF ALL THE SCHOOL'S STUDENTS...
...ONLY THESE EIGHT OF THE X-MEN WILL REMAIN ACTIVE.
THE REST, SHEPHERDED BY ARCHANGEL, WILL KEEP THE LOWEST OF PROFILES.
SUBJECT TO BASIC OVERSIGHT, THAT WORKS FOR ME.
YOU COULD ALWAYS REOPEN MANZANAR.
DON'T THINK INTERNMENT CAMPS HAVEN'T BEEN SUGGESTED, DOCTOR.
NICHOLAS, THEY'RE CHILDREN!
AND WHAT HAPPENS WHEN KIDS LOSE THEIR TEMPER?
OR EVEN WORSE, WHEN THEY REALIZE THEY HAVE NO FUTURE?
THESE ARE EARLY DAYS YET, MOIRA, THE SHOCK HASN'T WORN OFF, THE REALITY OF THEIR FUTURE-- OR LACK OF IT--HAS YET TO SINK IN. WHICH GIVES THE REST OF US A LITTLE BIT OF TIME TO GET READY.
THINK OF STORM, IF SHE DECIDES TO GET "EVEN" WITH THE WORLD. WE'VE ALREADY HAD A TASTE OF WHAT THAT MEANS...
...AND SHE'S JUST A SINGLE MUTANT.
D'YOU HAVE AN ANSWER FOR THAT THREAT?
BECAUSE I KNOW PEOPLE, DOCTOR. I GUARANTEE THAT SOMEONE'S GONNA DECIDE TO CROSS THE LINE--
--AND THEN, MY FRIENDS, THINGS ARE GOING TO GET BLOODY.

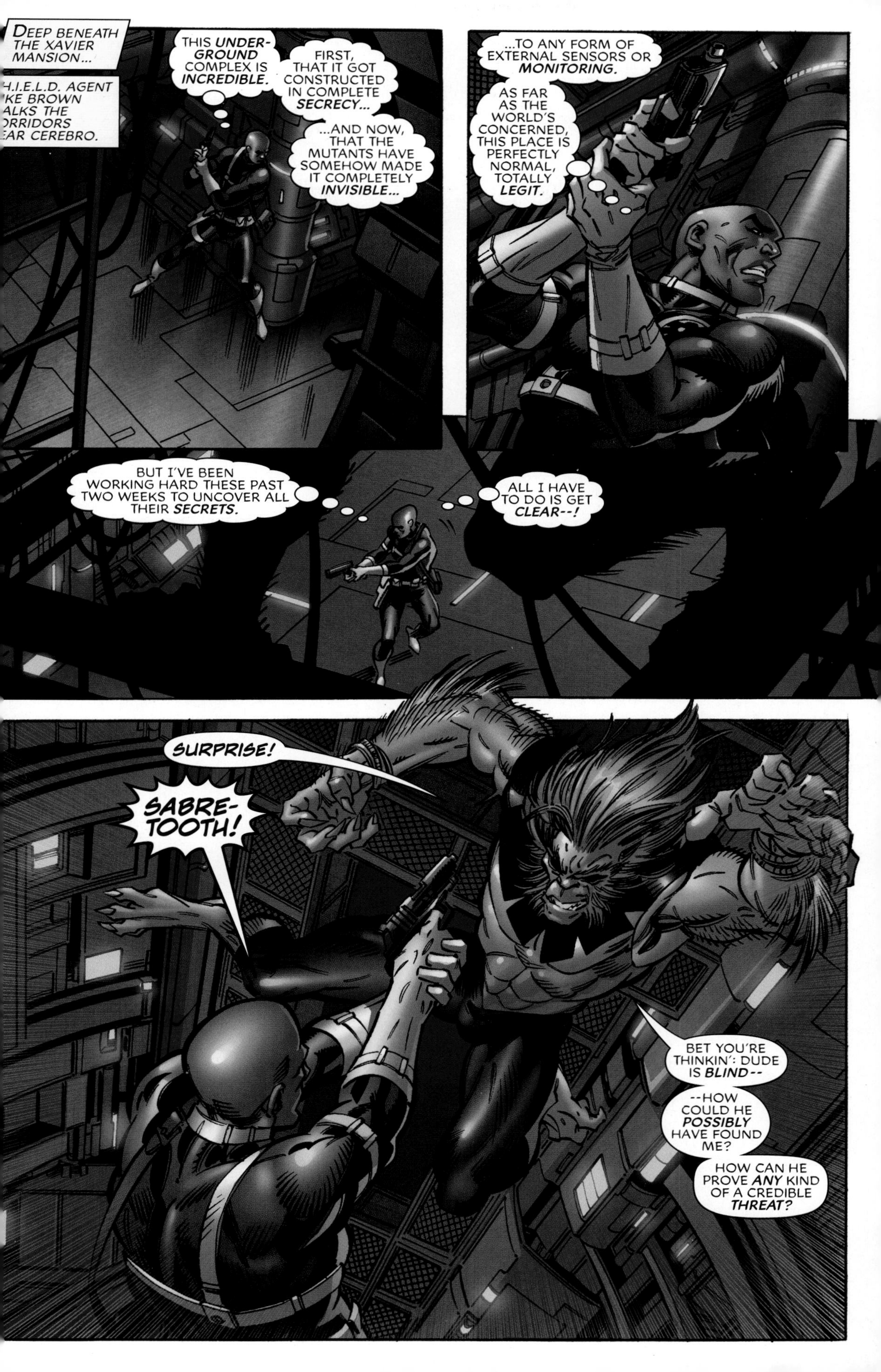
DEEP BENEATH THE XAVIER MANSION...
.H.I.E.L.D. AGENT IKE BROWN ALKS THE ORRIDORS EAR CEREBRO.
THIS UNDERGROUND COMPLEX IS INCREDIBLE.
FIRST, THAT IT GOT CONSTRUCTED IN COMPLETE SECRECY...
...AND NOW, THAT THE MUTANTS HAVE SOMEHOW MADE IT COMPLETELY INVISIBLE...
...TO ANY FORM OF EXTERNAL SENSORS OR MONITORING.
AS FAR AS THE WORLD'S CONCERNED, THIS PLACE IS PERFECTLY NORMAL, TOTALLY LEGIT.
BUT I'VE BEEN WORKING HARD THESE PAST TWO WEEKS TO UNCOVER ALL THEIR SECRETS.
ALL I HAVE TO DO IS GET CLEAR--!
SURPRISE!
SABRE-TOOTH!
BET YOU'RE THINKIN': DUDE IS BLIND--
--HOW COULD HE POSSIBLY HAVE FOUND ME?
HOW CAN HE PROVE ANY KIND OF A CREDIBLE THREAT?

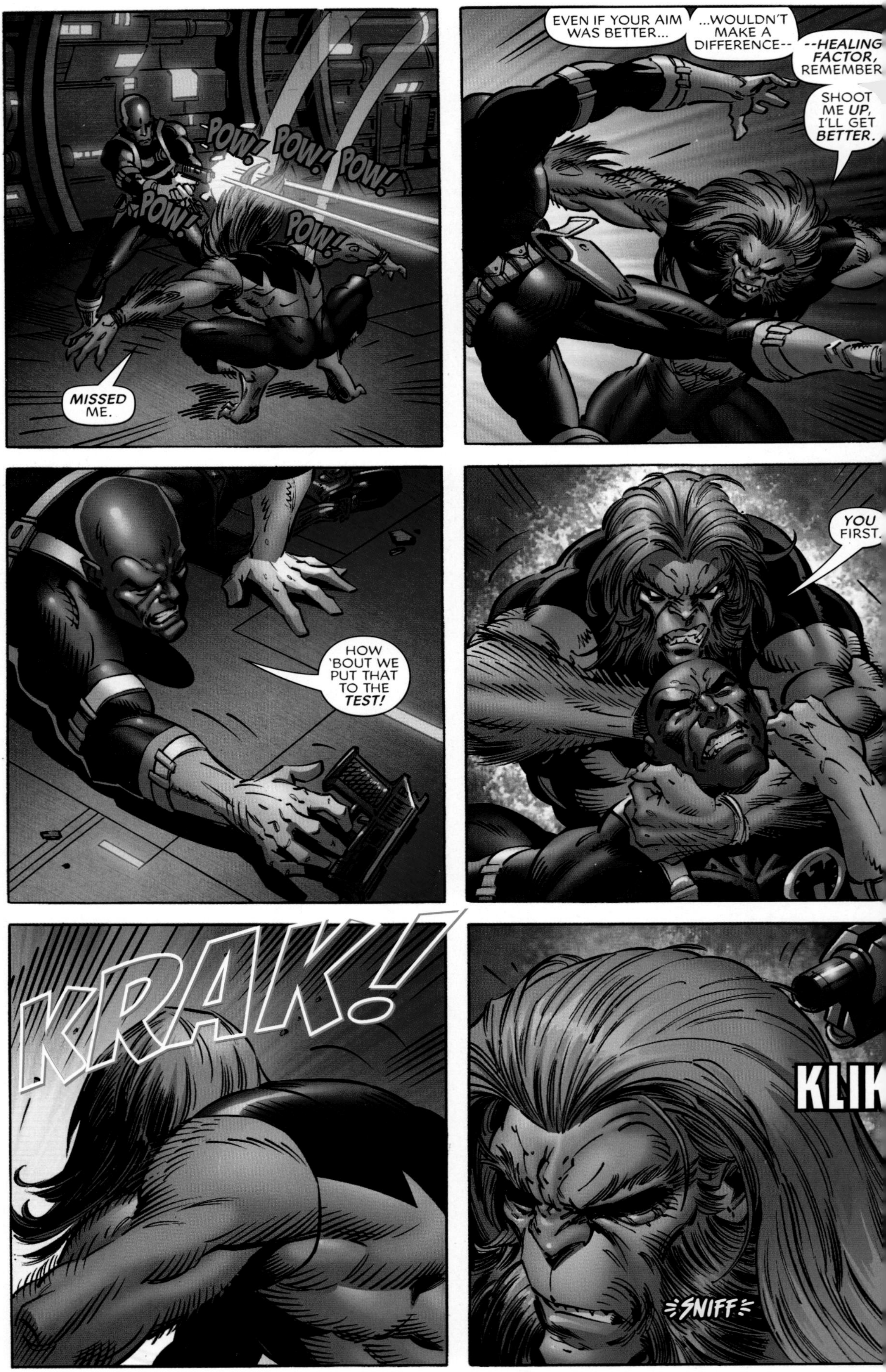
POW! POW! POW!
POW!
POW!
MISSED ME.
EVEN IF YOUR AIM WAS BETTER...
...WOULDN'T MAKE A DIFFERENCE--
--HEALING FACTOR, REMEMBER
SHOOT ME UP, I'LL GET BETTER.
HOW 'BOUT WE PUT THAT TO THE TEST!
YOU FIRST.
KRAK!
KLIK
SNIFF

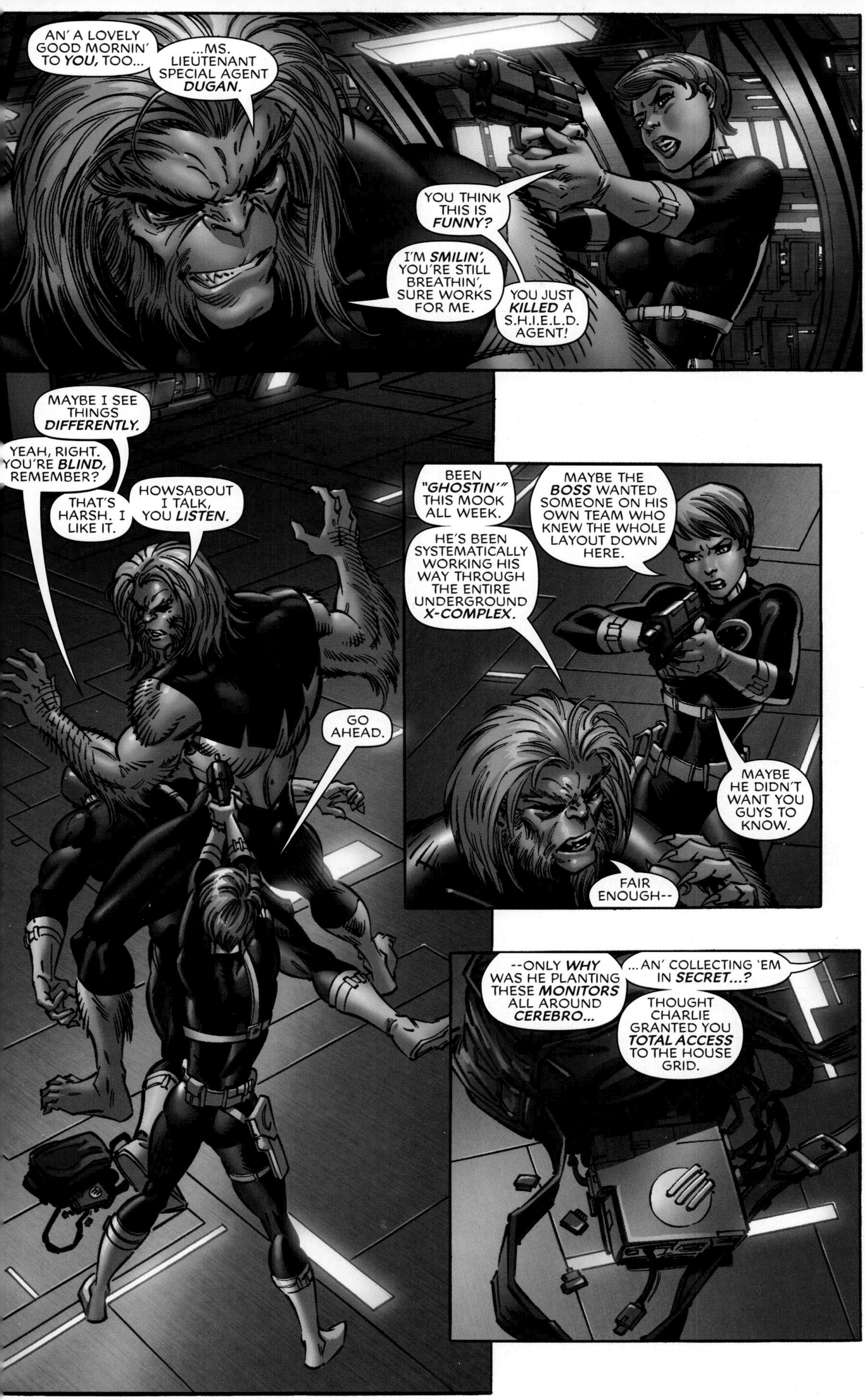
AN' A LOVELY GOOD MORNIN' TO YOU, TOO...
...MS. LIEUTENANT SPECIAL AGENT DUGAN.
YOU THINK THIS IS FUNNY?
I'M SMILIN', YOU'RE STILL BREATHIN', SURE WORKS FOR ME.
YOU JUST KILLED A S.H.I.E.L.D. AGENT!
MAYBE I SEE THINGS DIFFERENTLY.
YEAH, RIGHT. YOU'RE BLIND, REMEMBER?
THAT'S HARSH. I LIKE IT.
HOWSABOUT I TALK, YOU LISTEN.
GO AHEAD.
BEEN "GHOSTIN'" THIS MOOK ALL WEEK.
HE'S BEEN SYSTEMATICALLY WORKING HIS WAY THROUGH THE ENTIRE UNDERGROUND X-COMPLEX.
MAYBE THE BOSS WANTED SOMEONE ON HIS OWN TEAM WHO KNEW THE WHOLE LAYOUT DOWN HERE.
MAYBE HE DIDN'T WANT YOU GUYS TO KNOW.
FAIR ENOUGH--
--ONLY WHY WAS HE PLANTING THESE MONITORS ALL AROUND CEREBRO...
...AN' COLLECTING 'EM IN SECRET...?
THOUGHT CHARLIE GRANTED YOU TOTAL ACCESS TO THE HOUSE GRID.

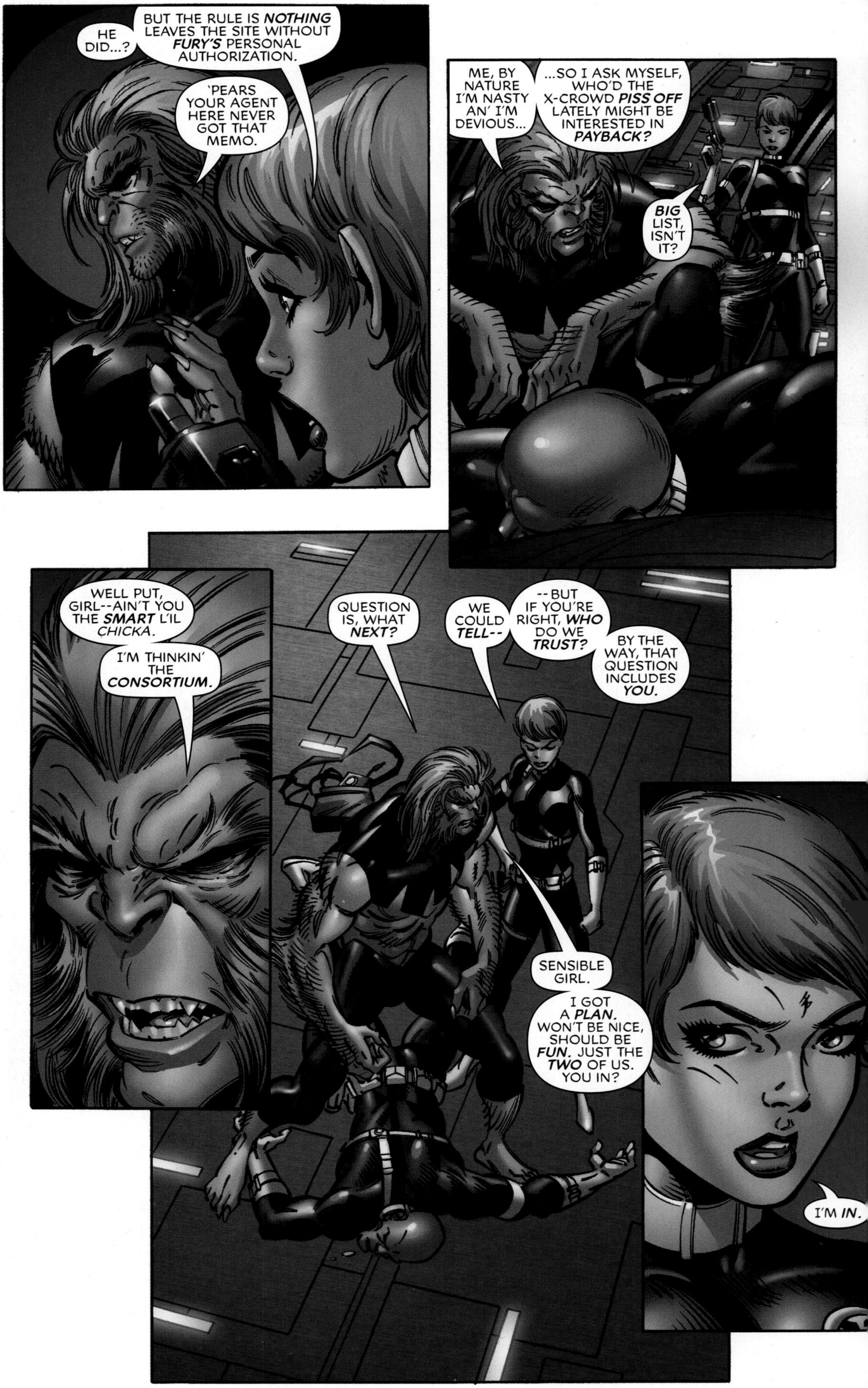
HE DID...?
BUT THE RULE IS NOTHING LEAVES THE SITE WITHOUT FURY'S PERSONAL AUTHORIZATION.
'PEARS YOUR AGENT HERE NEVER GOT THAT MEMO.
ME, BY NATURE I'M NASTY AN' I'M DEVIOUS...
...SO I ASK MYSELF, WHO'D THE X-CROWD PISS OFF LATELY MIGHT BE INTERESTED IN PAYBACK?
BIG LIST, ISN'T IT?
WELL PUT, GIRL--AIN'T YOU THE SMART L'IL CHICKA.
I'M THINKIN' THE CONSORTIUM.
QUESTION IS, WHAT NEXT?
WE COULD TELL--
--BUT IF YOU'RE RIGHT, WHO DO WE TRUST?
BY THE WAY, THAT QUESTION INCLUDES YOU.
SENSIBLE GIRL.
I GOT A PLAN. WON'T BE NICE, SHOULD BE FUN. JUST THE TWO OF US. YOU IN?
I'M IN.

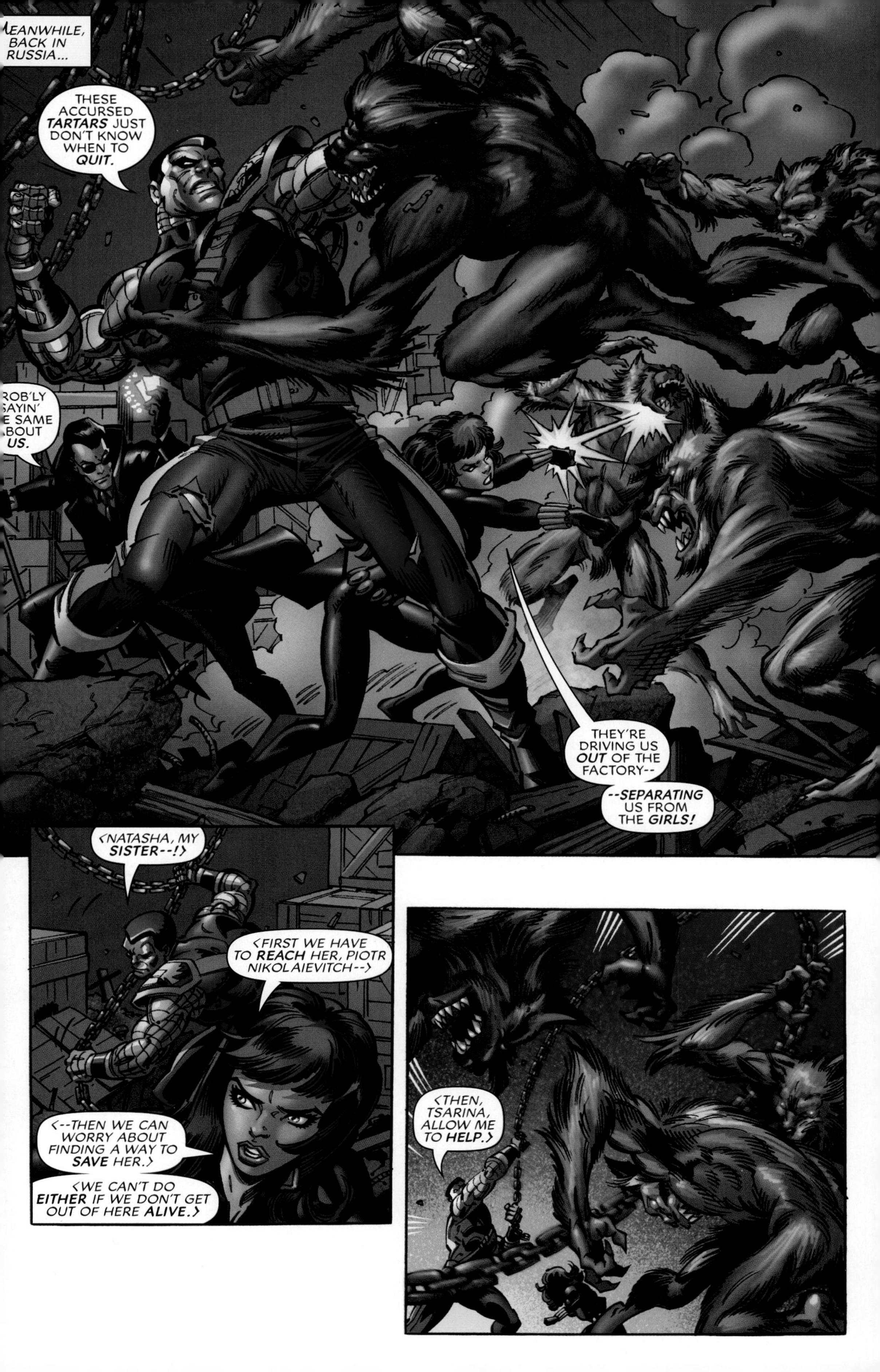

MEANWHILE, BACK IN RUSSIA...
THESE ACCURSED TARTARS JUST DON'T KNOW WHEN TO QUIT.
ROB'LY SAYIN' E SAME ABOUT US.
THEY'RE DRIVING US OUT OF THE FACTORY--
--SEPARATING US FROM THE GIRLS!
<NATASHA, MY SISTER--!>
<FIRST WE HAVE TO REACH HER, PIOTR NIKOLAIEVITCH-->
<--THEN WE CAN WORRY ABOUT FINDING A WAY TO SAVE HER.>
<WE CAN'T DO EITHER IF WE DON'T GET OUT OF HERE ALIVE.>
<THEN, TSARINA, ALLOW ME TO HELP.>

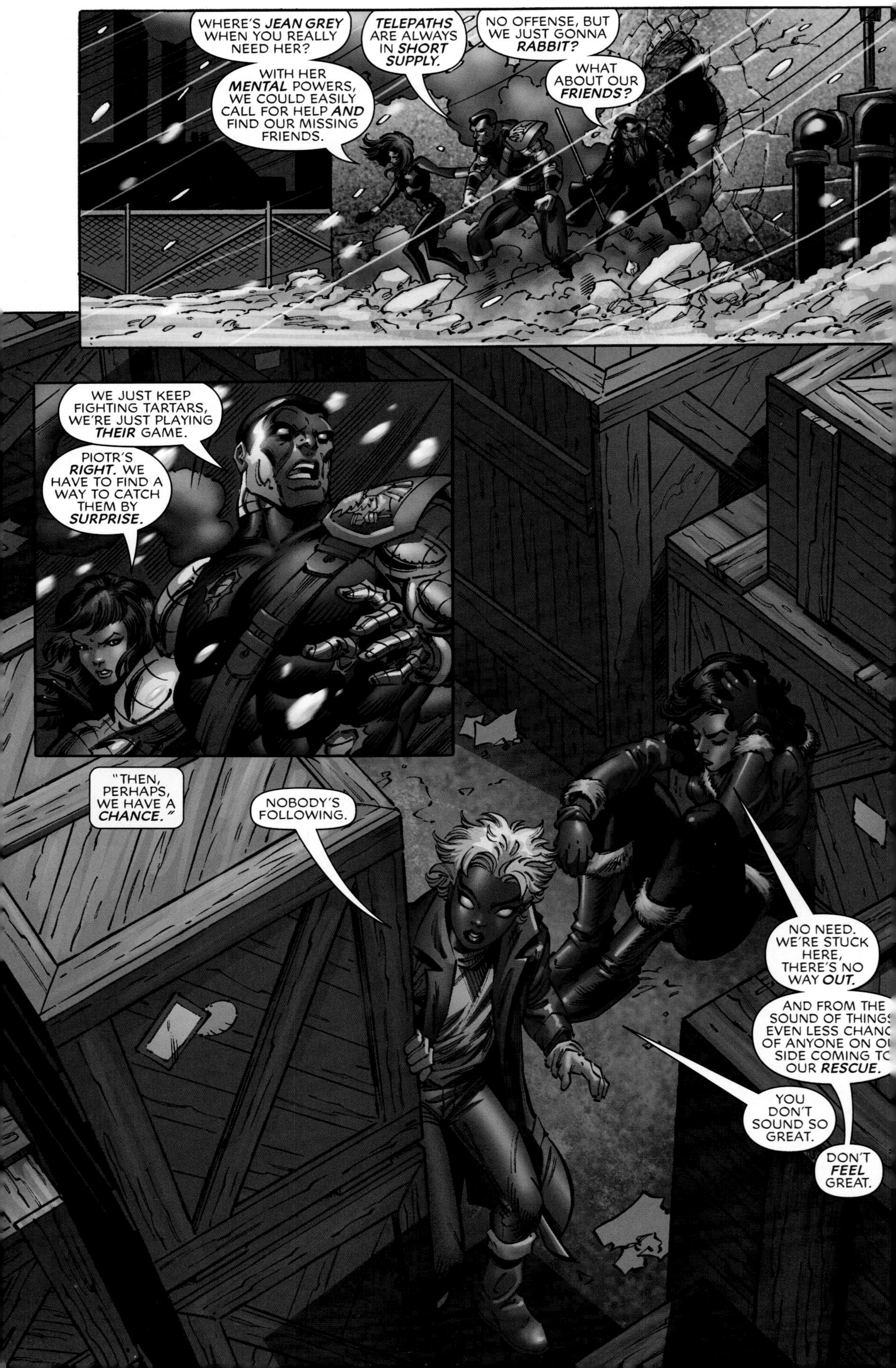
WHERE'S JEAN GREY WHEN YOU REALLY NEED HER?
WITH HER MENTAL POWERS, WE COULD EASILY CALL FOR HELP AND FIND OUR MISSING FRIENDS.
TELEPATHS ARE ALWAYS IN SHORT SUPPLY.
NO OFFENSE, BUT WE JUST GONNA RABBIT?
WHAT ABOUT OUR FRIENDS?
WE JUST KEEP FIGHTING TARTARS, WE'RE JUST PLAYING THEIR GAME.
PIOTR'S RIGHT. WE HAVE TO FIND A WAY TO CATCH THEM BY SURPRISE.
"THEN, PERHAPS, WE HAVE A CHANCE."
NOBODY'S FOLLOWING.
NO NEED. WE'RE STUCK HERE, THERE'S NO WAY OUT.
YOU DON'T SOUND SO GREAT.
DON'T FEEL GREAT.

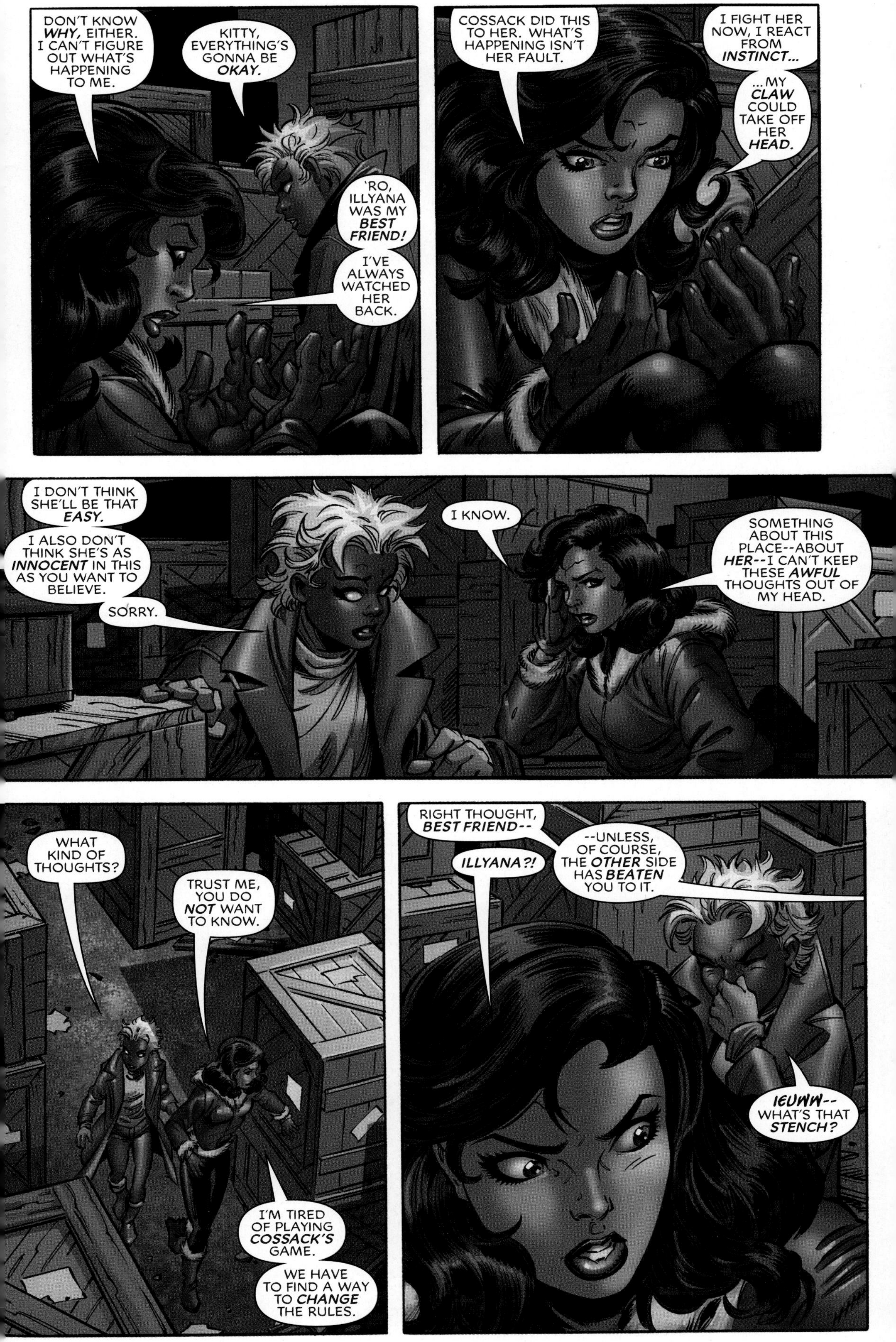
DON'T KNOW *WHY*, EITHER. I CAN'T FIGURE OUT WHAT'S HAPPENING TO ME.
KITTY, EVERYTHING'S GONNA BE *OKAY.*
'RO, ILLYANA WAS MY *BEST FRIEND!*
I'VE ALWAYS WATCHED HER BACK.
COSSACK DID THIS TO HER. WHAT'S HAPPENING ISN'T HER FAULT.
I FIGHT HER NOW, I REACT FROM *INSTINCT...*
...MY *CLAW* COULD TAKE OFF HER *HEAD.*
I DON'T THINK SHE'LL BE THAT *EASY.*
I ALSO DON'T THINK SHE'S AS *INNOCENT* IN THIS AS YOU WANT TO BELIEVE.
SORRY.
I KNOW.
SOMETHING ABOUT THIS PLACE--ABOUT *HER--*I CAN'T KEEP THESE *AWFUL* THOUGHTS OUT OF MY HEAD.
WHAT KIND OF THOUGHTS?
TRUST ME, YOU DO *NOT* WANT TO KNOW.
I'M TIRED OF PLAYING *COSSACK'S* GAME.
WE HAVE TO FIND A WAY TO *CHANGE* THE RULES.
RIGHT THOUGHT, *BEST FRIEND--*
--UNLESS, OF COURSE, THE *OTHER* SIDE HAS *BEATEN* YOU TO IT.
ILLYANA?!
IEUWW-- WHAT'S THAT *STENCH?*

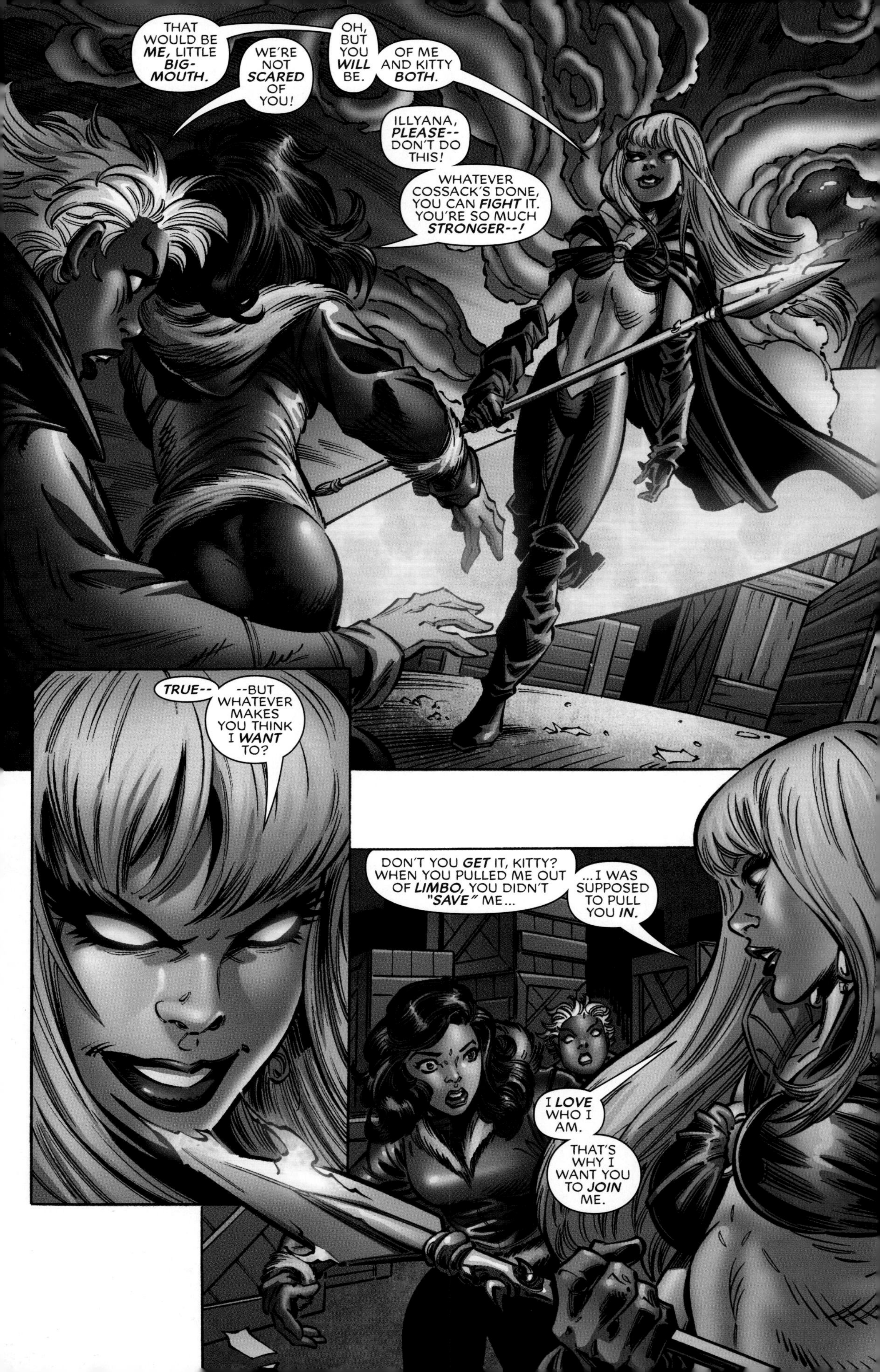

THAT WOULD BE ME, LITTLE BIG-MOUTH.
WE'RE NOT SCARED OF YOU!
OH, BUT YOU WILL BE.
OF ME AND KITTY BOTH.
ILLYANA, PLEASE-- DON'T DO THIS!
WHATEVER COSSACK'S DONE, YOU CAN FIGHT IT. YOU'RE SO MUCH STRONGER--!
TRUE--
--BUT WHATEVER MAKES YOU THINK I WANT TO?
DON'T YOU GET IT, KITTY? WHEN YOU PULLED ME OUT OF LIMBO, YOU DIDN'T "SAVE" ME...
...I WAS SUPPOSED TO PULL YOU IN.
I LOVE WHO I AM.
THAT'S WHY I WANT YOU TO JOIN ME.

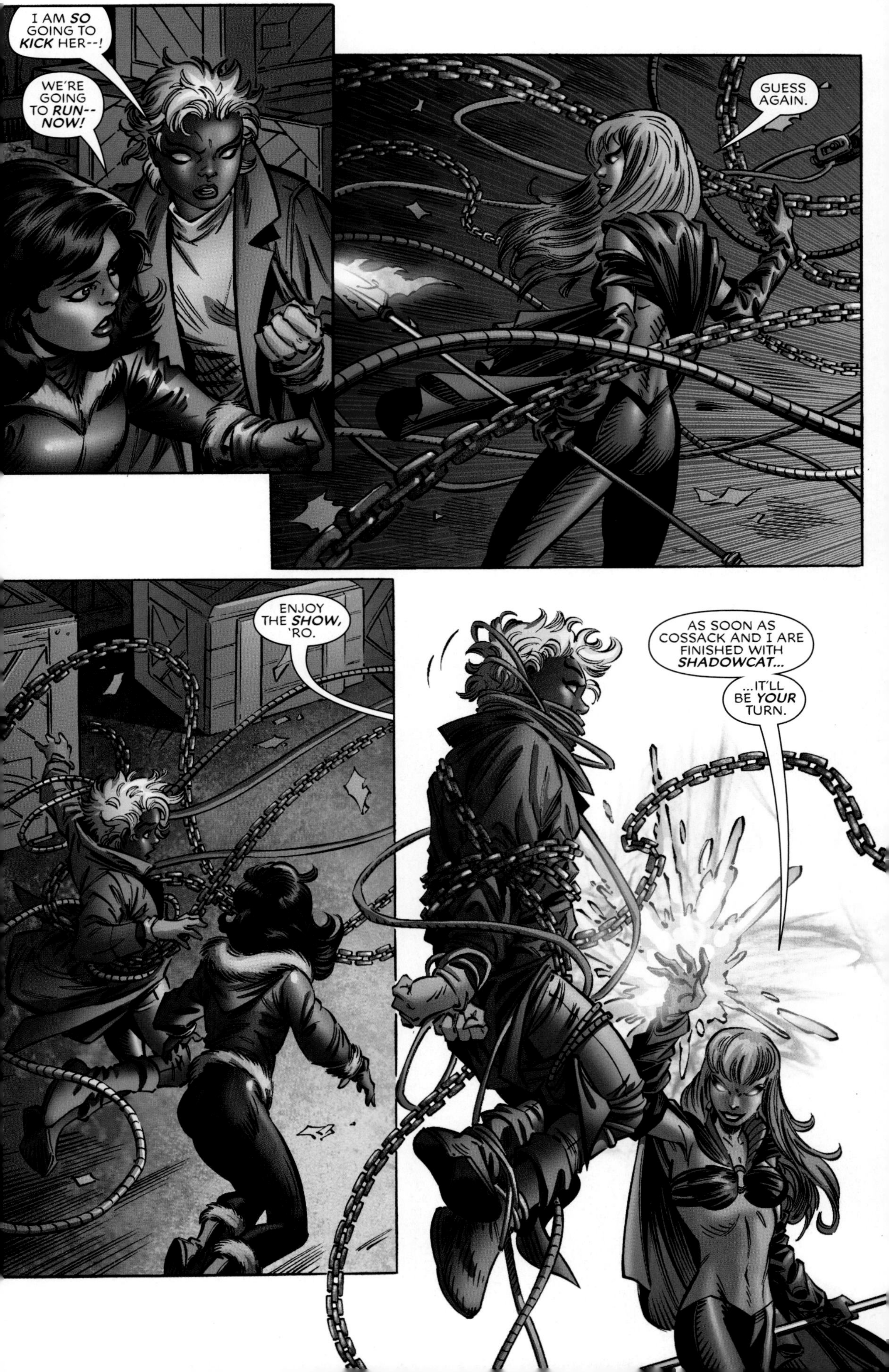
I AM SO GOING TO KICK HER--!
WE'RE GOING TO RUN-- NOW!
GUESS AGAIN.
ENJOY THE SHOW, 'RO.
AS SOON AS COSSACK AND I ARE FINISHED WITH SHADOWCAT...
...IT'LL BE YOUR TURN.

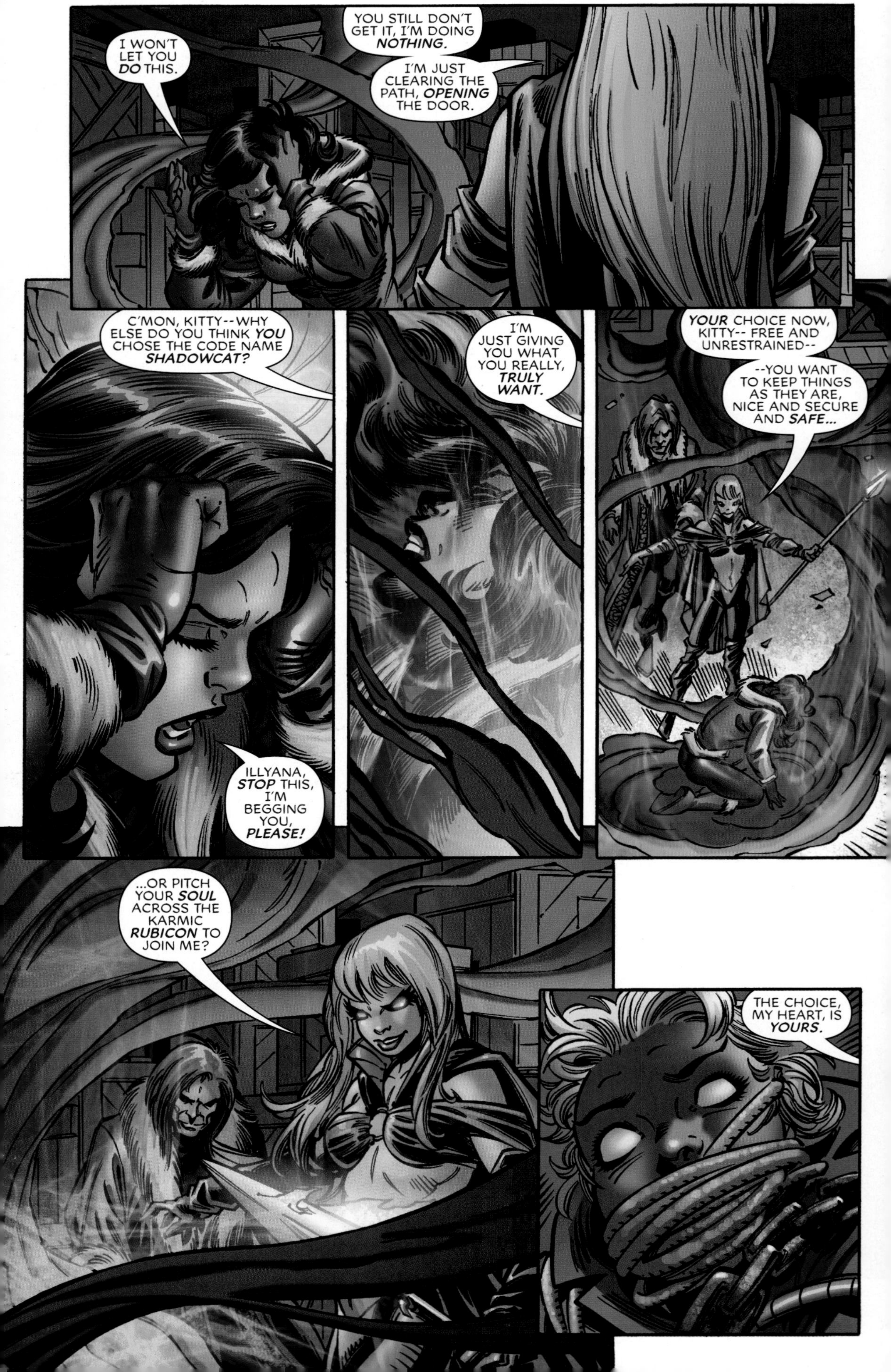
I WON'T LET YOU DO THIS.
YOU STILL DON'T GET IT, I'M DOING NOTHING.
I'M JUST CLEARING THE PATH, OPENING THE DOOR.
C'MON, KITTY--WHY ELSE DO YOU THINK YOU CHOSE THE CODE NAME SHADOWCAT?
ILLYANA, STOP THIS, I'M BEGGING YOU, PLEASE!
I'M JUST GIVING YOU WHAT YOU REALLY, TRULY WANT.
YOUR CHOICE NOW, KITTY-- FREE AND UNRESTRAINED--
--YOU WANT TO KEEP THINGS AS THEY ARE, NICE AND SECURE AND SAFE...
...OR PITCH YOUR SOUL ACROSS THE KARMIC RUBICON TO JOIN ME?
THE CHOICE, MY HEART, IS YOURS.

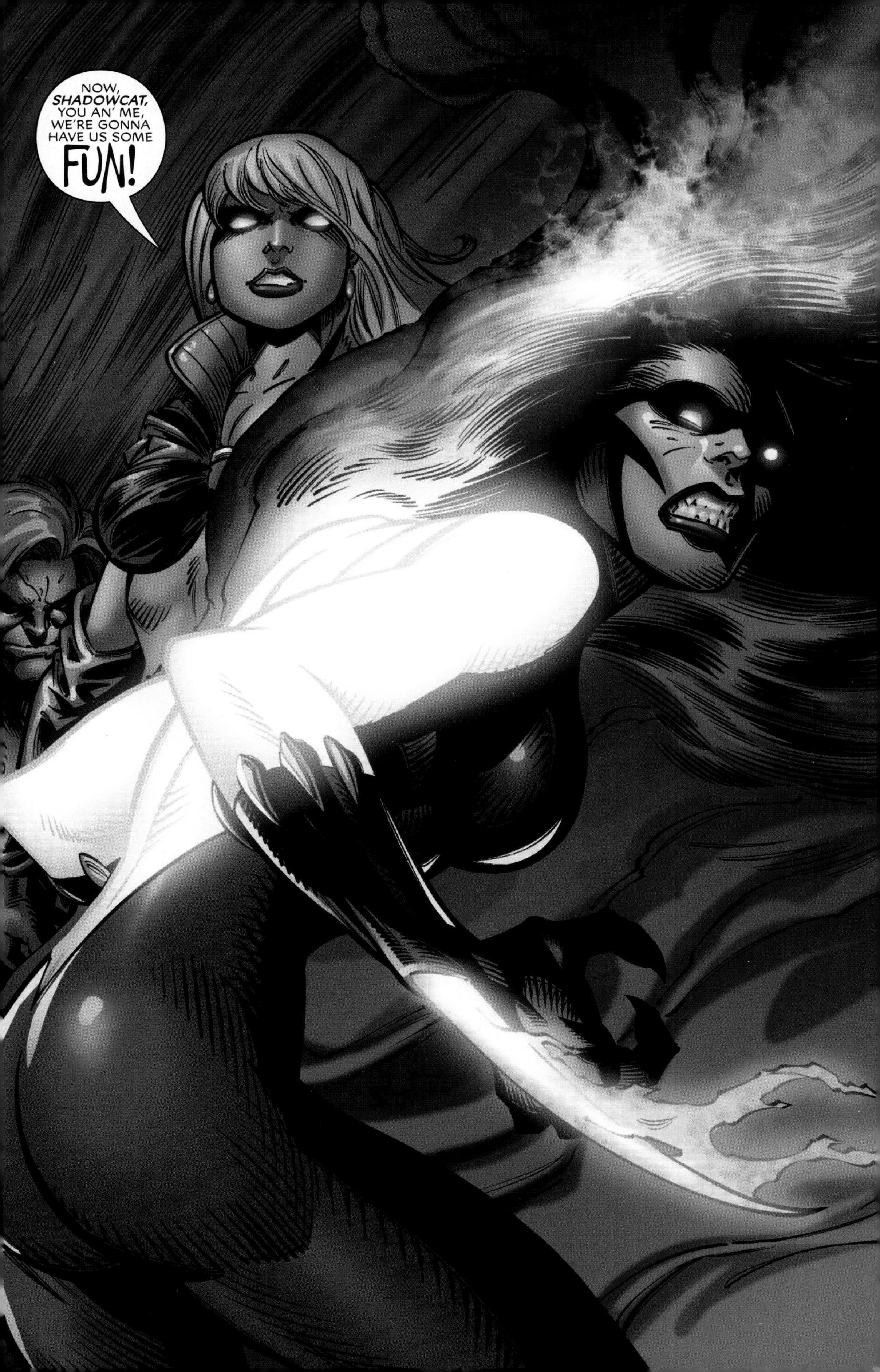
NOW, SHADOWCAT, YOU AN' ME, WE'RE GONNA HAVE US SOME FUN!

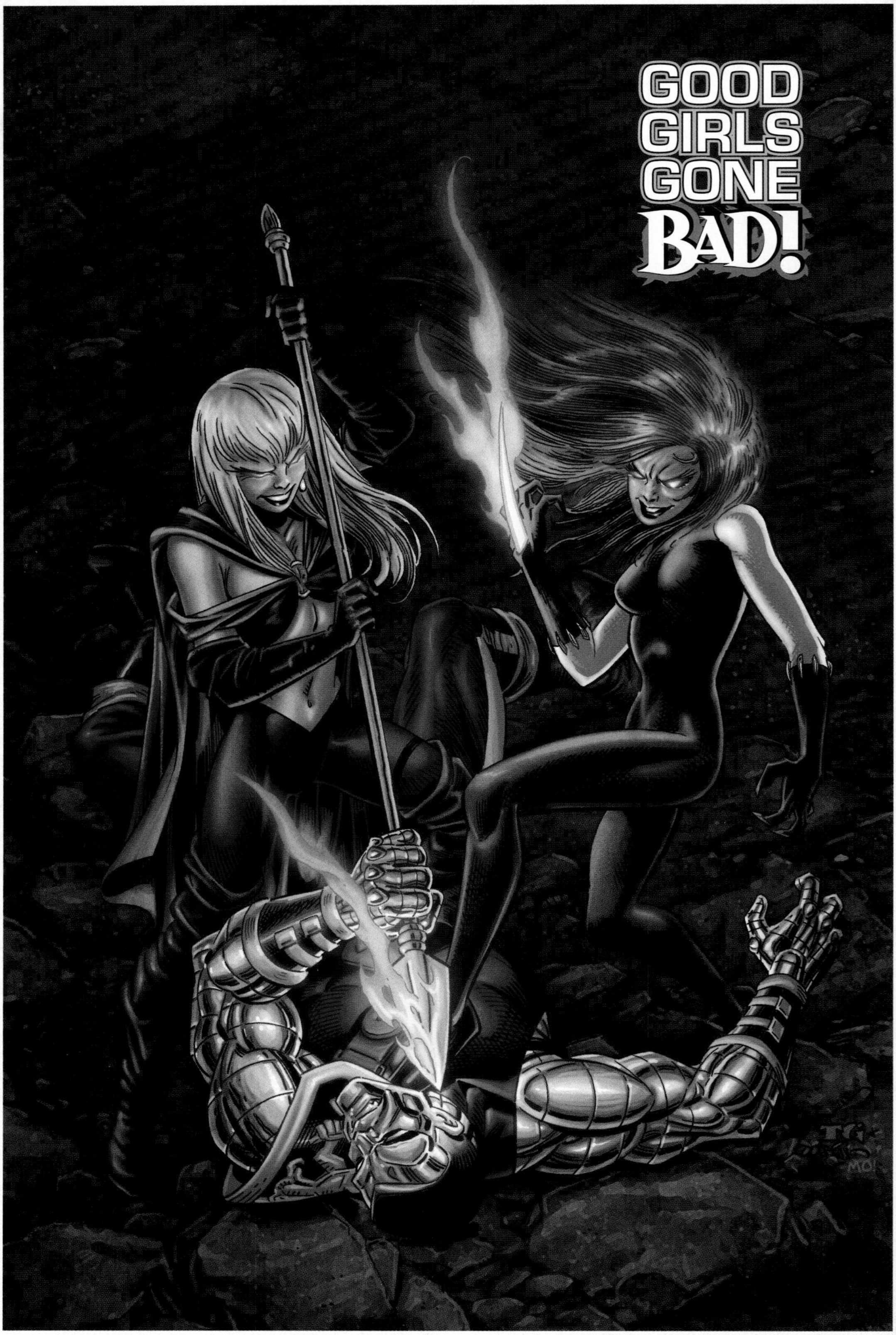
GOOD GIRLS GONE BAD!

FOURTEEN

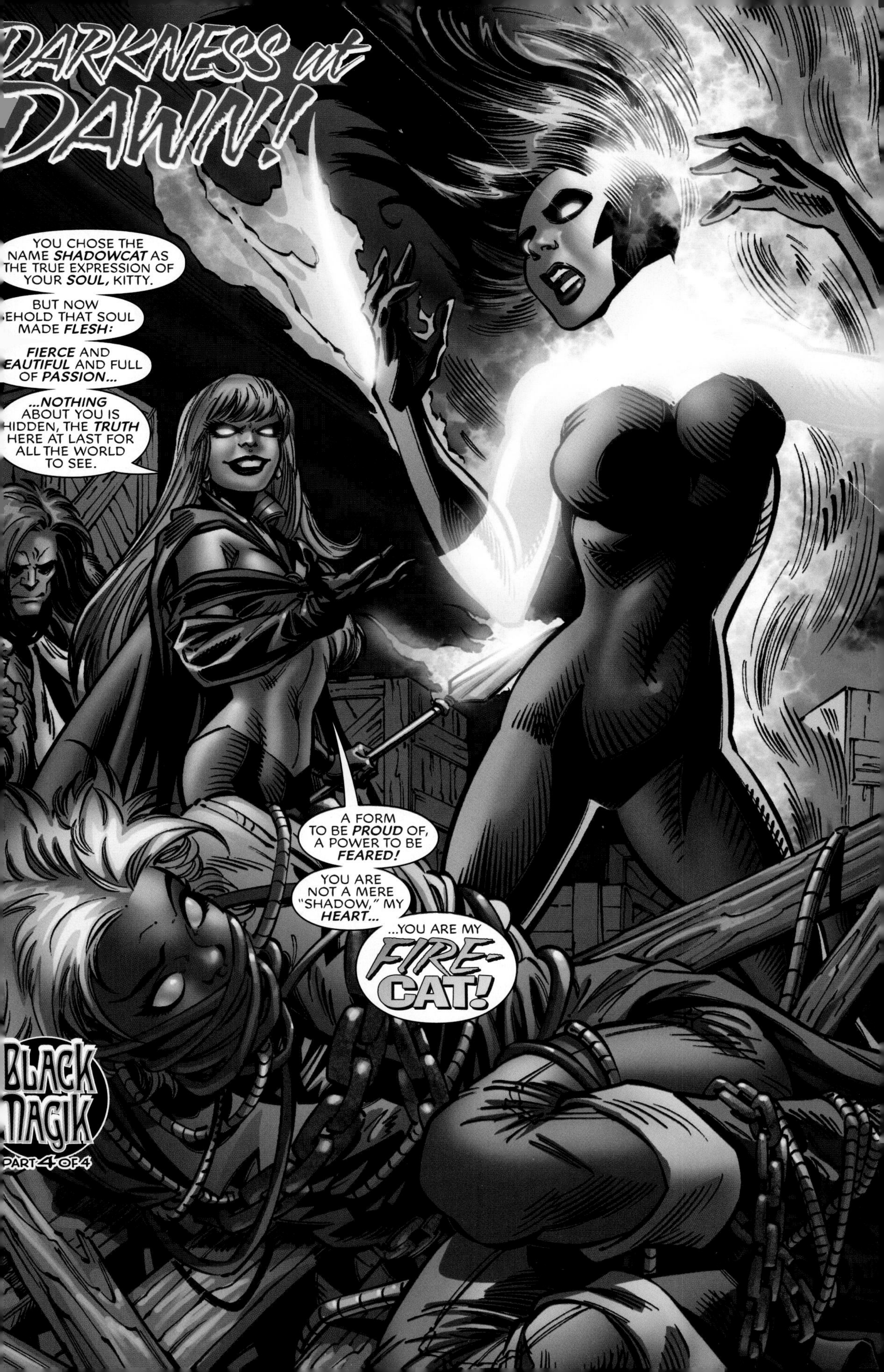
DARKNESS at DAWN!
YOU CHOSE THE NAME SHADOWCAT AS THE TRUE EXPRESSION OF YOUR SOUL, KITTY.
BUT NOW EHOLD THAT SOUL MADE FLESH:
FIERCE AND EAUTIFUL AND FULL OF PASSION...
...NOTHING ABOUT YOU IS HIDDEN, THE TRUTH HERE AT LAST FOR ALL THE WORLD TO SEE.
A FORM TO BE PROUD OF, A POWER TO BE FEARED!
YOU ARE NOT A MERE "SHADOW," MY HEART...
...YOU ARE MY FIRE-CAT!
BLACK MAGIK
PART 4 OF 4

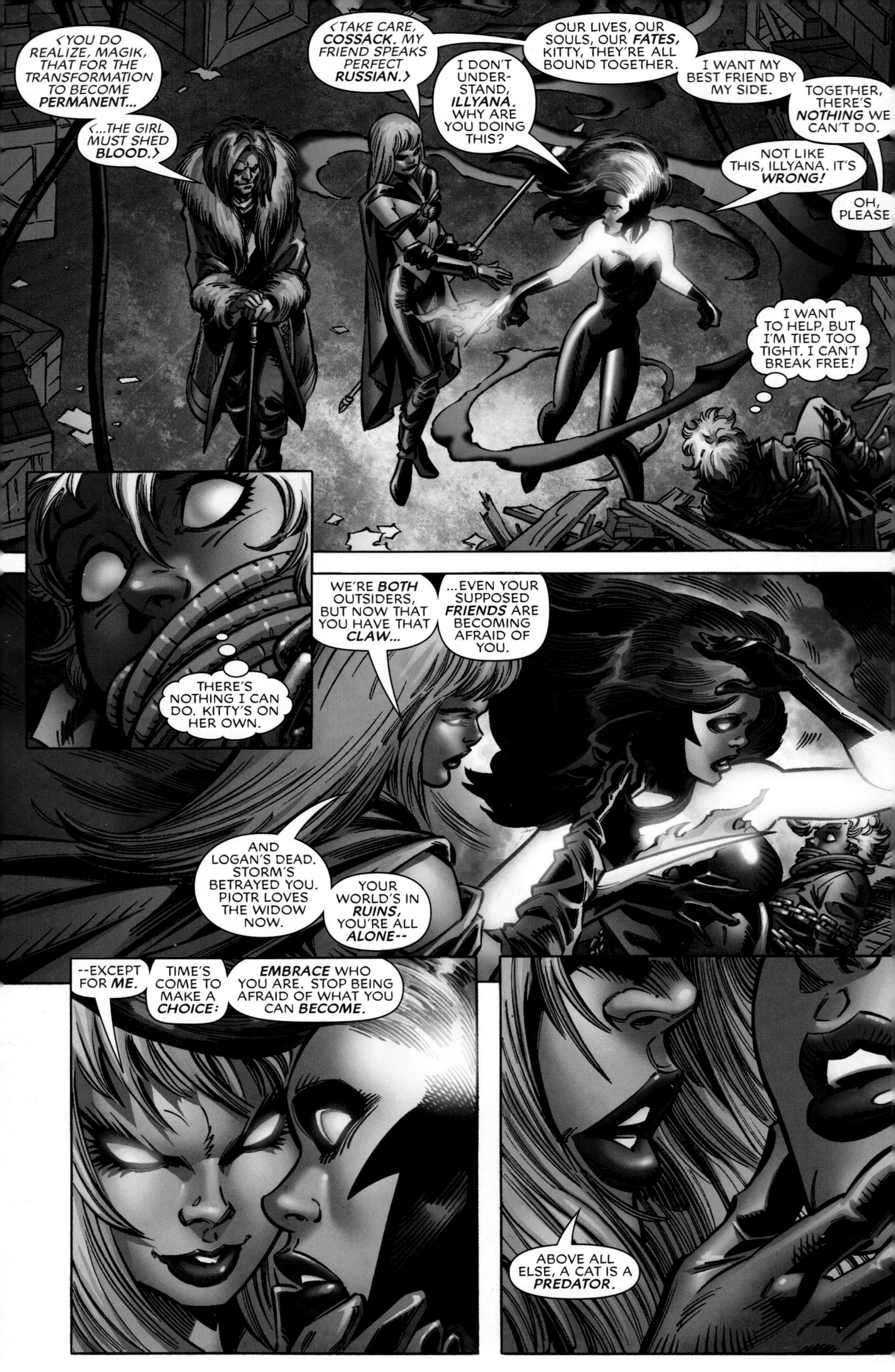

‹YOU DO REALIZE, MAGIK, THAT FOR THE TRANSFORMATION TO BECOME PERMANENT...
‹...THE GIRL MUST SHED BLOOD.›
‹TAKE CARE, COSSACK. MY FRIEND SPEAKS PERFECT RUSSIAN.›
I DON'T UNDER-STAND, ILLYANA. WHY ARE YOU DOING THIS?
OUR LIVES, OUR SOULS, OUR FATES, KITTY, THEY'RE ALL BOUND TOGETHER.
I WANT MY BEST FRIEND BY MY SIDE.
TOGETHER, THERE'S NOTHING WE CAN'T DO.
NOT LIKE THIS, ILLYANA. IT'S WRONG!
OH, PLEASE
I WANT TO HELP, BUT I'M TIED TOO TIGHT. I CAN'T BREAK FREE!
THERE'S NOTHING I CAN DO. KITTY'S ON HER OWN.
WE'RE BOTH OUTSIDERS, BUT NOW THAT YOU HAVE THAT CLAW...
...EVEN YOUR SUPPOSED FRIENDS ARE BECOMING AFRAID OF YOU.
AND LOGAN'S DEAD. STORM'S BETRAYED YOU. PIOTR LOVES THE WIDOW NOW.
YOUR WORLD'S IN RUINS, YOU'RE ALL ALONE--
--EXCEPT FOR ME.
TIME'S COME TO MAKE A CHOICE:
EMBRACE WHO YOU ARE. STOP BEING AFRAID OF WHAT YOU CAN BECOME.
ABOVE ALL ELSE, A CAT IS A PREDATOR.

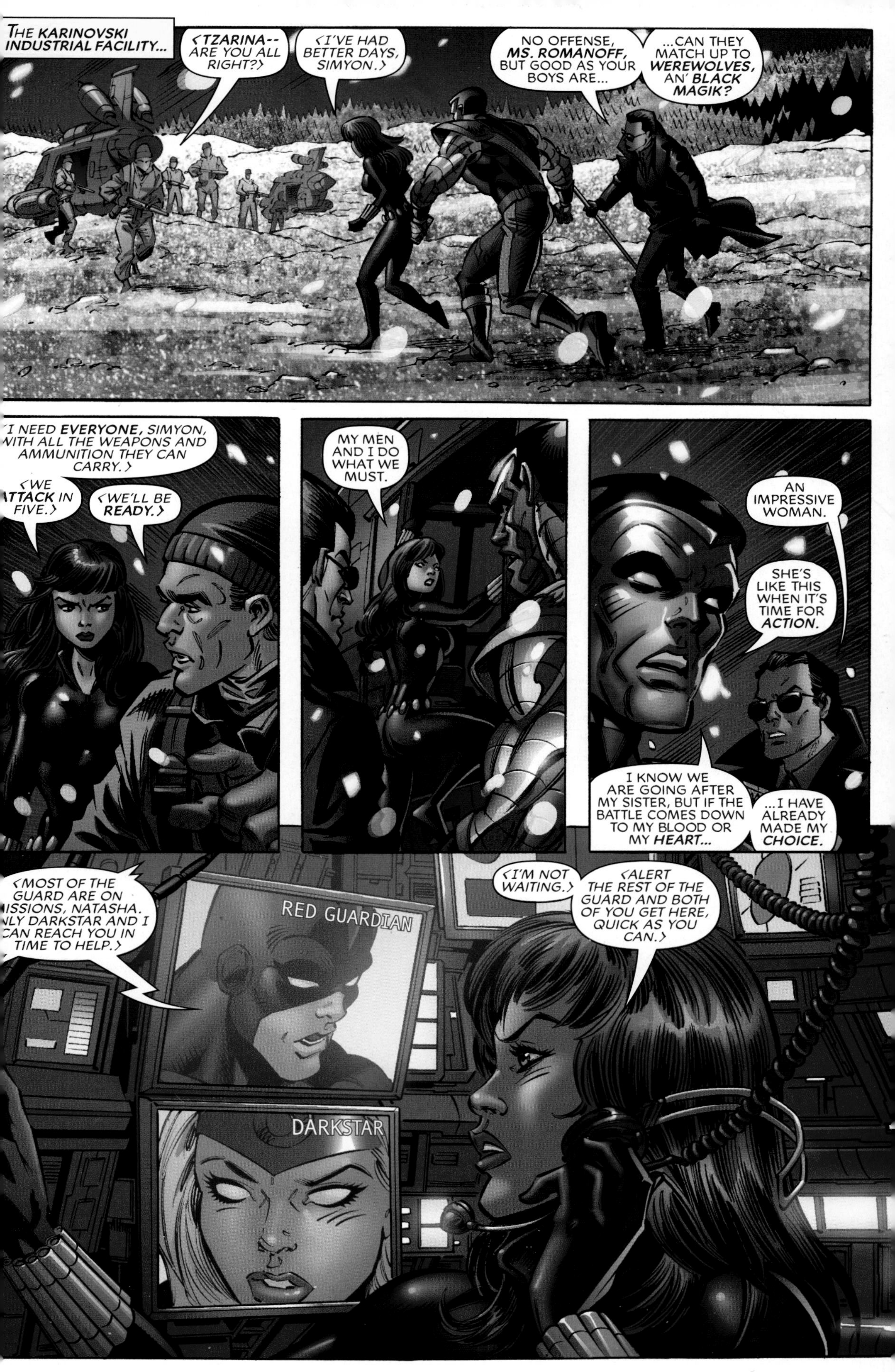
THE KARINOVSKI INDUSTRIAL FACILITY...
<TZARINA-- ARE YOU ALL RIGHT?>
<I'VE HAD BETTER DAYS, SIMYON.>
NO OFFENSE, MS. ROMANOFF, BUT GOOD AS YOUR BOYS ARE...
...CAN THEY MATCH UP TO WEREWOLVES, AN' BLACK MAGIK?
<I NEED EVERYONE, SIMYON, WITH ALL THE WEAPONS AND AMMUNITION THEY CAN CARRY.>
<WE ATTACK IN FIVE.>
<WE'LL BE READY.>
MY MEN AND I DO WHAT WE MUST.
AN IMPRESSIVE WOMAN.
SHE'S LIKE THIS WHEN IT'S TIME FOR ACTION.
I KNOW WE ARE GOING AFTER MY SISTER, BUT IF THE BATTLE COMES DOWN TO MY BLOOD OR MY HEART...
...I HAVE ALREADY MADE MY CHOICE.
<MOST OF THE GUARD ARE ON MISSIONS, NATASHA. ONLY DARKSTAR AND I CAN REACH YOU IN TIME TO HELP.>
RED GUARDIAN
DARKSTAR
<I'M NOT WAITING.>
<ALERT THE REST OF THE GUARD AND BOTH OF YOU GET HERE, QUICK AS YOU CAN.>

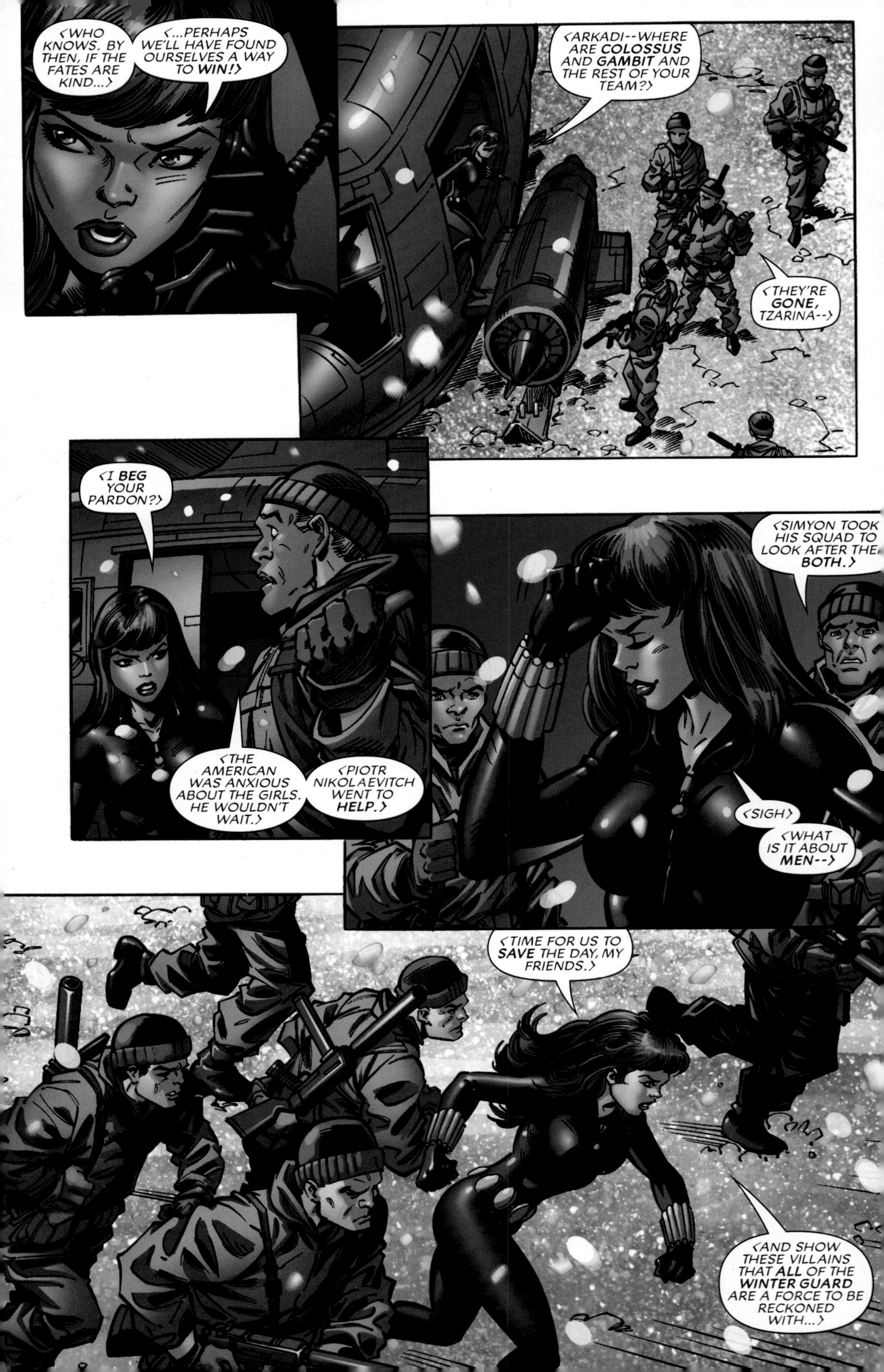
‹WHO KNOWS. BY THEN, IF THE FATES ARE KIND...›
‹...PERHAPS WE'LL HAVE FOUND OURSELVES A WAY TO WIN!›
‹ARKADI--WHERE ARE COLOSSUS AND GAMBIT AND THE REST OF YOUR TEAM?›
‹THEY'RE GONE, TZARINA--›
‹I BEG YOUR PARDON?›
‹THE AMERICAN WAS ANXIOUS ABOUT THE GIRLS. HE WOULDN'T WAIT.›
‹PIOTR NIKOLAEVITCH WENT TO HELP.›
‹SIMYON TOOK HIS SQUAD TO LOOK AFTER THEM BOTH.›
‹SIGH›
‹WHAT IS IT ABOUT MEN--›
‹TIME FOR US TO SAVE THE DAY, MY FRIENDS.›
‹AND SHOW THESE VILLAINS THAT ALL OF THE WINTER GUARD ARE A FORCE TO BE RECKONED WITH...›

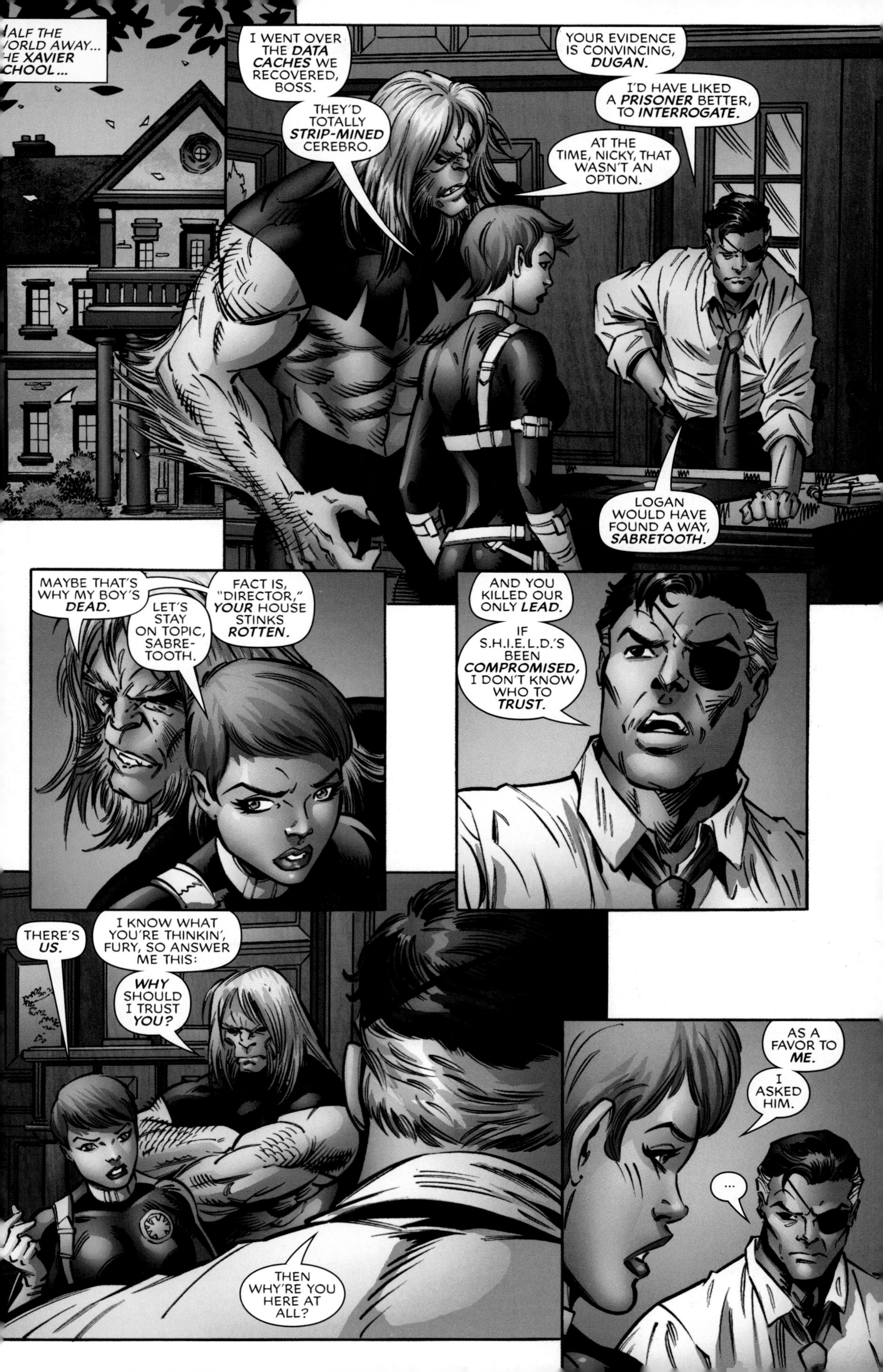

HALF THE WORLD AWAY... THE XAVIER SCHOOL...
I WENT OVER THE DATA CACHES WE RECOVERED, BOSS.
THEY'D TOTALLY STRIP-MINED CEREBRO.
YOUR EVIDENCE IS CONVINCING, DUGAN.
I'D HAVE LIKED A PRISONER BETTER, TO INTERROGATE.
AT THE TIME, NICKY, THAT WASN'T AN OPTION.
LOGAN WOULD HAVE FOUND A WAY, SABRETOOTH.
MAYBE THAT'S WHY MY BOY'S DEAD.
LET'S STAY ON TOPIC, SABRE-TOOTH.
FACT IS, "DIRECTOR," YOUR HOUSE STINKS ROTTEN.
AND YOU KILLED OUR ONLY LEAD.
IF S.H.I.E.L.D.'S BEEN COMPROMISED, I DON'T KNOW WHO TO TRUST.
THERE'S US.
I KNOW WHAT YOU'RE THINKIN', FURY, SO ANSWER ME THIS:
WHY SHOULD I TRUST YOU?
THEN WHY'RE YOU HERE AT ALL?
AS A FAVOR TO ME.
I ASKED HIM.
...

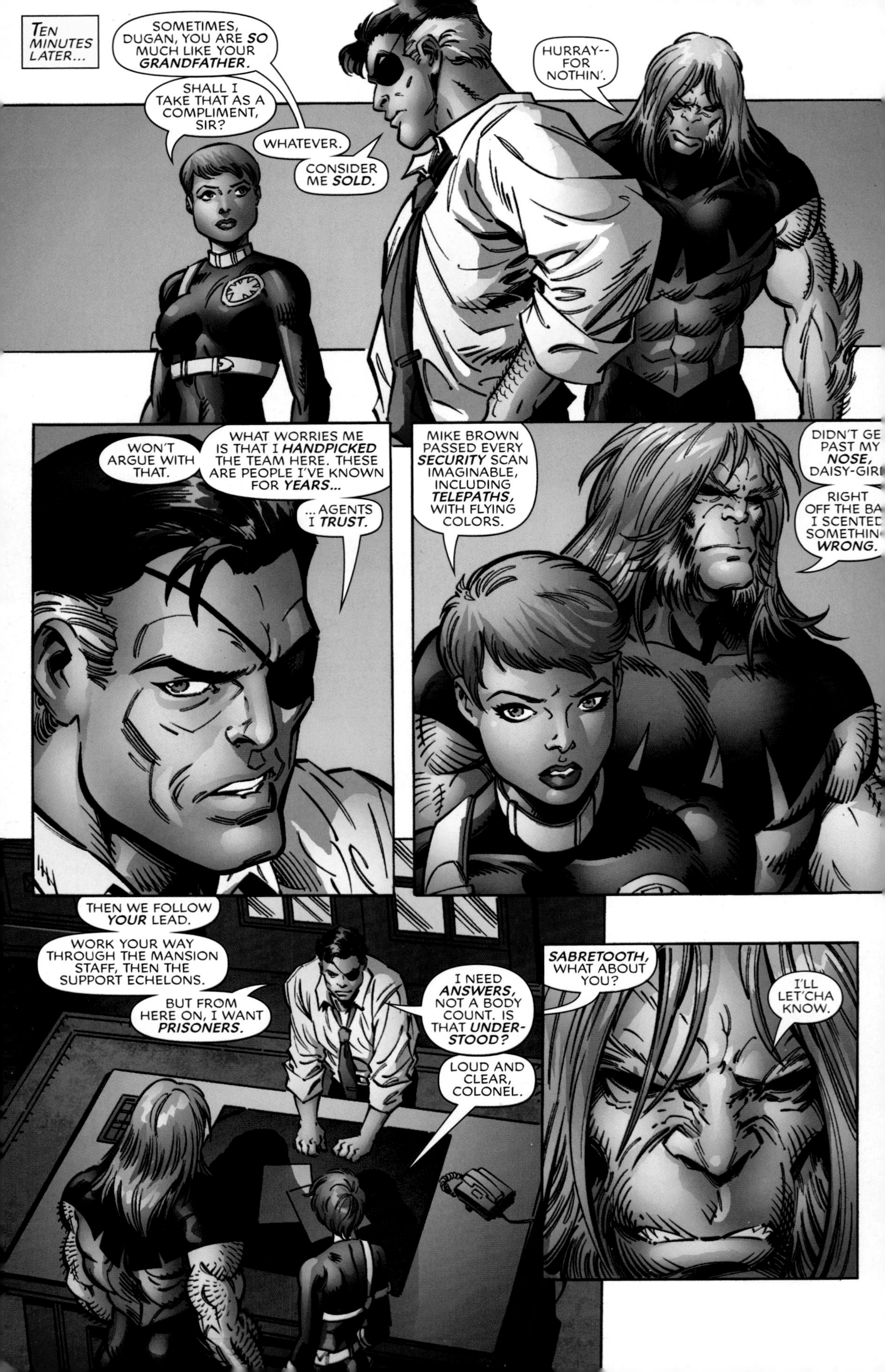
TEN MINUTES LATER...
SOMETIMES, DUGAN, YOU ARE SO MUCH LIKE YOUR GRANDFATHER.
SHALL I TAKE THAT AS A COMPLIMENT, SIR?
WHATEVER.
CONSIDER ME SOLD.
HURRAY-- FOR NOTHIN'.
WON'T ARGUE WITH THAT.
WHAT WORRIES ME IS THAT I HANDPICKED THE TEAM HERE. THESE ARE PEOPLE I'VE KNOWN FOR YEARS...
...AGENTS I TRUST.
MIKE BROWN PASSED EVERY SECURITY SCAN IMAGINABLE, INCLUDING TELEPATHS, WITH FLYING COLORS.
DIDN'T GE PAST MY NOSE, DAISY-GIR
RIGHT OFF THE BA I SCENTED SOMETHIN WRONG.
THEN WE FOLLOW YOUR LEAD.
WORK YOUR WAY THROUGH THE MANSION STAFF, THEN THE SUPPORT ECHELONS.
BUT FROM HERE ON, I WANT PRISONERS.
I NEED ANSWERS, NOT A BODY COUNT. IS THAT UNDER-STOOD?
LOUD AND CLEAR, COLONEL.
SABRETOOTH, WHAT ABOUT YOU?
I'LL LET'CHA KNOW.

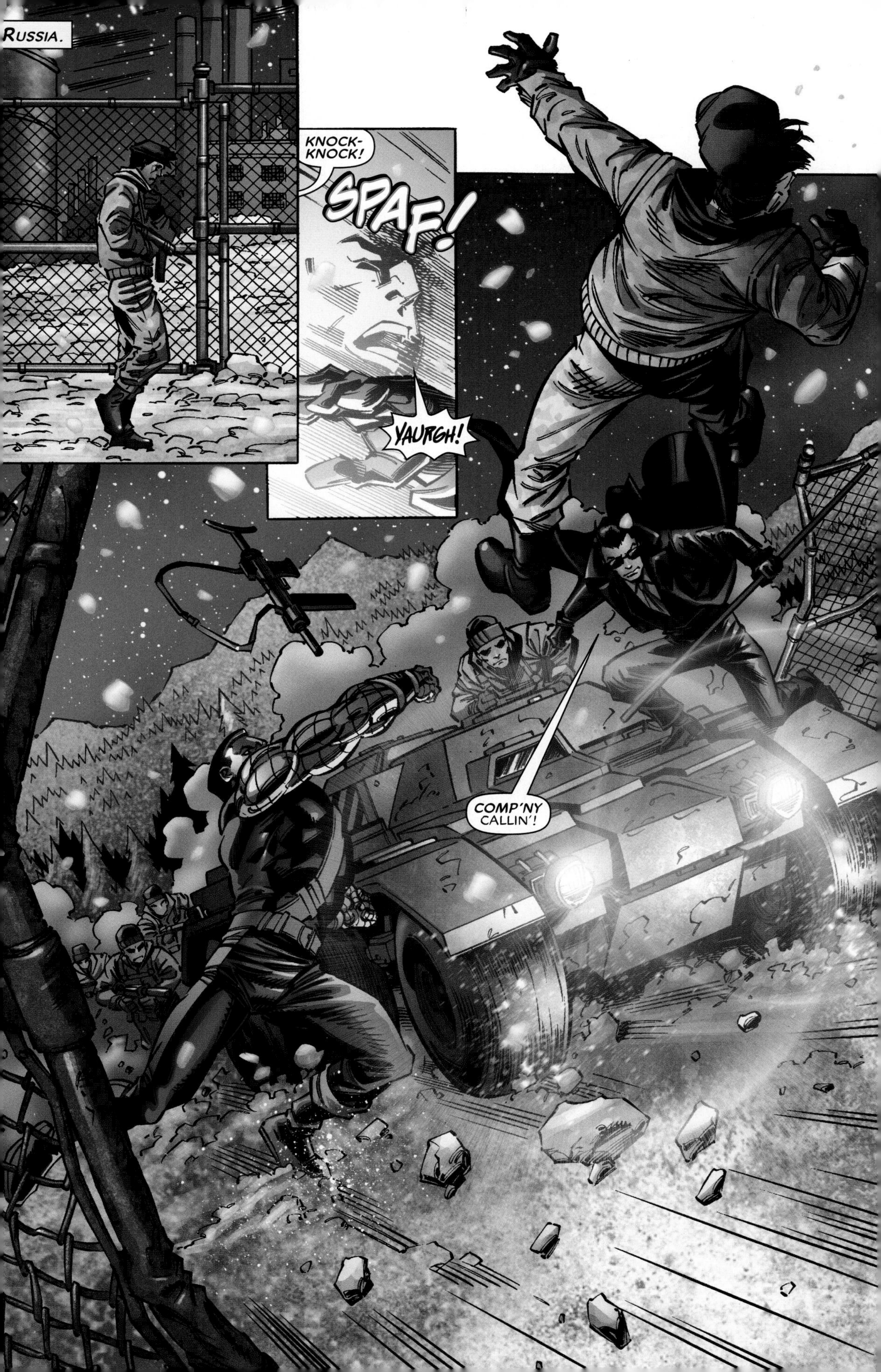
RUSSIA.
KNOCK-KNOCK!
SPAF!
YAURGH!
COMP'NY CALLIN'!

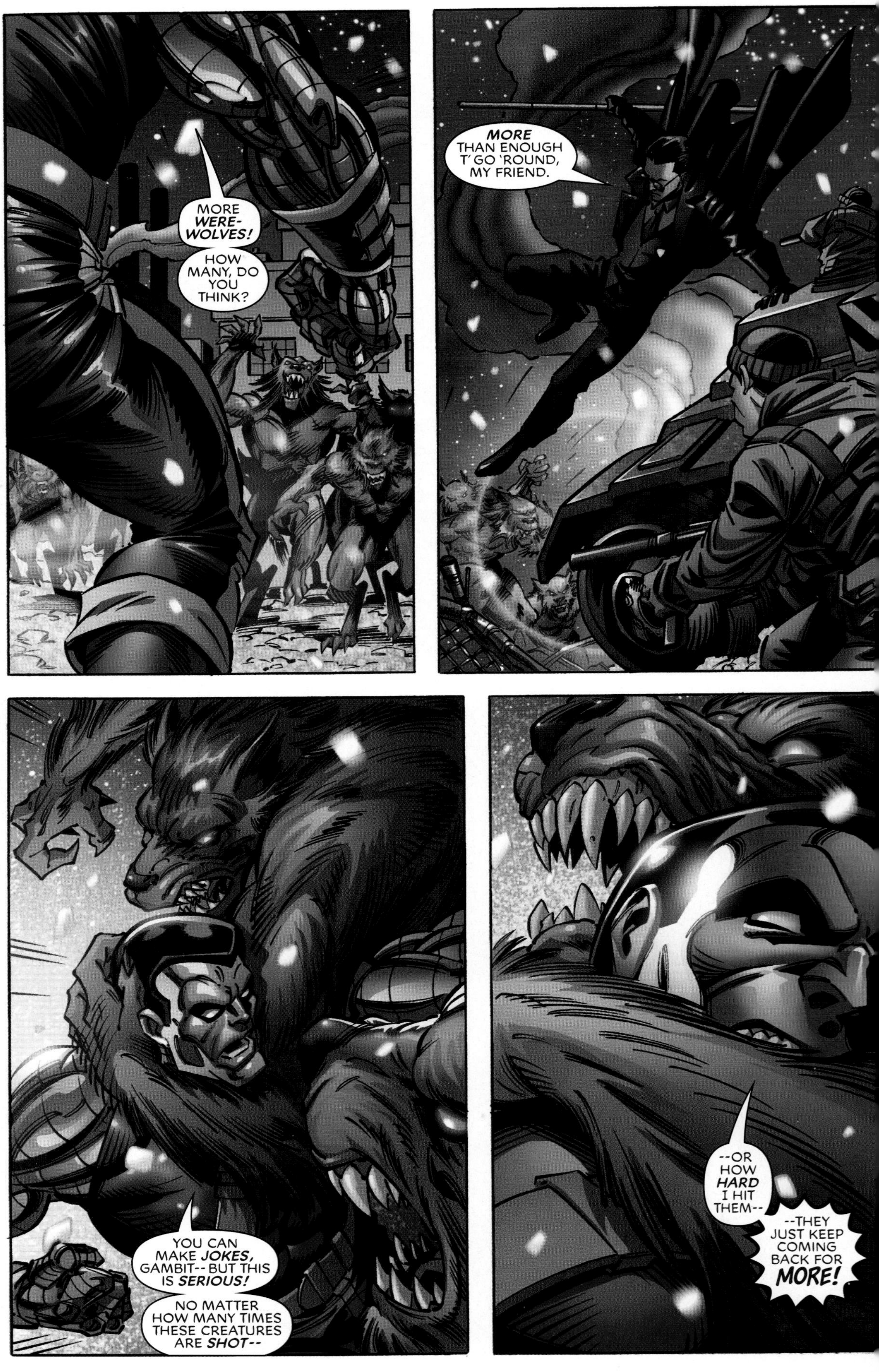
MORE WERE-WOLVES!
HOW MANY, DO YOU THINK?
MORE THAN ENOUGH T' GO 'ROUND, MY FRIEND.
YOU CAN MAKE JOKES, GAMBIT-- BUT THIS IS SERIOUS!
NO MATTER HOW MANY TIMES THESE CREATURES ARE SHOT--
--OR HOW HARD I HIT THEM--
--THEY JUST KEEP COMING BACK FOR MORE!

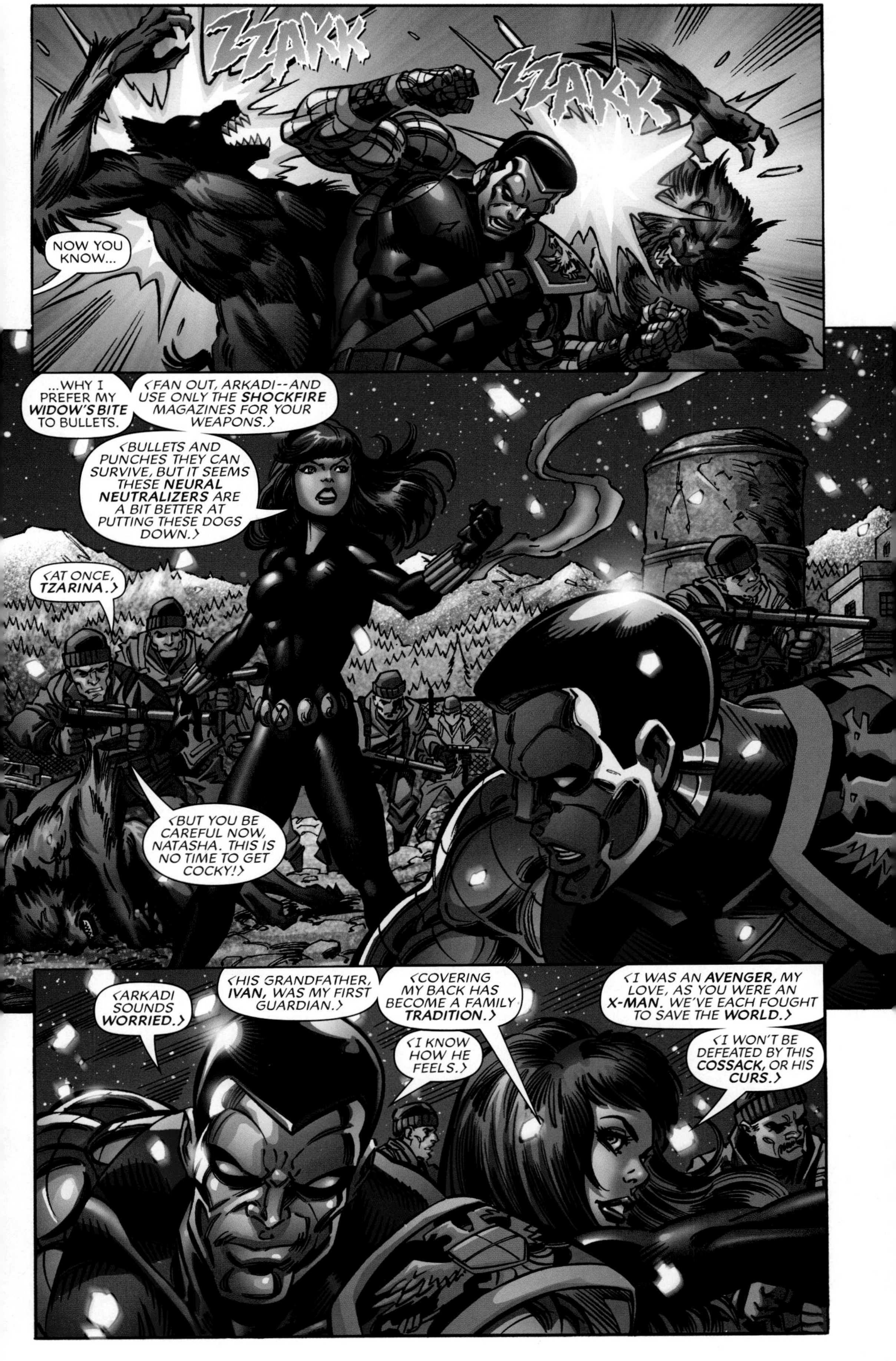

ZZAKK
ZZAKK
NOW YOU KNOW...
...WHY I PREFER MY **WIDOW'S BITE** TO BULLETS.
<FAN OUT, ARKADI--AND USE ONLY THE **SHOCKFIRE** MAGAZINES FOR YOUR WEAPONS.>
<BULLETS AND PUNCHES THEY CAN SURVIVE, BUT IT SEEMS THESE **NEURAL NEUTRALIZERS** ARE A BIT BETTER AT PUTTING THESE DOGS DOWN.>
<AT ONCE, **TZARINA**.>
<BUT YOU BE CAREFUL NOW, NATASHA. THIS IS NO TIME TO GET COCKY!>
<ARKADI SOUNDS **WORRIED**.>
<HIS GRANDFATHER, **IVAN**, WAS MY FIRST GUARDIAN.>
<COVERING MY BACK HAS BECOME A FAMILY **TRADITION**.>
<I KNOW HOW HE FEELS.>
<I WAS AN **AVENGER**, MY LOVE, AS YOU WERE AN **X-MAN**. WE'VE EACH FOUGHT TO SAVE THE **WORLD**.>
<I WON'T BE DEFEATED BY THIS **COSSACK**, OR HIS **CURS**.>

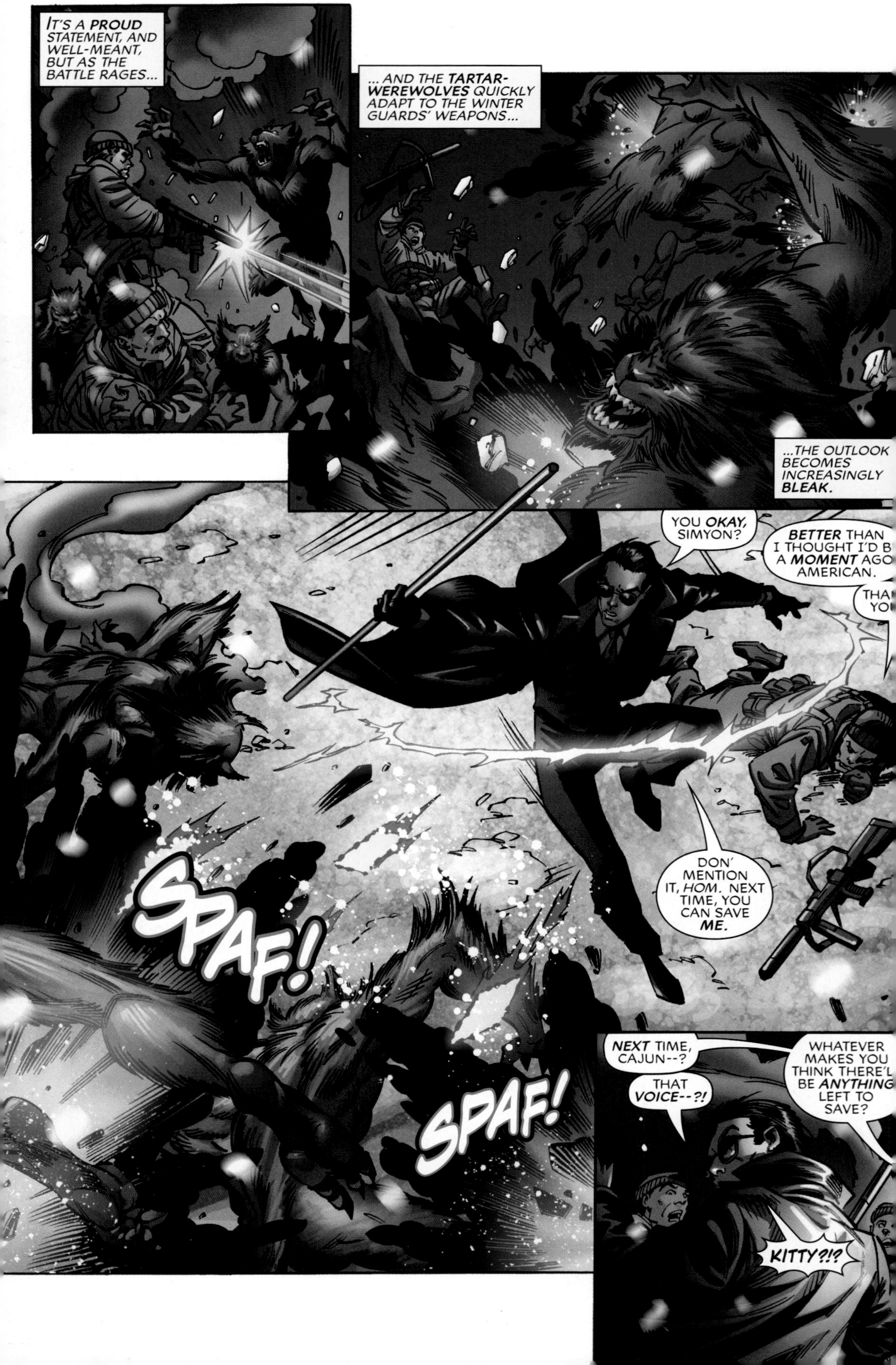
IT'S A PROUD STATEMENT, AND WELL-MEANT, BUT AS THE BATTLE RAGES...
...AND THE TARTAR-WEREWOLVES QUICKLY ADAPT TO THE WINTER GUARDS' WEAPONS...
...THE OUTLOOK BECOMES INCREASINGLY BLEAK.
YOU OKAY, SIMYON?
BETTER THAN I THOUGHT I'D B A MOMENT AGO AMERICAN.
DON' MENTION IT, HOM. NEXT TIME, YOU CAN SAVE ME.
SPAF!
SPAF!
NEXT TIME, CAJUN--?
THAT VOICE--?!
WHATEVER MAKES YOU THINK THERE'L BE ANYTHING LEFT TO SAVE?
KITTY?!?

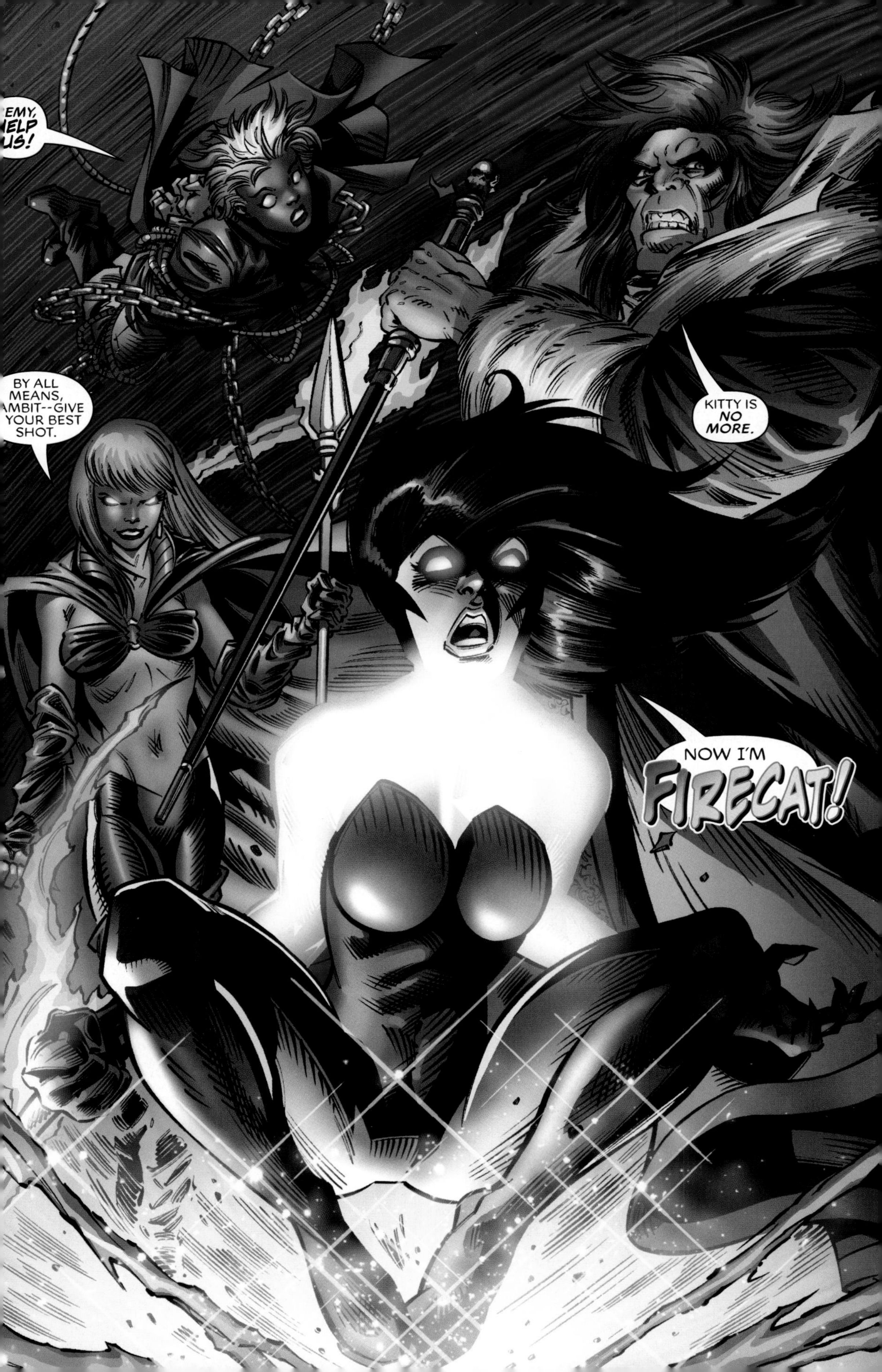
EMY, ELP US!
BY ALL MEANS, AMBIT--GIVE YOUR BEST SHOT.
KITTY IS NO MORE.
NOW I'M FIRECAT!

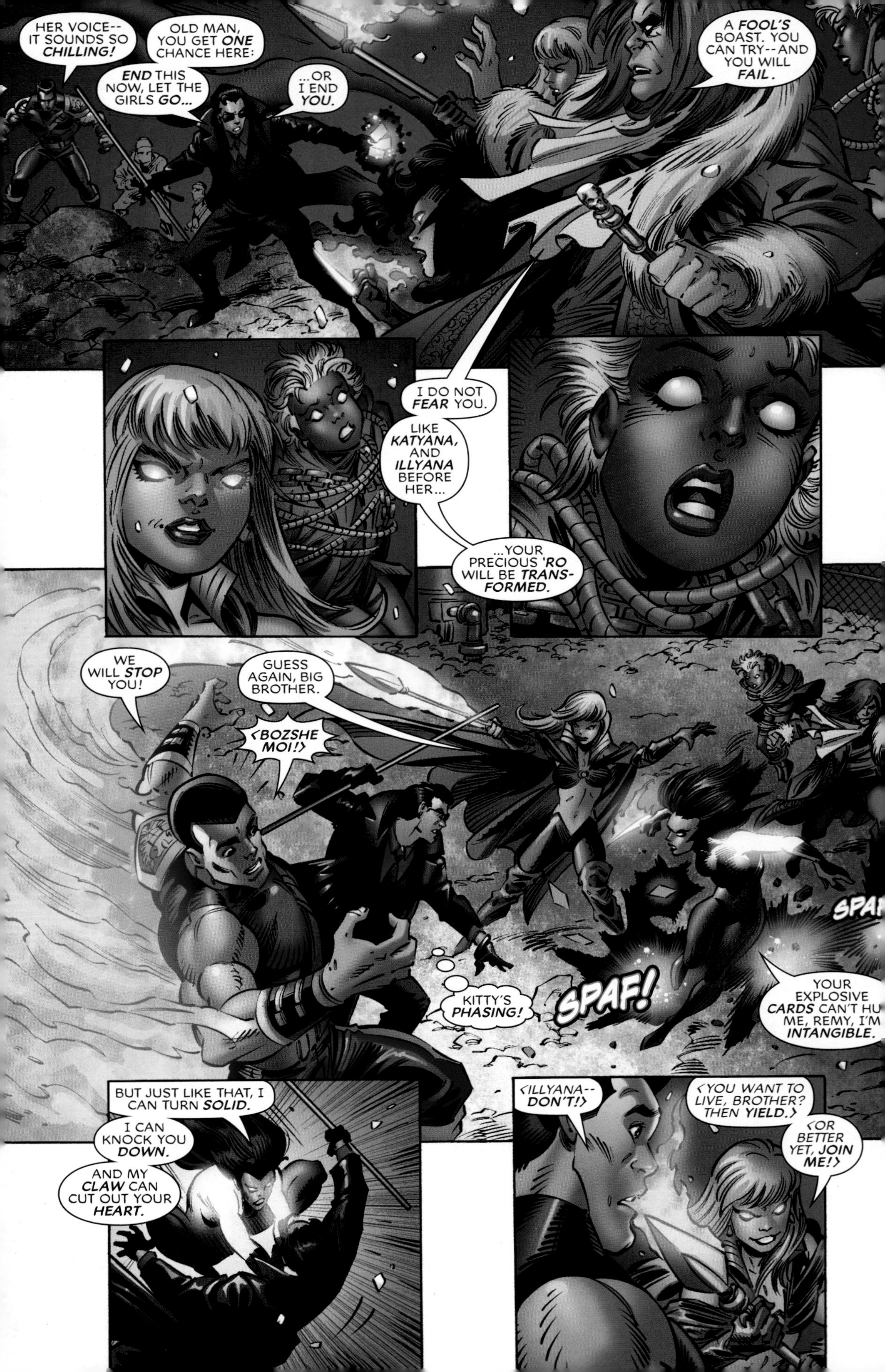

HER VOICE-- IT SOUNDS SO CHILLING!
OLD MAN, YOU GET ONE CHANCE HERE:
END THIS NOW, LET THE GIRLS GO...
...OR I END YOU.
A FOOL'S BOAST. YOU CAN TRY--AND YOU WILL FAIL.
I DO NOT FEAR YOU.
LIKE KATYANA, AND ILLYANA BEFORE HER...
...YOUR PRECIOUS 'RO WILL BE TRANS-FORMED.
WE WILL STOP YOU!
GUESS AGAIN, BIG BROTHER.
<BOZSHE MOI!>
KITTY'S PHASING!
SPAF!
SPAF
YOUR EXPLOSIVE CARDS CAN'T HU ME, REMY, I'M INTANGIBLE.
BUT JUST LIKE THAT, I CAN TURN SOLID.
I CAN KNOCK YOU DOWN.
AND MY CLAW CAN CUT OUT YOUR HEART.
<ILLYANA-- DON'T!>
<YOU WANT TO LIVE, BROTHER? THEN YIELD.>
<OR BETTER YET, JOIN ME!>

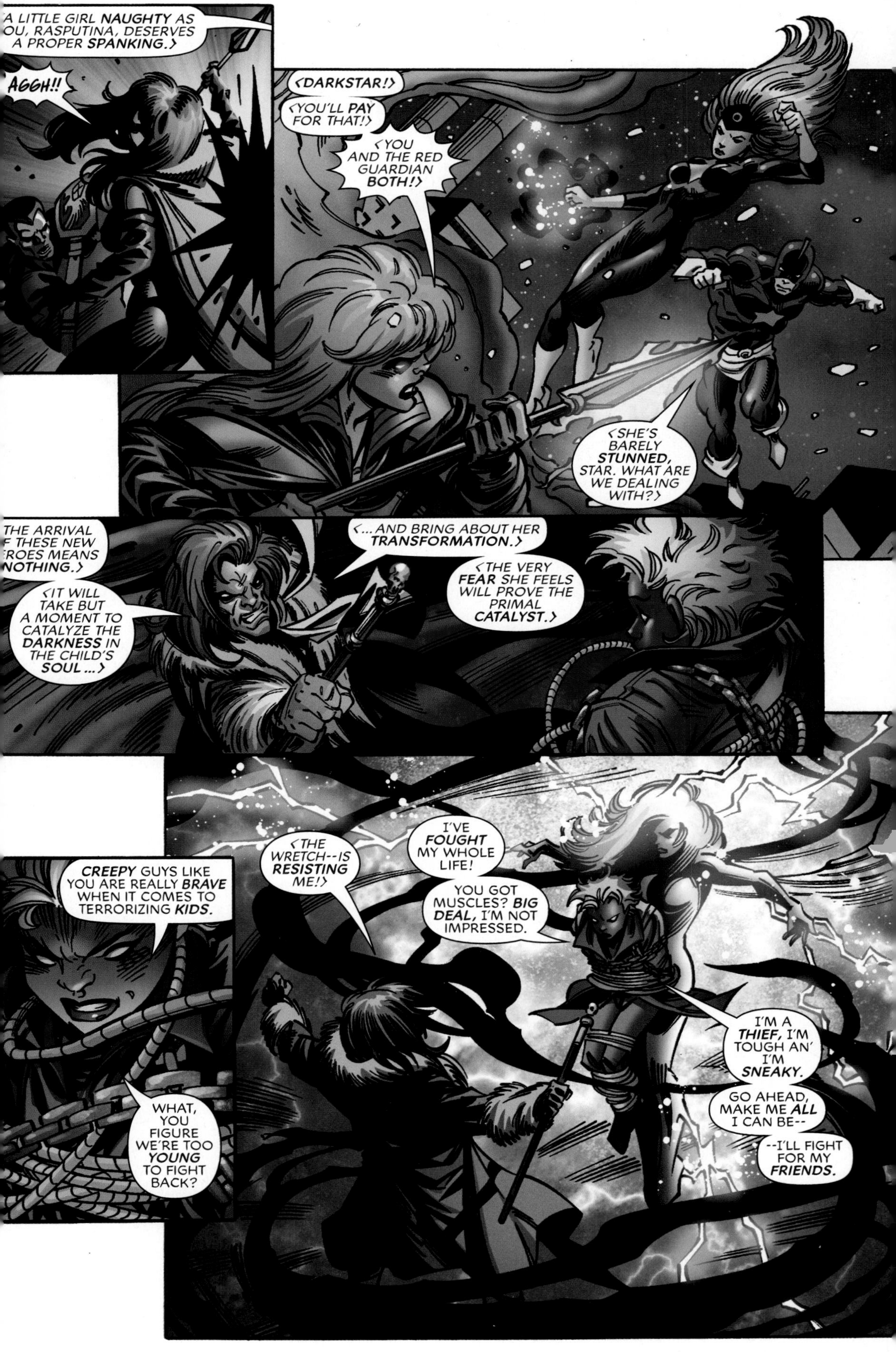

A LITTLE GIRL NAUGHTY AS OU, RASPUTINA, DESERVES A PROPER SPANKING.›
AGGH!!
‹DARKSTAR!›
‹YOU'LL PAY FOR THAT!›
‹YOU AND THE RED GUARDIAN BOTH!›
‹SHE'S BARELY STUNNED, STAR. WHAT ARE WE DEALING WITH?›
THE ARRIVAL F THESE NEW EROES MEANS NOTHING.›
‹IT WILL TAKE BUT A MOMENT TO CATALYZE THE DARKNESS IN THE CHILD'S SOUL...›
‹...AND BRING ABOUT HER TRANSFORMATION.›
‹THE VERY FEAR SHE FEELS WILL PROVE THE PRIMAL CATALYST.›
CREEPY GUYS LIKE YOU ARE REALLY BRAVE WHEN IT COMES TO TERRORIZING KIDS.
WHAT, YOU FIGURE WE'RE TOO YOUNG TO FIGHT BACK?
‹THE WRETCH--IS RESISTING ME!›
I'VE FOUGHT MY WHOLE LIFE!
YOU GOT MUSCLES? BIG DEAL, I'M NOT IMPRESSED.
I'M A THIEF, I'M TOUGH AN' I'M SNEAKY.
GO AHEAD, MAKE ME ALL I CAN BE--
--I'LL FIGHT FOR MY FRIENDS.

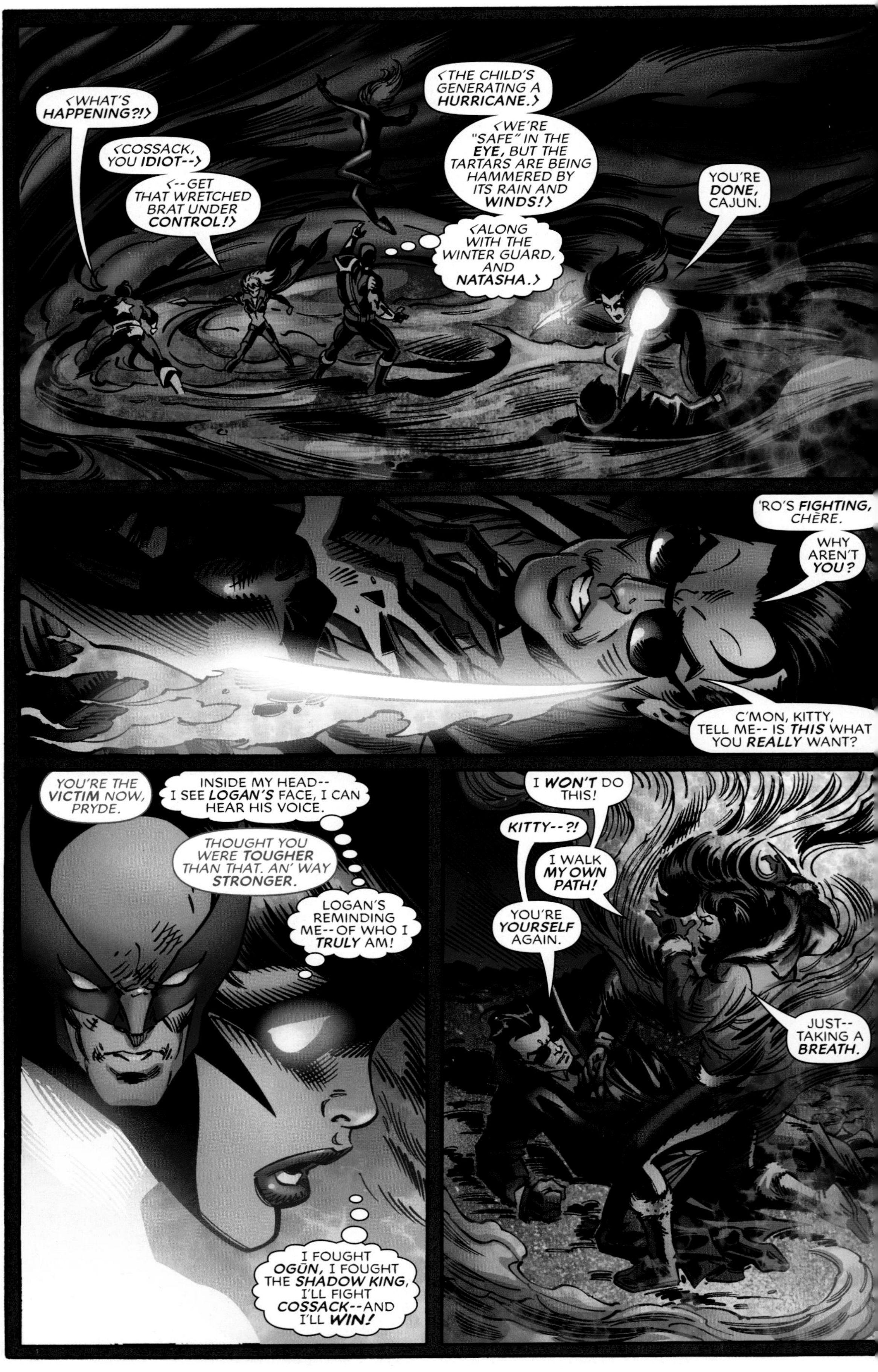

‹WHAT'S HAPPENING?!›
‹COSSACK, YOU IDIOT--›
‹--GET THAT WRETCHED BRAT UNDER CONTROL!›
‹THE CHILD'S GENERATING A HURRICANE.›
‹WE'RE "SAFE" IN THE EYE, BUT THE TARTARS ARE BEING HAMMERED BY ITS RAIN AND WINDS!›
‹ALONG WITH THE WINTER GUARD, AND NATASHA.›
YOU'RE DONE, CAJUN.
'RO'S FIGHTING, CHÈRE.
WHY AREN'T YOU?
C'MON, KITTY, TELL ME-- IS THIS WHAT YOU REALLY WANT?
YOU'RE THE VICTIM NOW, PRYDE.
INSIDE MY HEAD-- I SEE LOGAN'S FACE, I CAN HEAR HIS VOICE.
THOUGHT YOU WERE TOUGHER THAN THAT. AN' WAY STRONGER.
LOGAN'S REMINDING ME-- OF WHO I TRULY AM!
I FOUGHT OGŪN, I FOUGHT THE SHADOW KING, I'LL FIGHT COSSACK--AND I'LL WIN!
I WON'T DO THIS!
KITTY--?!
I WALK MY OWN PATH!
YOU'RE YOURSELF AGAIN.
JUST-- TAKING A BREATH.

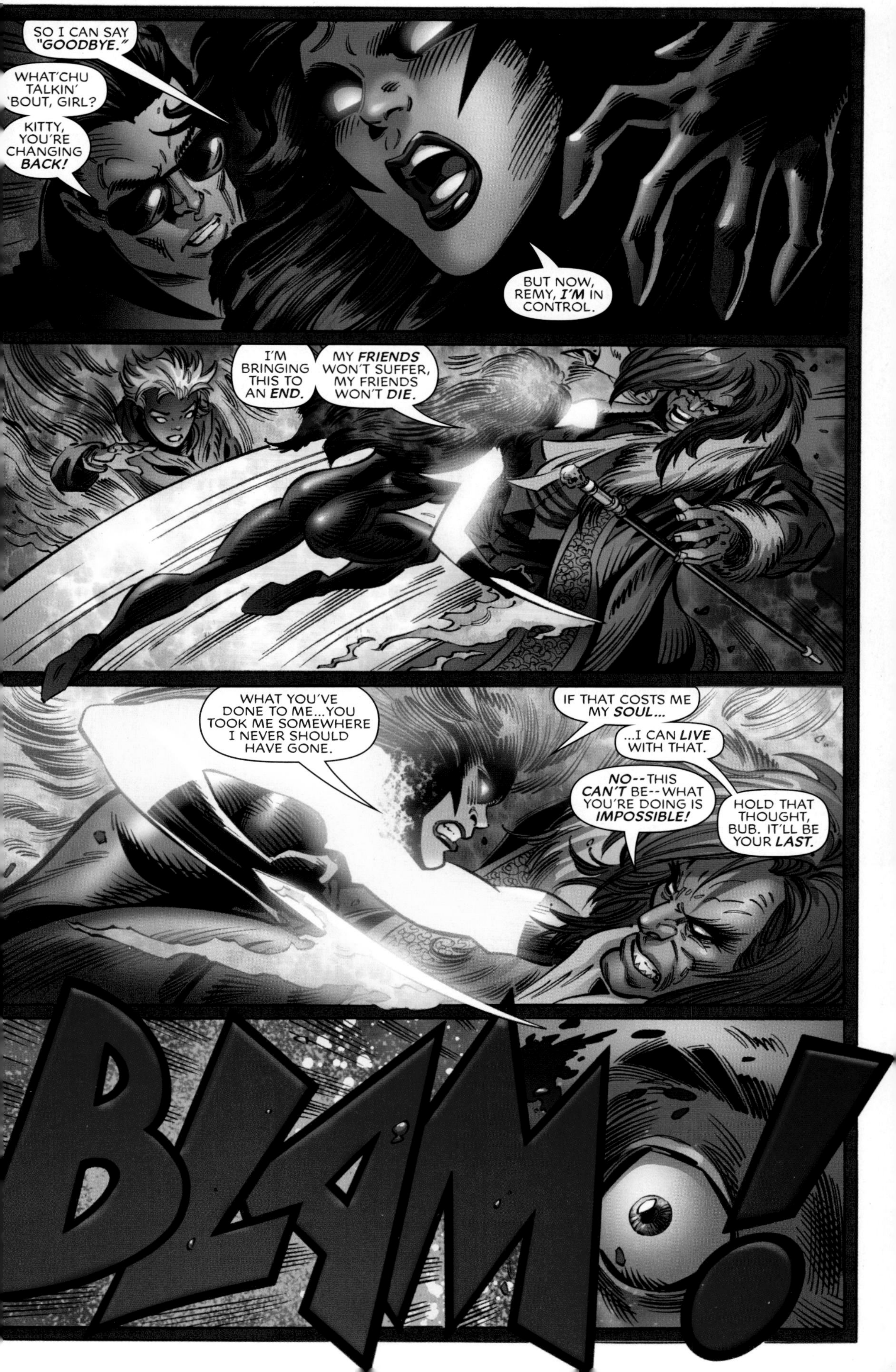
SO I CAN SAY "GOODBYE."
WHAT'CHU TALKIN' 'BOUT, GIRL?
KITTY, YOU'RE CHANGING BACK!
BUT NOW, REMY, I'M IN CONTROL.
I'M BRINGING THIS TO AN END.
MY FRIENDS WON'T SUFFER, MY FRIENDS WON'T DIE.
WHAT YOU'VE DONE TO ME...YOU TOOK ME SOMEWHERE I NEVER SHOULD HAVE GONE.
IF THAT COSTS ME MY SOUL...
...I CAN LIVE WITH THAT.
NO--THIS CAN'T BE--WHAT YOU'RE DOING IS IMPOSSIBLE!
HOLD THAT THOUGHT, BUB. IT'LL BE YOUR LAST.
BLAM!

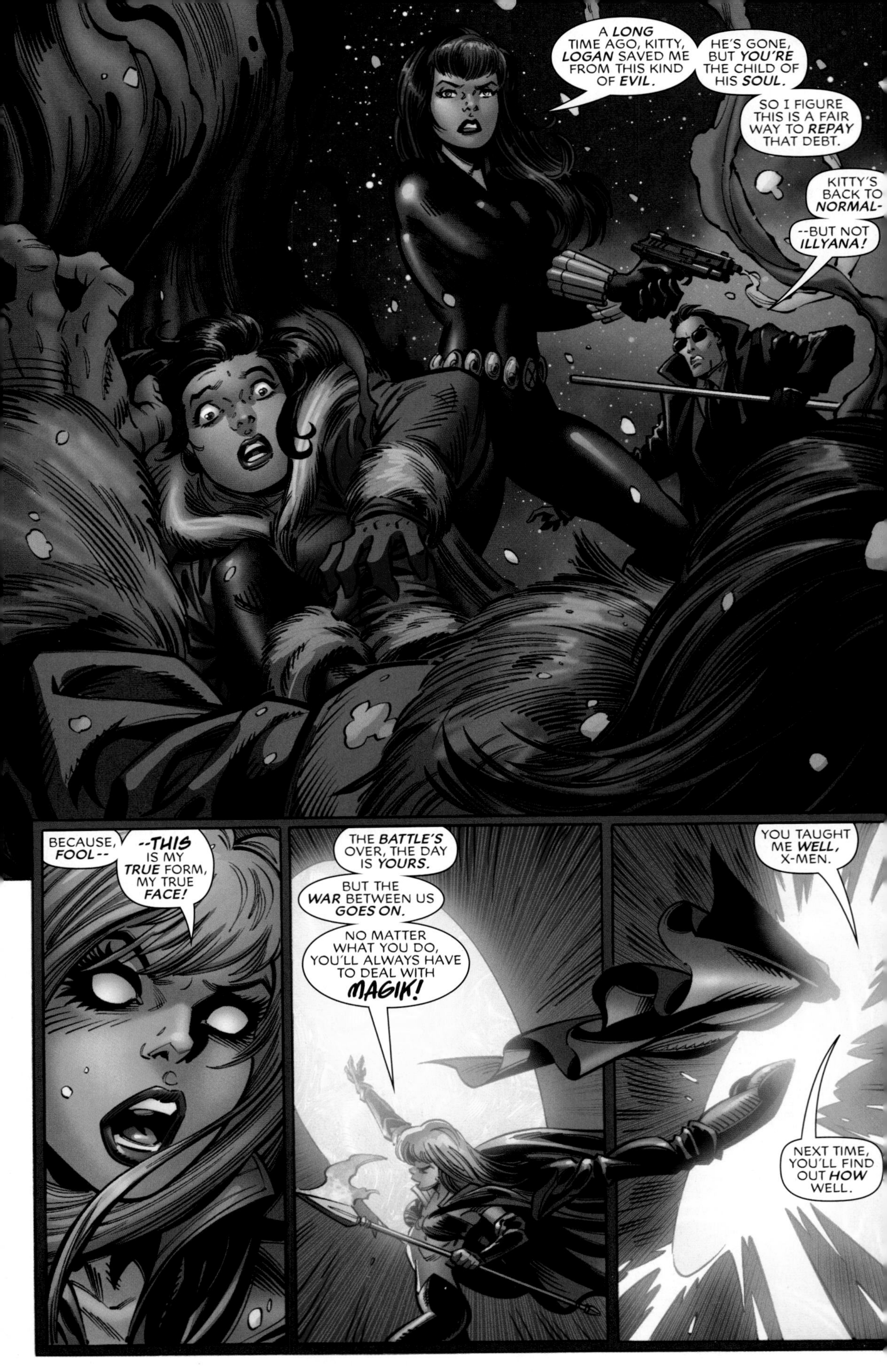
A LONG TIME AGO, KITTY, LOGAN SAVED ME FROM THIS KIND OF EVIL.
HE'S GONE, BUT YOU'RE THE CHILD OF HIS SOUL.
SO I FIGURE THIS IS A FAIR WAY TO REPAY THAT DEBT.
KITTY'S BACK TO NORMAL-
--BUT NOT ILLYANA!
BECAUSE, FOOL--
--THIS IS MY TRUE FORM, MY TRUE FACE!
THE BATTLE'S OVER, THE DAY IS YOURS.
BUT THE WAR BETWEEN US GOES ON.
NO MATTER WHAT YOU DO, YOU'LL ALWAYS HAVE TO DEAL WITH MAGIK!
YOU TAUGHT ME WELL, X-MEN.
NEXT TIME, YOU'LL FIND OUT HOW WELL.

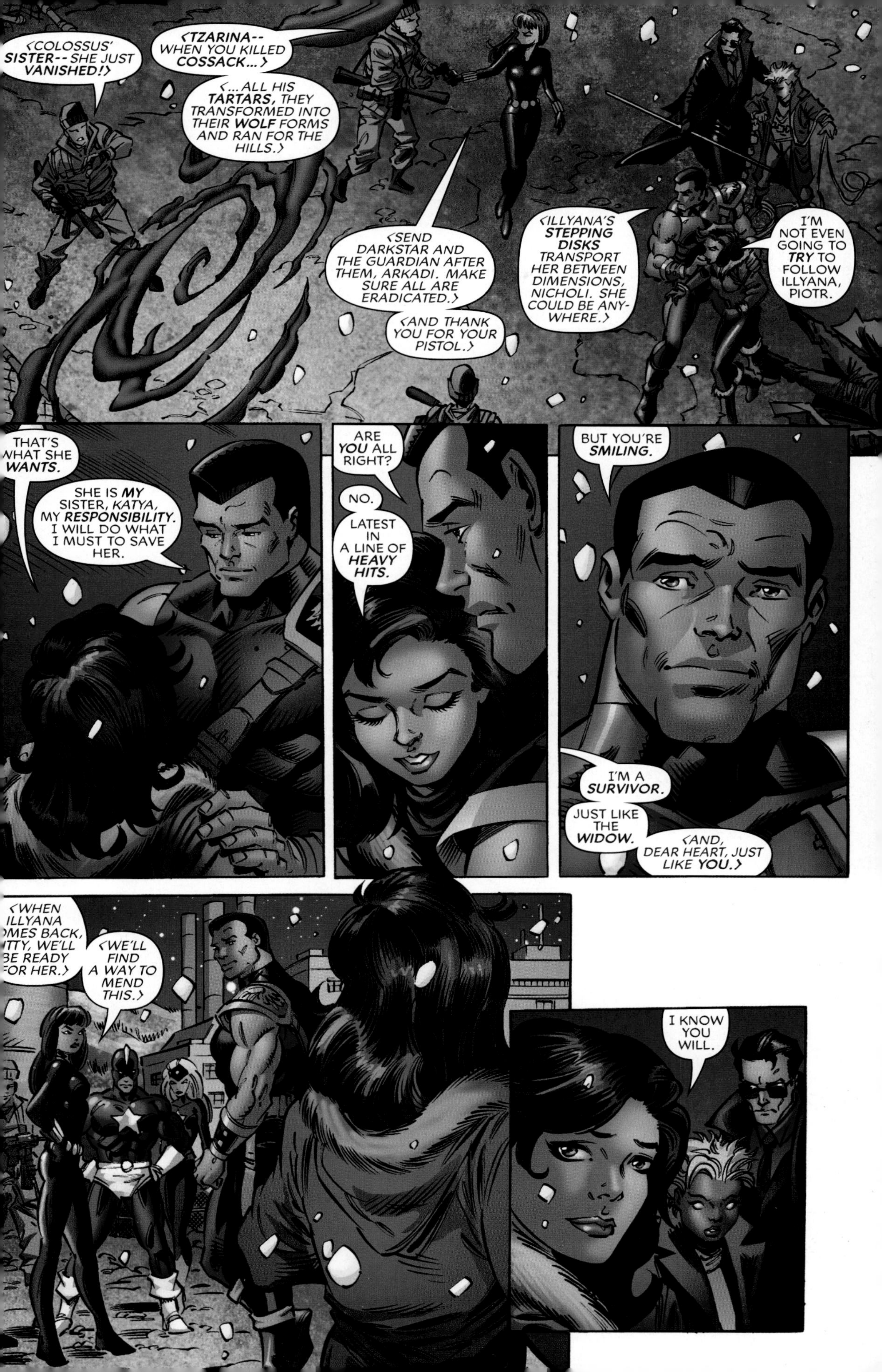
‹COLOSSUS' SISTER-- SHE JUST VANISHED!›
‹TZARINA-- WHEN YOU KILLED COSSACK...›
‹...ALL HIS TARTARS, THEY TRANSFORMED INTO THEIR WOLF FORMS AND RAN FOR THE HILLS.›
‹SEND DARKSTAR AND THE GUARDIAN AFTER THEM, ARKADI. MAKE SURE ALL ARE ERADICATED.›
‹AND THANK YOU FOR YOUR PISTOL.›
‹ILLYANA'S STEPPING DISKS TRANSPORT HER BETWEEN DIMENSIONS, NICHOLI. SHE COULD BE ANY-WHERE.›
I'M NOT EVEN GOING TO TRY TO FOLLOW ILLYANA, PIOTR.
THAT'S WHAT SHE WANTS.
SHE IS MY SISTER, KATYA, MY RESPONSIBILITY. I WILL DO WHAT I MUST TO SAVE HER.
ARE YOU ALL RIGHT?
NO.
LATEST IN A LINE OF HEAVY HITS.
BUT YOU'RE SMILING.
I'M A SURVIVOR.
JUST LIKE THE WIDOW.
‹AND, DEAR HEART, JUST LIKE YOU.›
‹WHEN ILLYANA OMES BACK, ITTY, WE'LL BE READY FOR HER.›
‹WE'LL FIND A WAY TO MEND THIS.›
I KNOW YOU WILL.

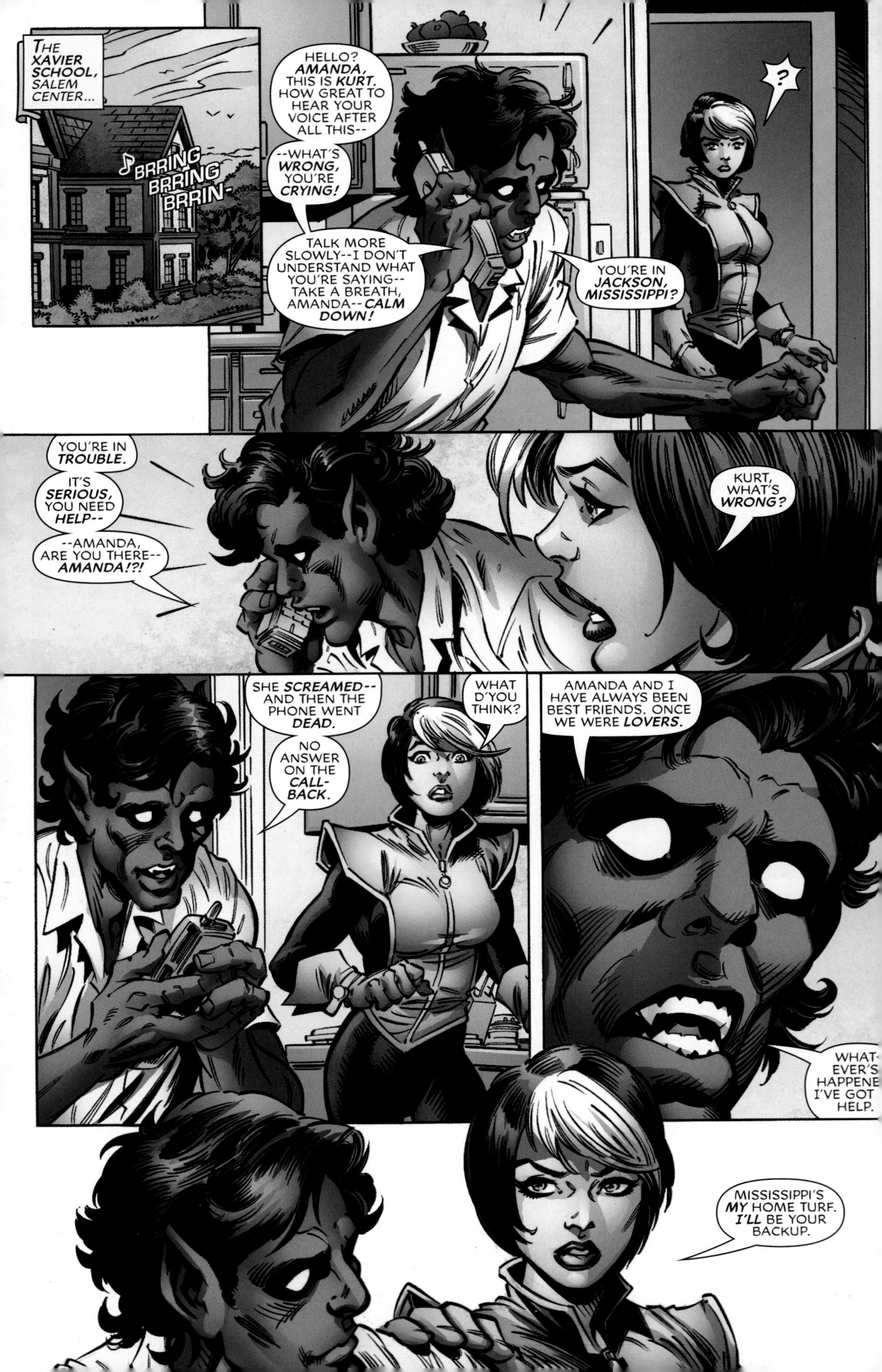
THE XAVIER SCHOOL, SALEM CENTER...
BRRING BRRING BRRIN-
HELLO? AMANDA, THIS IS KURT. HOW GREAT TO HEAR YOUR VOICE AFTER ALL THIS--
--WHAT'S WRONG, YOU'RE CRYING!
TALK MORE SLOWLY--I DON'T UNDERSTAND WHAT YOU'RE SAYING--TAKE A BREATH, AMANDA--CALM DOWN!
?
YOU'RE IN JACKSON, MISSISSIPPI?
YOU'RE IN TROUBLE.
IT'S SERIOUS, YOU NEED HELP--
--AMANDA, ARE YOU THERE--AMANDA!?!
KURT, WHAT'S WRONG?
SHE SCREAMED--AND THEN THE PHONE WENT DEAD.
NO ANSWER ON THE CALL-BACK.
WHAT D'YOU THINK?
AMANDA AND I HAVE ALWAYS BEEN BEST FRIENDS. ONCE WE WERE LOVERS.
MISSISSIPPI'S MY HOME TURF. I'LL BE YOUR BACKUP.

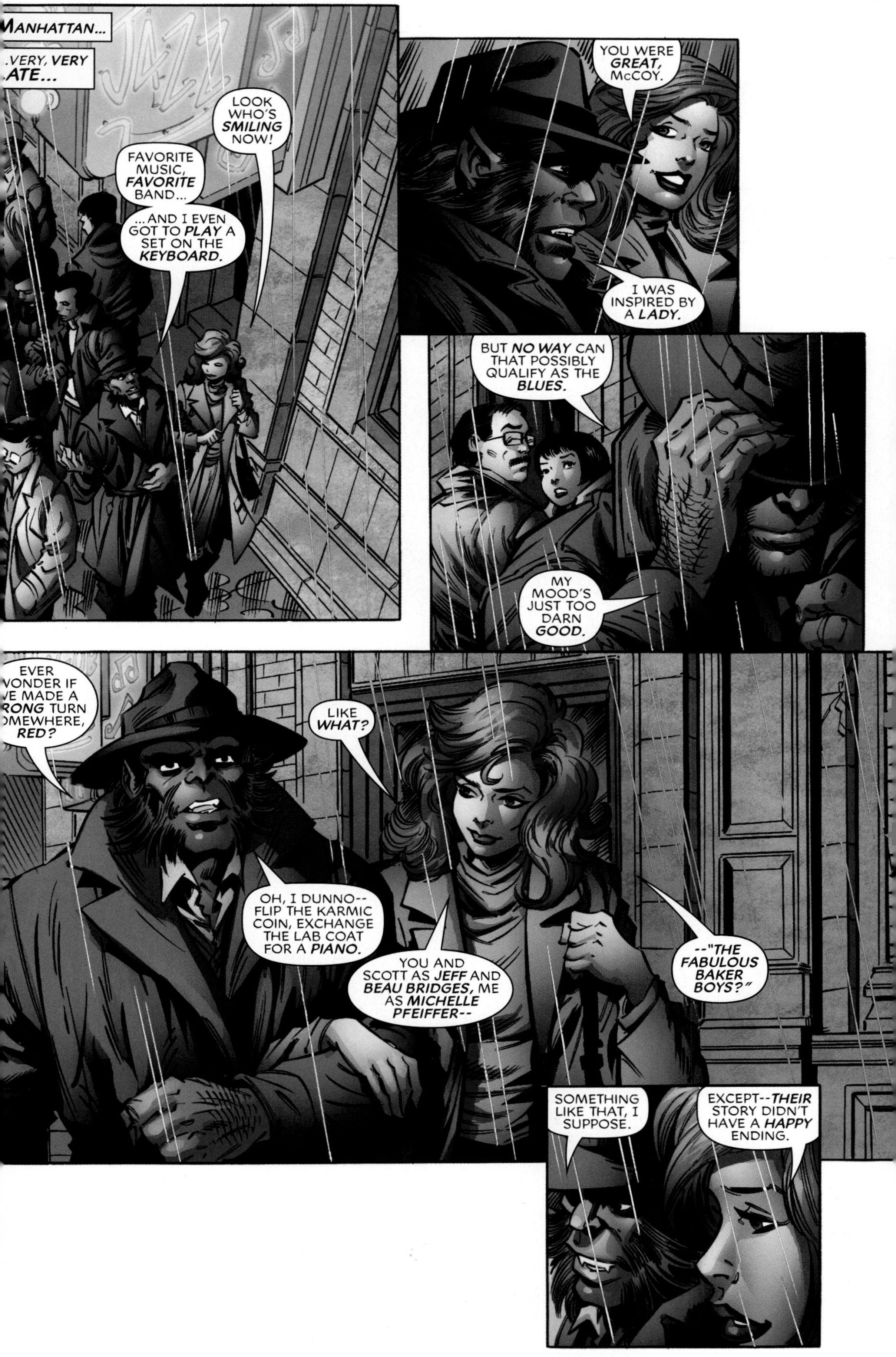
MANHATTAN...
...VERY, VERY LATE...
FAVORITE MUSIC, FAVORITE BAND...
...AND I EVEN GOT TO PLAY A SET ON THE KEYBOARD.
LOOK WHO'S SMILING NOW!
YOU WERE GREAT, McCOY.
I WAS INSPIRED BY A LADY.
BUT NO WAY CAN THAT POSSIBLY QUALIFY AS THE BLUES.
MY MOOD'S JUST TOO DARN GOOD.
EVER WONDER IF WE MADE A WRONG TURN SOMEWHERE, RED?
LIKE WHAT?
OH, I DUNNO-- FLIP THE KARMIC COIN, EXCHANGE THE LAB COAT FOR A PIANO.
YOU AND SCOTT AS JEFF AND BEAU BRIDGES, ME AS MICHELLE PFEIFFER--
--"THE FABULOUS BAKER BOYS?"
SOMETHING LIKE THAT, I SUPPOSE.
EXCEPT--THEIR STORY DIDN'T HAVE A HAPPY ENDING.

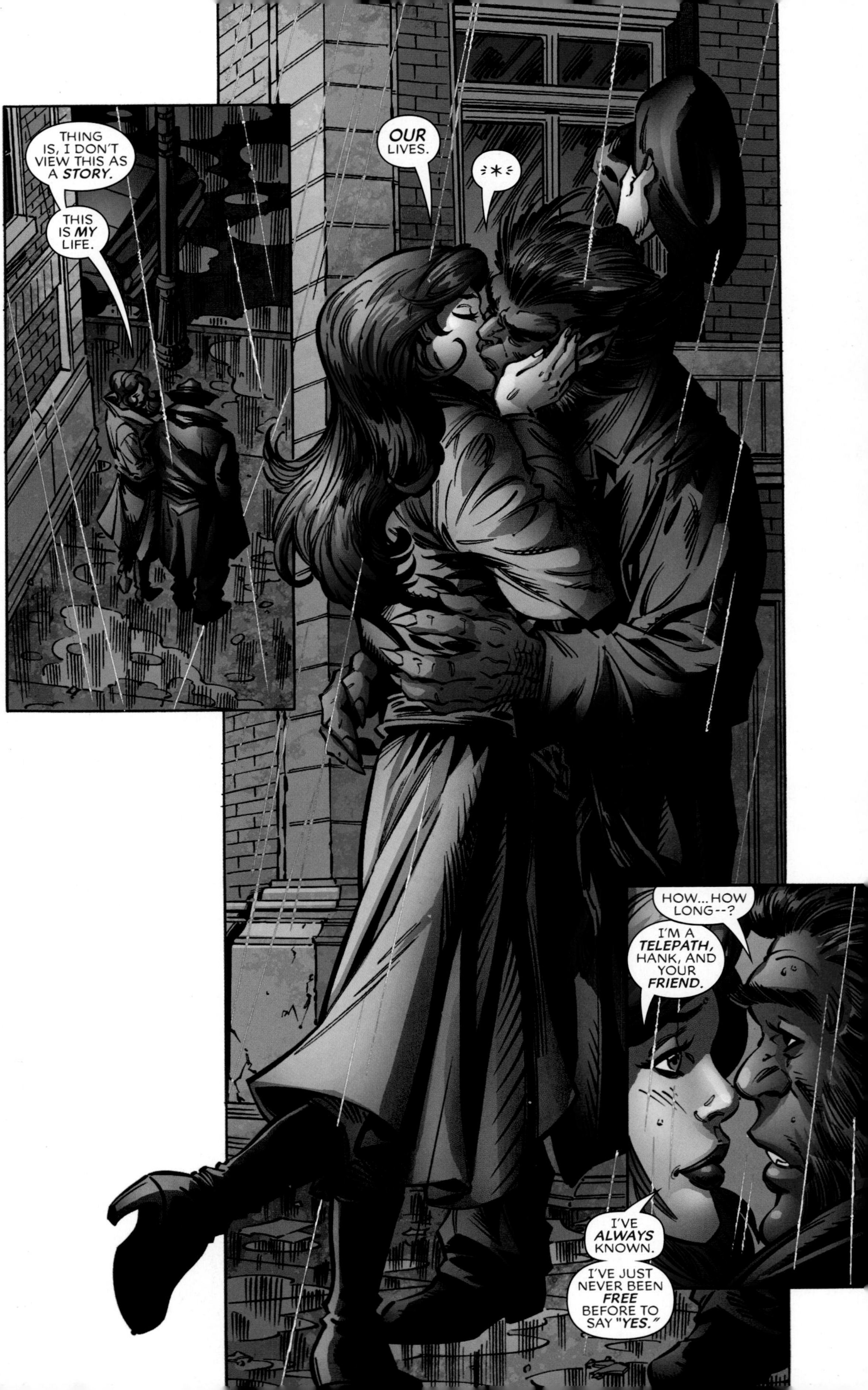
THING IS, I DON'T VIEW THIS AS A STORY.
THIS IS MY LIFE.
OUR LIVES.
*
HOW... HOW LONG--?
I'M A TELEPATH, HANK, AND YOUR FRIEND.
I'VE ALWAYS KNOWN.
I'VE JUST NEVER BEEN FREE BEFORE TO SAY "YES."

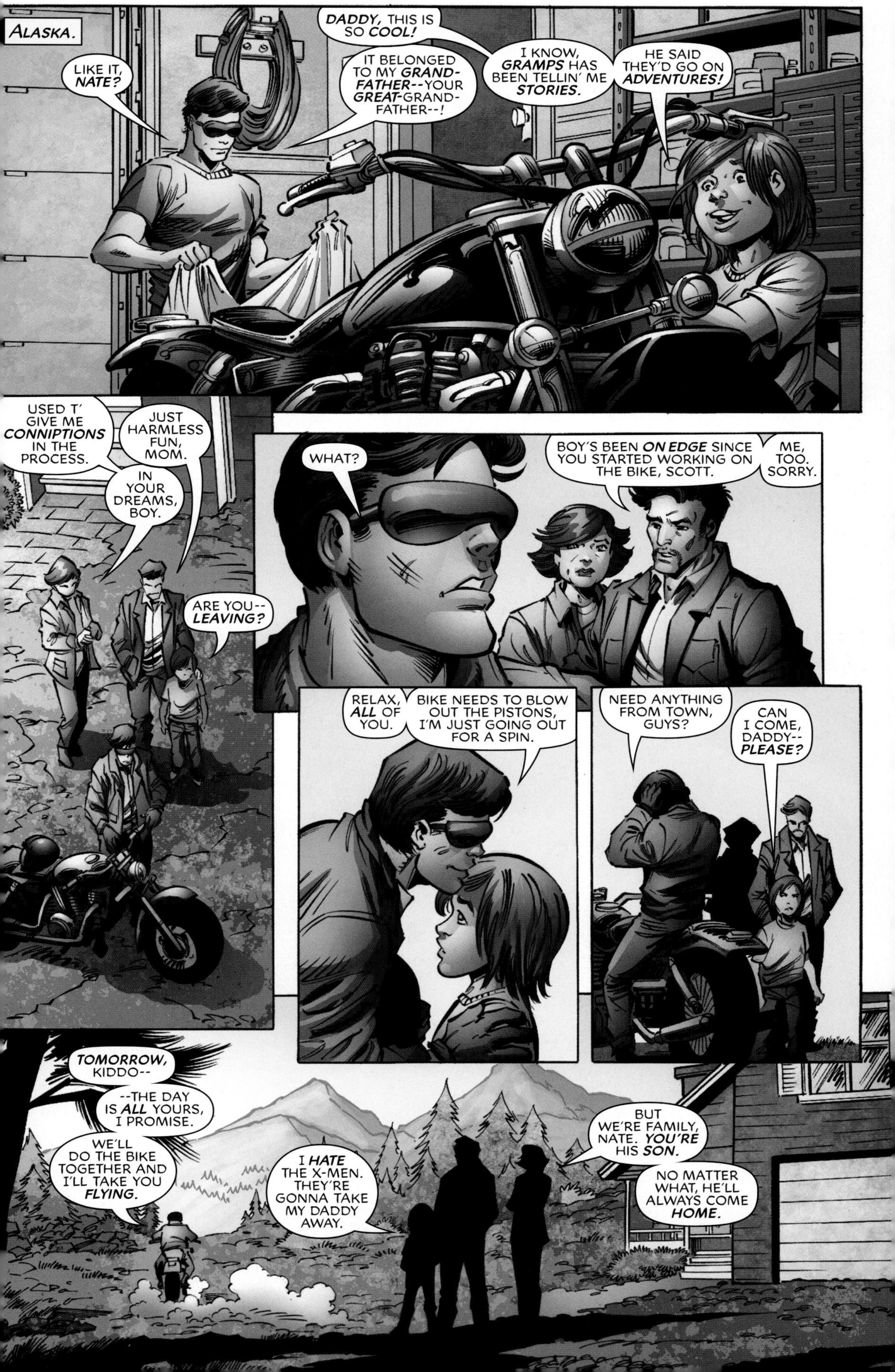
ALASKA.
LIKE IT, NATE?
DADDY, THIS IS SO COOL!
IT BELONGED TO MY GRAND-FATHER--YOUR GREAT-GRAND-FATHER--!
I KNOW, GRAMPS HAS BEEN TELLIN' ME STORIES.
HE SAID THEY'D GO ON ADVENTURES!
USED T' GIVE ME CONNIPTIONS IN THE PROCESS.
JUST HARMLESS FUN, MOM.
IN YOUR DREAMS, BOY.
ARE YOU--LEAVING?
WHAT?
BOY'S BEEN ON EDGE SINCE YOU STARTED WORKING ON THE BIKE, SCOTT.
ME, TOO. SORRY.
RELAX, ALL OF YOU.
BIKE NEEDS TO BLOW OUT THE PISTONS, I'M JUST GOING OUT FOR A SPIN.
NEED ANYTHING FROM TOWN, GUYS?
CAN I COME, DADDY--PLEASE?
TOMORROW, KIDDO--
--THE DAY IS ALL YOURS, I PROMISE.
WE'LL DO THE BIKE TOGETHER AND I'LL TAKE YOU FLYING.
I HATE THE X-MEN. THEY'RE GONNA TAKE MY DADDY AWAY.
BUT WE'RE FAMILY, NATE. YOU'RE HIS SON.
NO MATTER WHAT, HE'LL ALWAYS COME HOME.

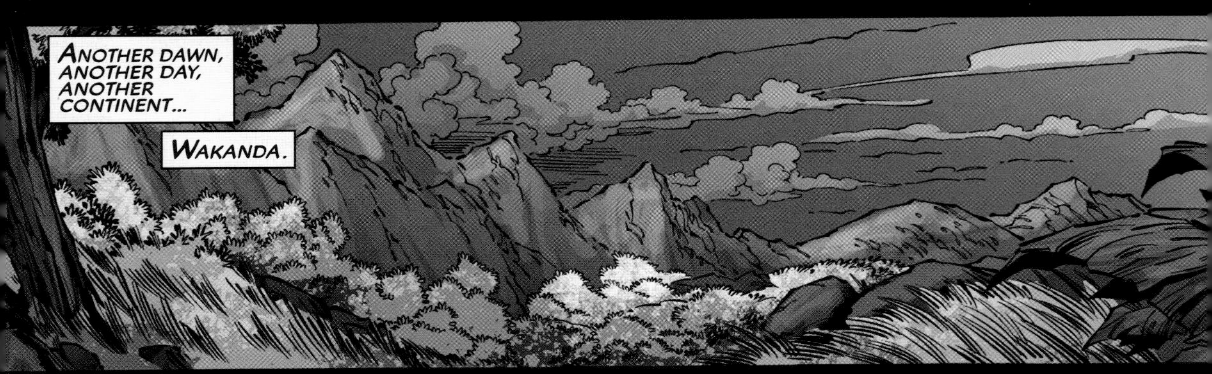
ANOTHER DAWN, ANOTHER DAY, ANOTHER CONTINENT...
WAKANDA.

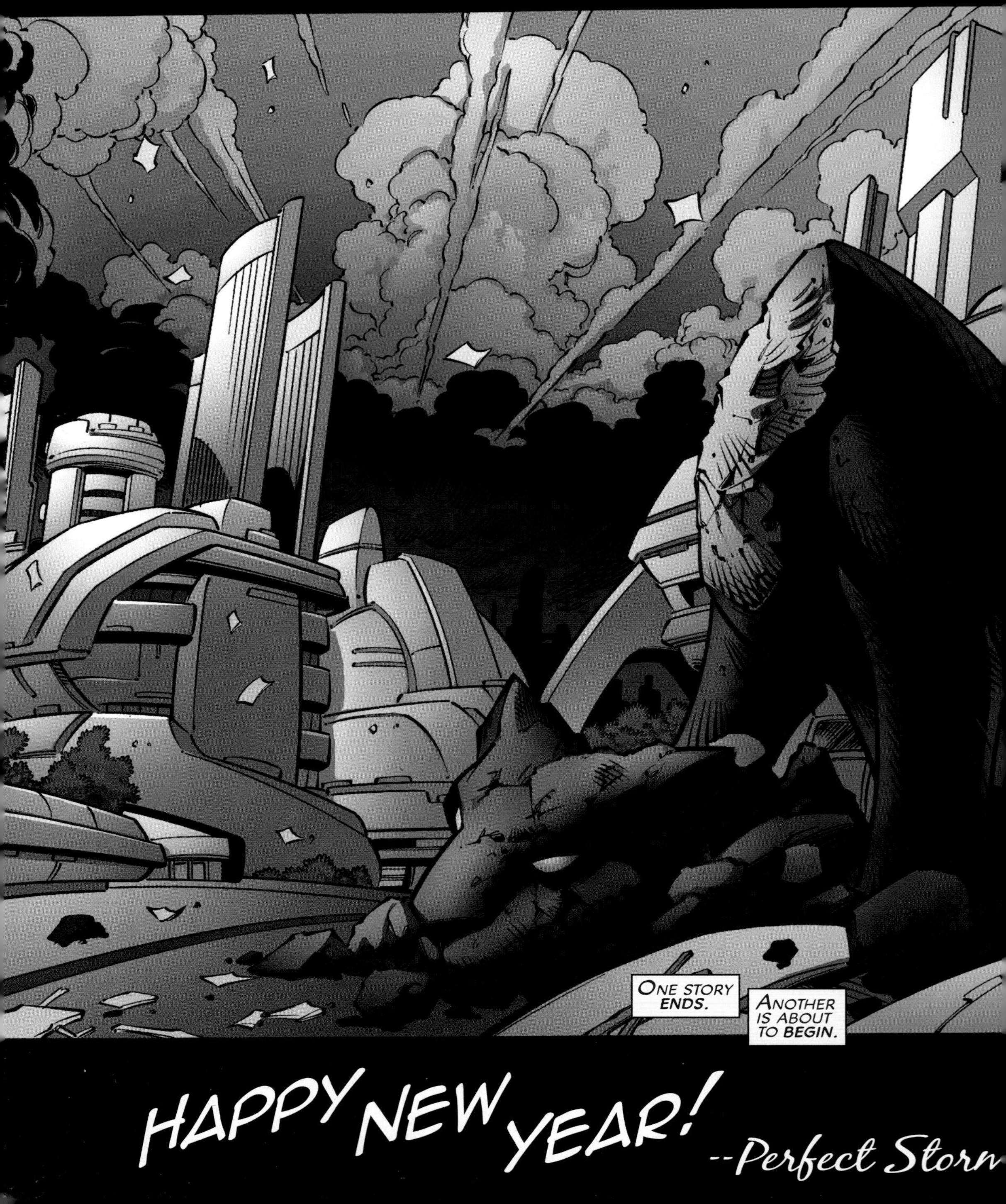
ONE STORY ENDS.
ANOTHER IS ABOUT TO BEGIN.

HAPPY NEW YEAR! --Perfect Storm

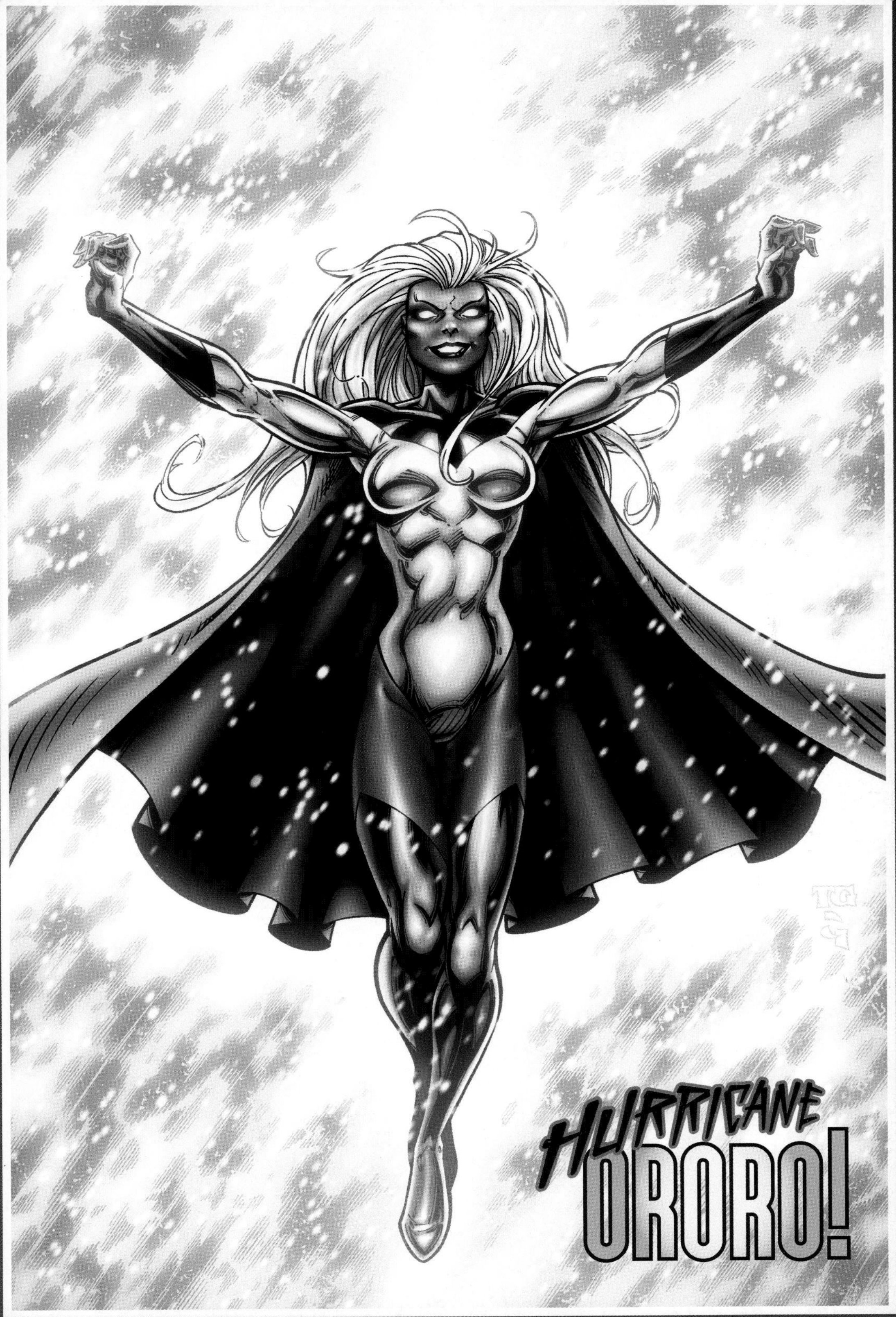
HURRICANE
ORORO!

FIFTEEN

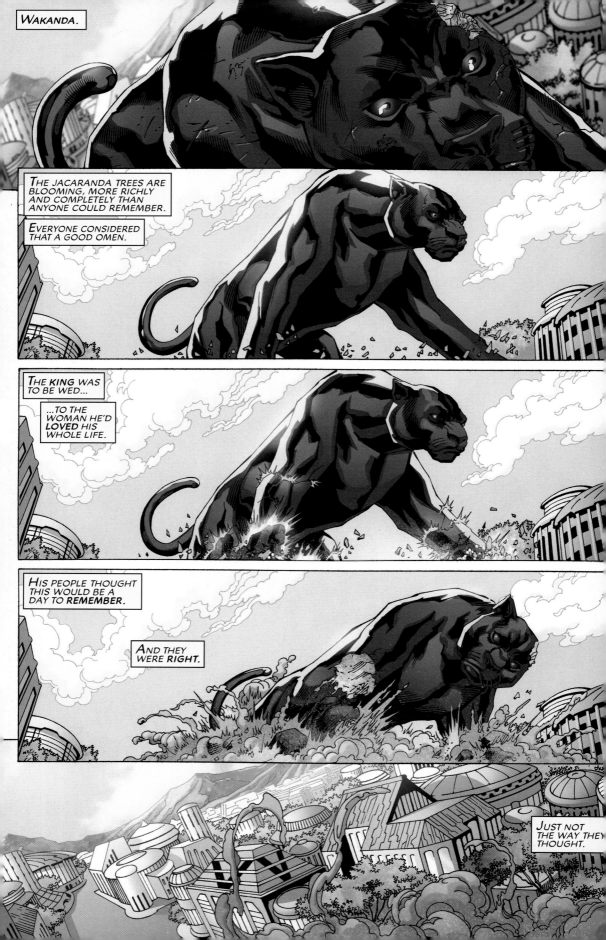

WAKANDA.

THE JACARANDA TREES ARE BLOOMING, MORE RICHLY AND COMPLETELY THAN ANYONE COULD REMEMBER.

EVERYONE CONSIDERED THAT A GOOD OMEN.

THE KING WAS TO BE WED...

...TO THE WOMAN HE'D LOVED HIS WHOLE LIFE.

HIS PEOPLE THOUGHT THIS WOULD BE A DAY TO REMEMBER.

AND THEY WERE RIGHT.

JUST NOT THE WAY THEY THOUGHT.

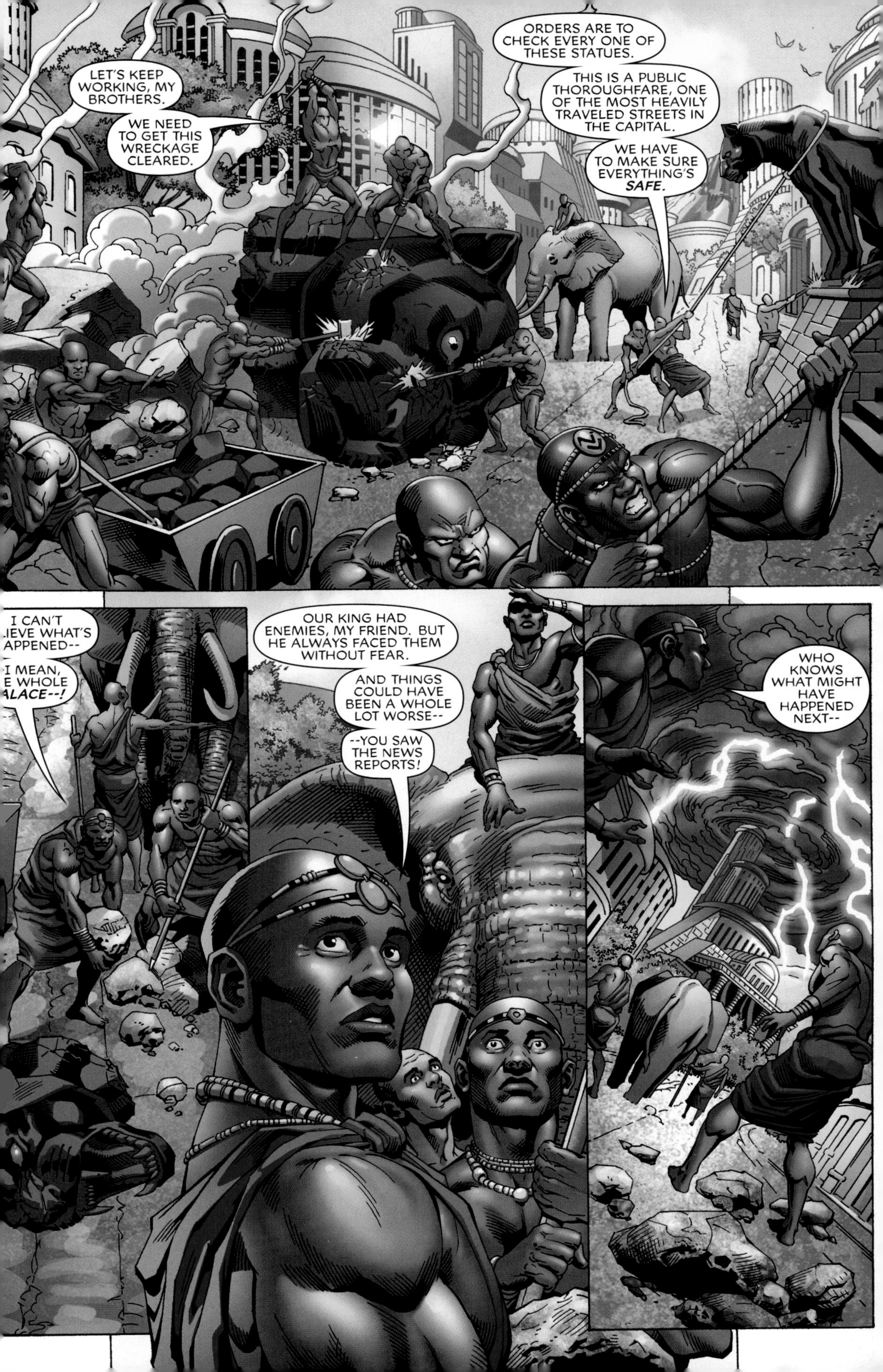
LET'S KEEP WORKING, MY BROTHERS.
WE NEED TO GET THIS WRECKAGE CLEARED.
ORDERS ARE TO CHECK EVERY ONE OF THESE STATUES.
THIS IS A PUBLIC THOROUGHFARE, ONE OF THE MOST HEAVILY TRAVELED STREETS IN THE CAPITAL.
WE HAVE TO MAKE SURE EVERYTHING'S *SAFE*.
I CAN'T
IEVE WHAT'S
APPENED--
I MEAN,
E WHOLE
ALACE--!
OUR KING HAD ENEMIES, MY FRIEND. BUT HE ALWAYS FACED THEM WITHOUT FEAR.
AND THINGS COULD HAVE BEEN A WHOLE LOT WORSE--
--YOU SAW THE NEWS REPORTS!
WHO KNOWS WHAT MIGHT HAVE HAPPENED NEXT--

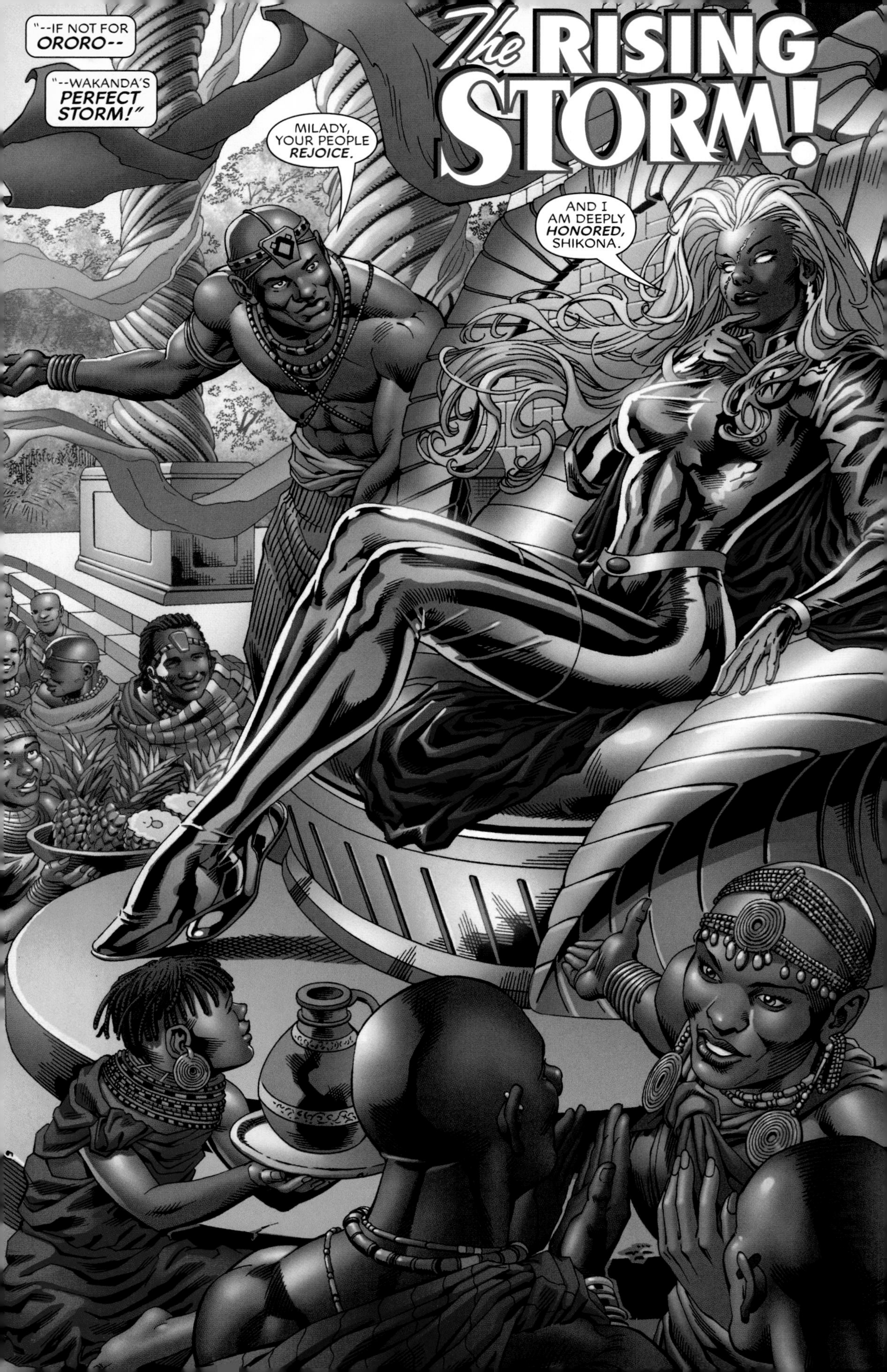

"--IF NOT FOR ORORO--
"--WAKANDA'S PERFECT STORM!"
The RISING STORM!
MILADY, YOUR PEOPLE REJOICE.
AND I AM DEEPLY HONORED, SHIKONA.

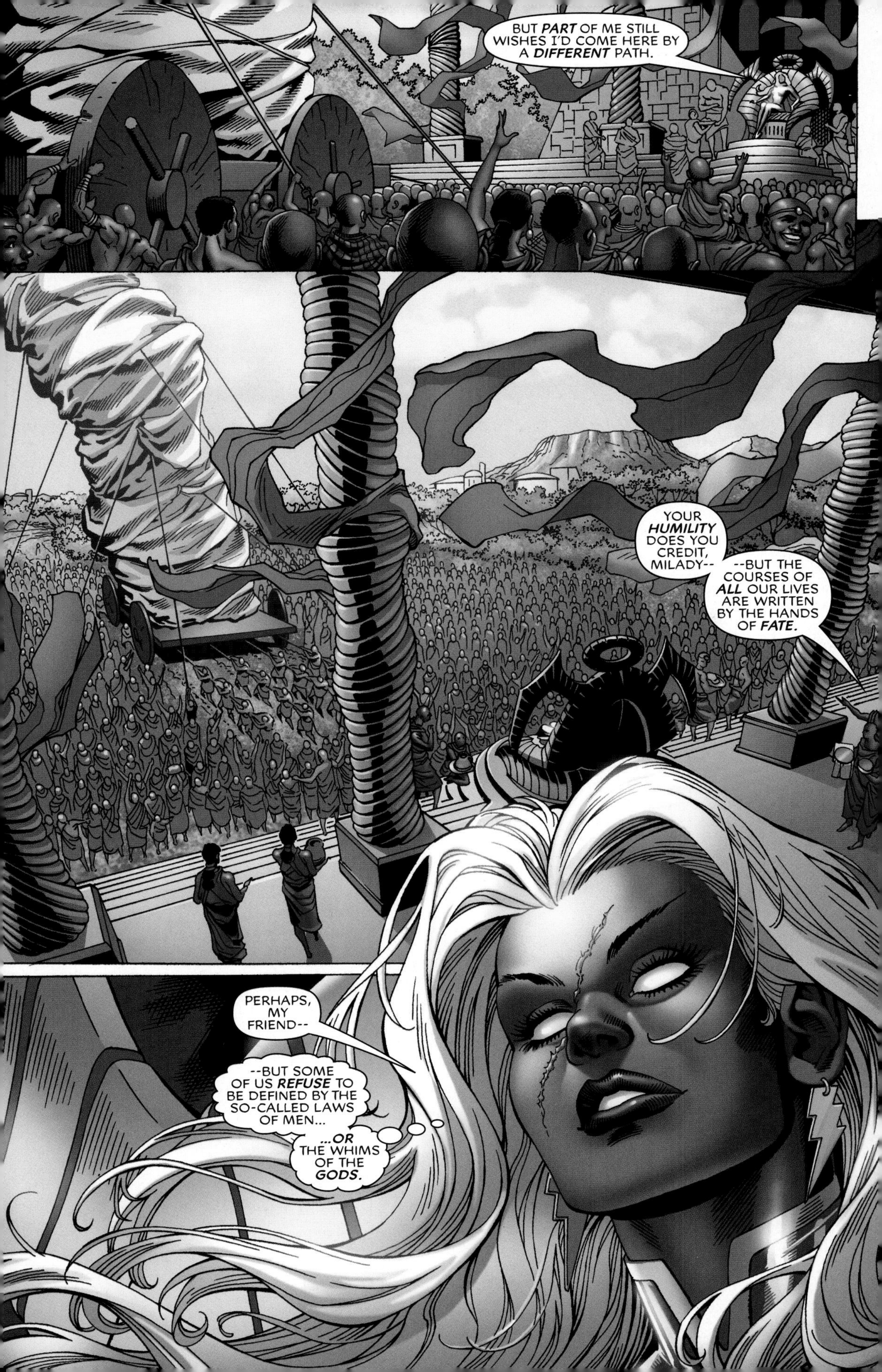
BUT *PART* OF ME STILL WISHES I'D COME HERE BY A *DIFFERENT* PATH.
YOUR *HUMILITY* DOES YOU CREDIT, MILADY--
--BUT THE COURSES OF *ALL* OUR LIVES ARE WRITTEN BY THE HANDS OF *FATE.*
PERHAPS, MY FRIEND--
--BUT SOME OF US *REFUSE* TO BE DEFINED BY THE SO-CALLED LAWS OF MEN...
...OR THE WHIMS OF THE *GODS.*

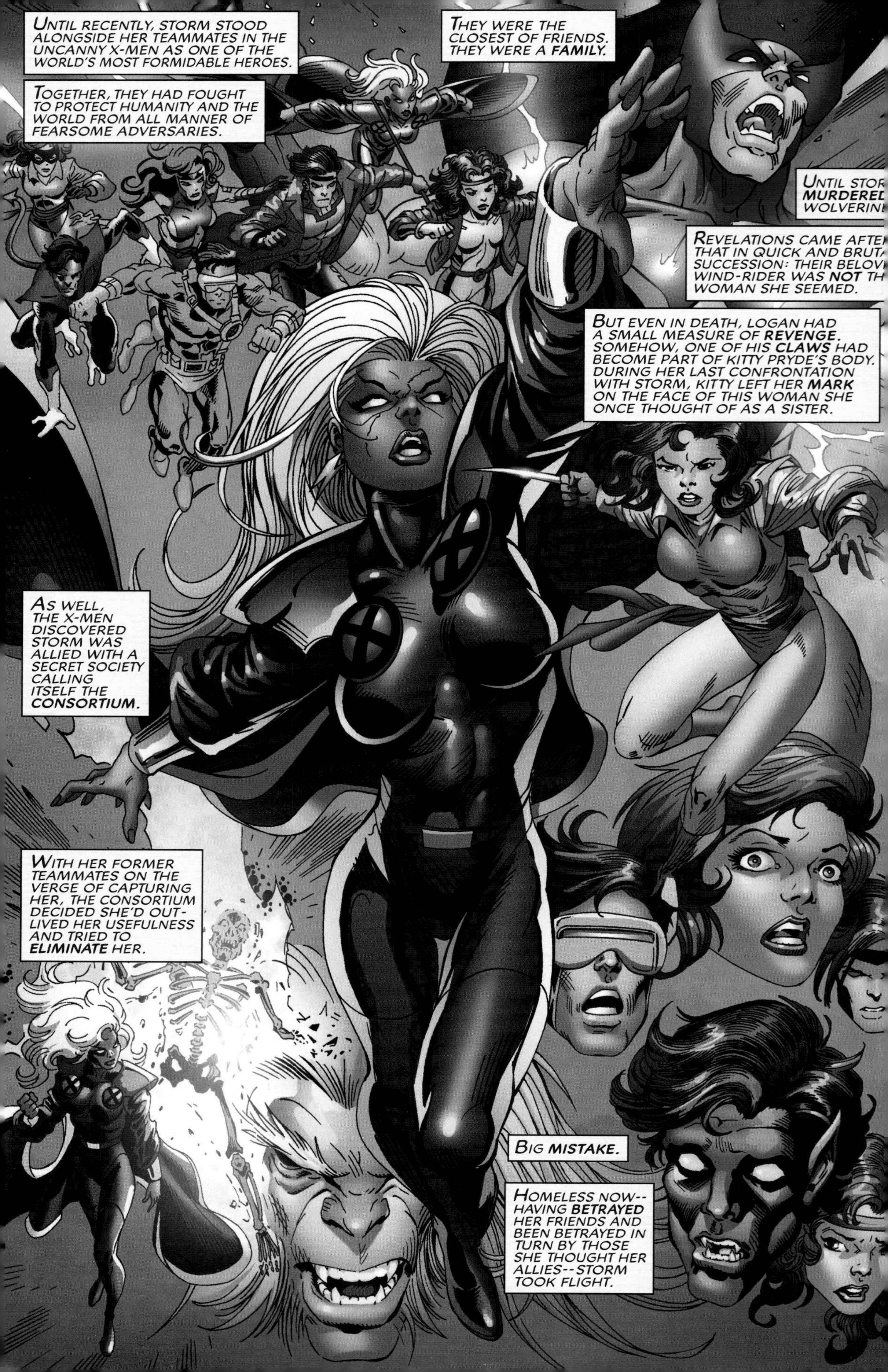
UNTIL RECENTLY, STORM STOOD ALONGSIDE HER TEAMMATES IN THE UNCANNY X-MEN AS ONE OF THE WORLD'S MOST FORMIDABLE HEROES.
TOGETHER, THEY HAD FOUGHT TO PROTECT HUMANITY AND THE WORLD FROM ALL MANNER OF FEARSOME ADVERSARIES.
THEY WERE THE CLOSEST OF FRIENDS. THEY WERE A FAMILY.
UNTIL STOR MURDERED WOLVERIN
REVELATIONS CAME AFTE THAT IN QUICK AND BRUT SUCCESSION: THEIR BELOV WIND-RIDER WAS NOT TH WOMAN SHE SEEMED.
BUT EVEN IN DEATH, LOGAN HAD A SMALL MEASURE OF REVENGE. SOMEHOW, ONE OF HIS CLAWS HAD BECOME PART OF KITTY PRYDE'S BODY. DURING HER LAST CONFRONTATION WITH STORM, KITTY LEFT HER MARK ON THE FACE OF THIS WOMAN SHE ONCE THOUGHT OF AS A SISTER.
AS WELL, THE X-MEN DISCOVERED STORM WAS ALLIED WITH A SECRET SOCIETY CALLING ITSELF THE CONSORTIUM.
WITH HER FORMER TEAMMATES ON THE VERGE OF CAPTURING HER, THE CONSORTIUM DECIDED SHE'D OUT-LIVED HER USEFULNESS AND TRIED TO ELIMINATE HER.
BIG MISTAKE.
HOMELESS NOW-- HAVING BETRAYED HER FRIENDS AND BEEN BETRAYED IN TURN BY THOSE SHE THOUGHT HER ALLIES-- STORM TOOK FLIGHT.

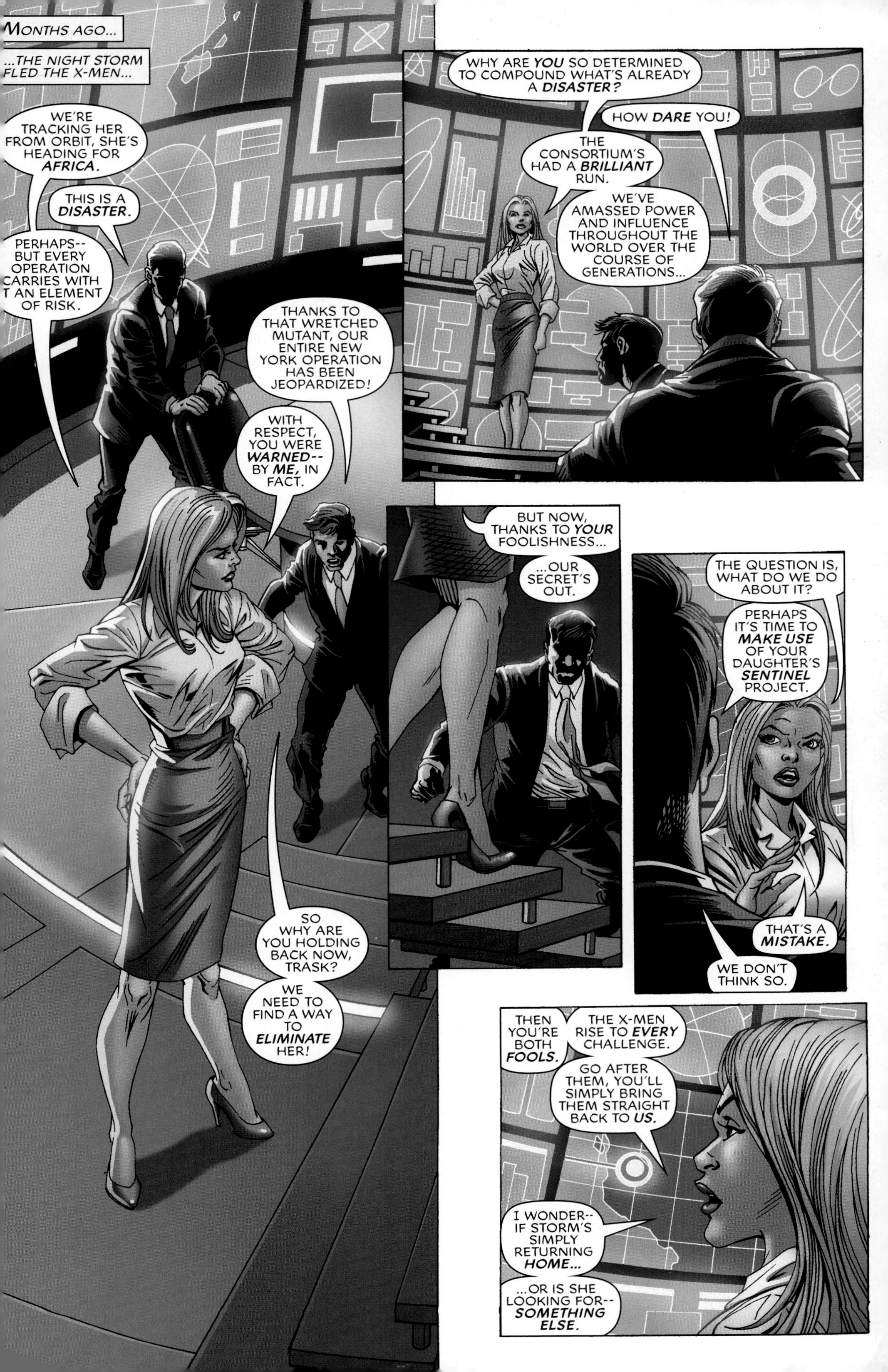
MONTHS AGO...
...THE NIGHT STORM FLED THE X-MEN...
WE'RE TRACKING HER FROM ORBIT, SHE'S HEADING FOR AFRICA.
THIS IS A DISASTER.
PERHAPS-- BUT EVERY OPERATION CARRIES WITH IT AN ELEMENT OF RISK.
THANKS TO THAT WRETCHED MUTANT, OUR ENTIRE NEW YORK OPERATION HAS BEEN JEOPARDIZED!
WITH RESPECT, YOU WERE WARNED-- BY ME, IN FACT.
SO WHY ARE YOU HOLDING BACK NOW, TRASK?
WE NEED TO FIND A WAY TO ELIMINATE HER!
WHY ARE YOU SO DETERMINED TO COMPOUND WHAT'S ALREADY A DISASTER?
HOW DARE YOU!
THE CONSORTIUM'S HAD A BRILLIANT RUN.
WE'VE AMASSED POWER AND INFLUENCE THROUGHOUT THE WORLD OVER THE COURSE OF GENERATIONS...
BUT NOW, THANKS TO YOUR FOOLISHNESS...
...OUR SECRET'S OUT.
THE QUESTION IS, WHAT DO WE DO ABOUT IT?
PERHAPS IT'S TIME TO MAKE USE OF YOUR DAUGHTER'S SENTINEL PROJECT.
THAT'S A MISTAKE.
WE DON'T THINK SO.
THEN YOU'RE BOTH FOOLS.
THE X-MEN RISE TO EVERY CHALLENGE.
GO AFTER THEM, YOU'LL SIMPLY BRING THEM STRAIGHT BACK TO US.
I WONDER-- IF STORM'S SIMPLY RETURNING HOME...
...OR IS SHE LOOKING FOR-- SOMETHING ELSE.

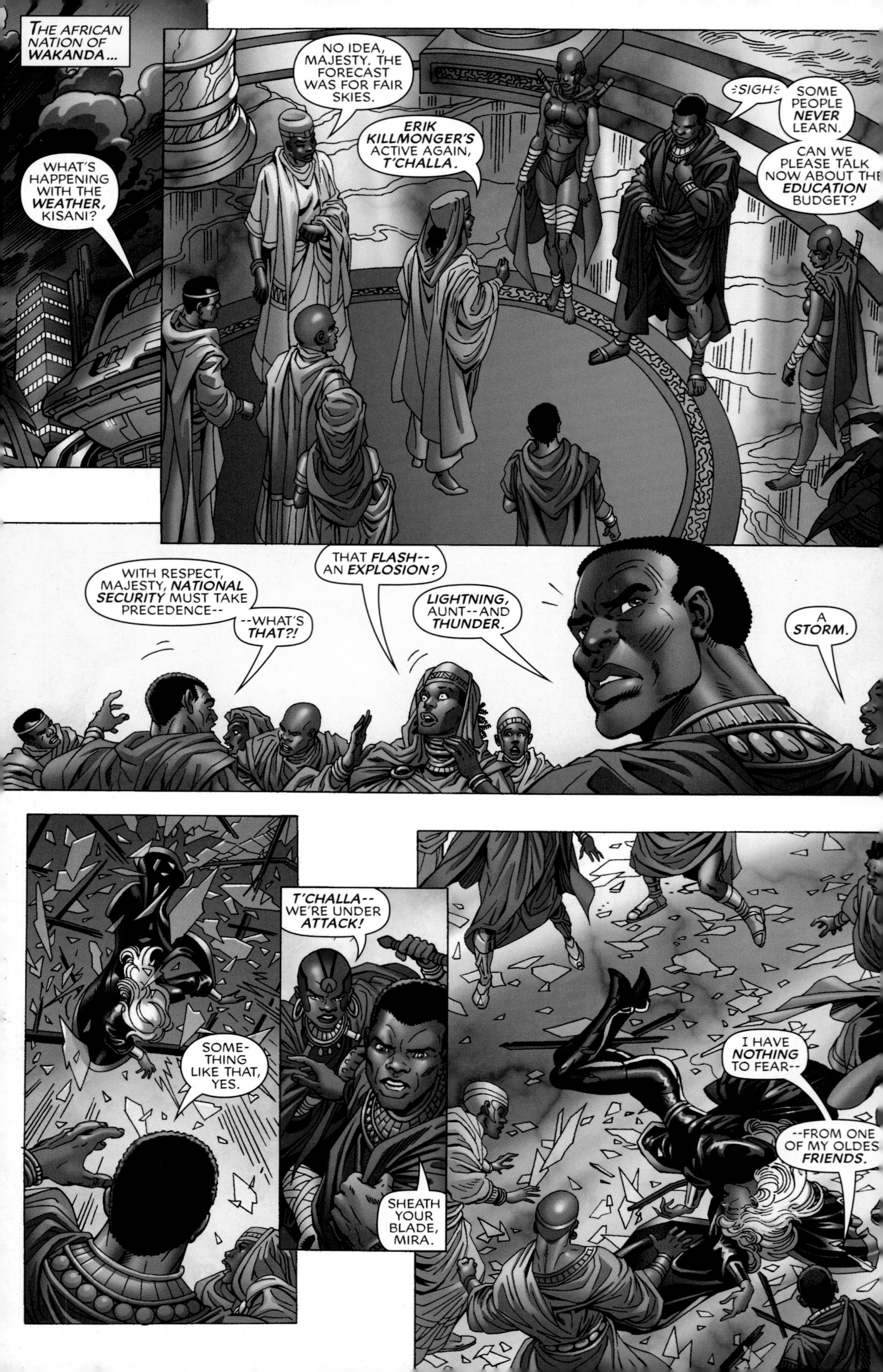
THE AFRICAN NATION OF WAKANDA...
WHAT'S HAPPENING WITH THE WEATHER, KISANI?
NO IDEA, MAJESTY. THE FORECAST WAS FOR FAIR SKIES.
ERIK KILLMONGER'S ACTIVE AGAIN, T'CHALLA.
SIGH
SOME PEOPLE NEVER LEARN.
CAN WE PLEASE TALK NOW ABOUT THE EDUCATION BUDGET?
WITH RESPECT, MAJESTY, NATIONAL SECURITY MUST TAKE PRECEDENCE--
--WHAT'S THAT?!
THAT FLASH--AN EXPLOSION?
LIGHTNING, AUNT--AND THUNDER.
A STORM.
SOME-THING LIKE THAT, YES.
T'CHALLA--WE'RE UNDER ATTACK!
SHEATH YOUR BLADE, MIRA.
I HAVE NOTHING TO FEAR--
--FROM ONE OF MY OLDES FRIENDS.

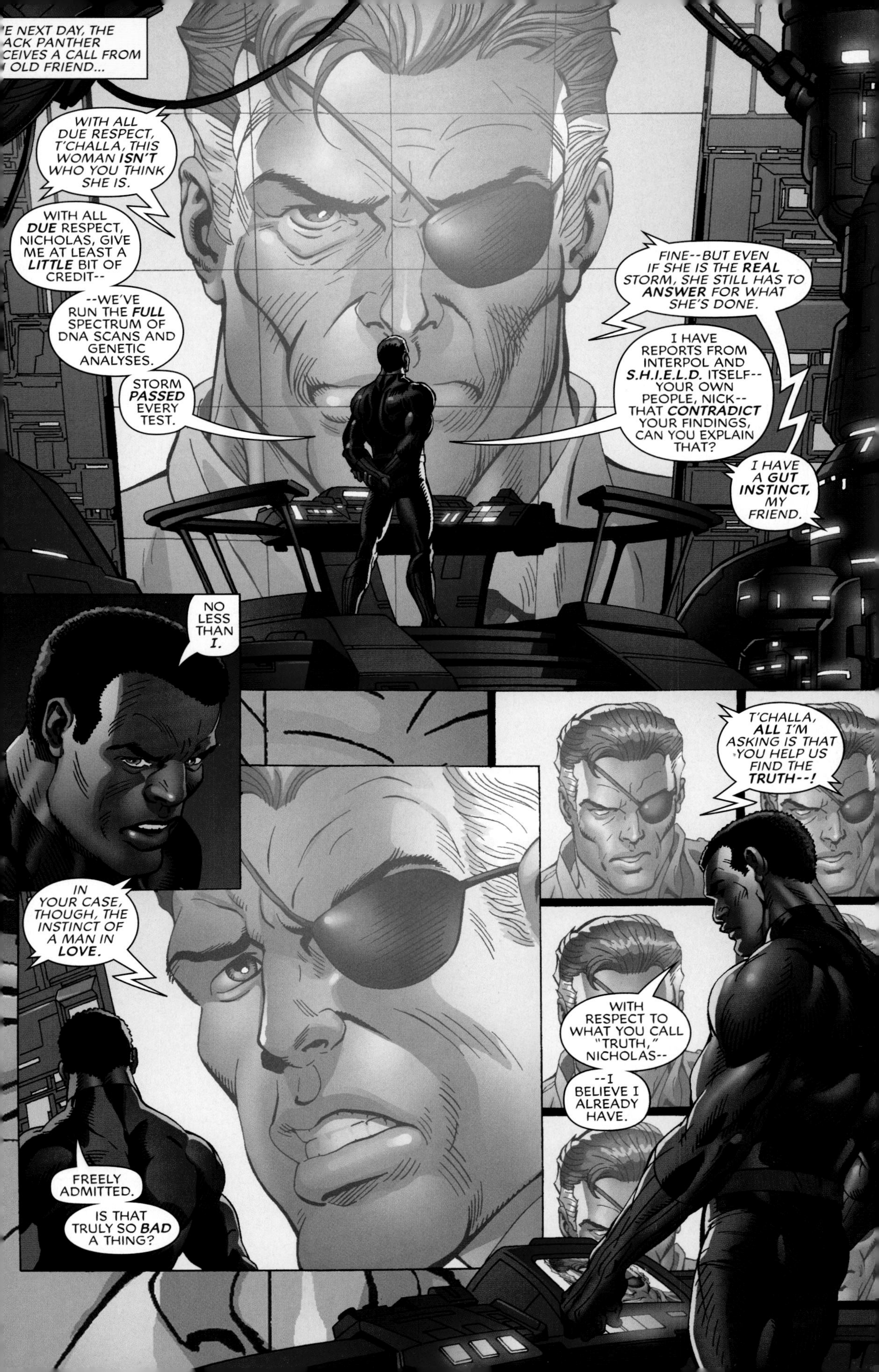
'E NEXT DAY, THE
ACK PANTHER
CEIVES A CALL FROM
I OLD FRIEND...
WITH ALL DUE RESPECT, T'CHALLA, THIS WOMAN ISN'T WHO YOU THINK SHE IS.
WITH ALL DUE RESPECT, NICHOLAS, GIVE ME AT LEAST A LITTLE BIT OF CREDIT--
--WE'VE RUN THE FULL SPECTRUM OF DNA SCANS AND GENETIC ANALYSES.
STORM PASSED EVERY TEST.
FINE--BUT EVEN IF SHE IS THE REAL STORM, SHE STILL HAS TO ANSWER FOR WHAT SHE'S DONE.
I HAVE REPORTS FROM INTERPOL AND S.H.I.E.L.D. ITSELF--YOUR OWN PEOPLE, NICK--THAT CONTRADICT YOUR FINDINGS, CAN YOU EXPLAIN THAT?
I HAVE A GUT INSTINCT, MY FRIEND.
NO LESS THAN I.
IN YOUR CASE, THOUGH, THE INSTINCT OF A MAN IN LOVE.
FREELY ADMITTED.
IS THAT TRULY SO BAD A THING?
T'CHALLA, ALL I'M ASKING IS THAT YOU HELP US FIND THE TRUTH--!
WITH RESPECT TO WHAT YOU CALL "TRUTH," NICHOLAS--
--I BELIEVE I ALREADY HAVE.

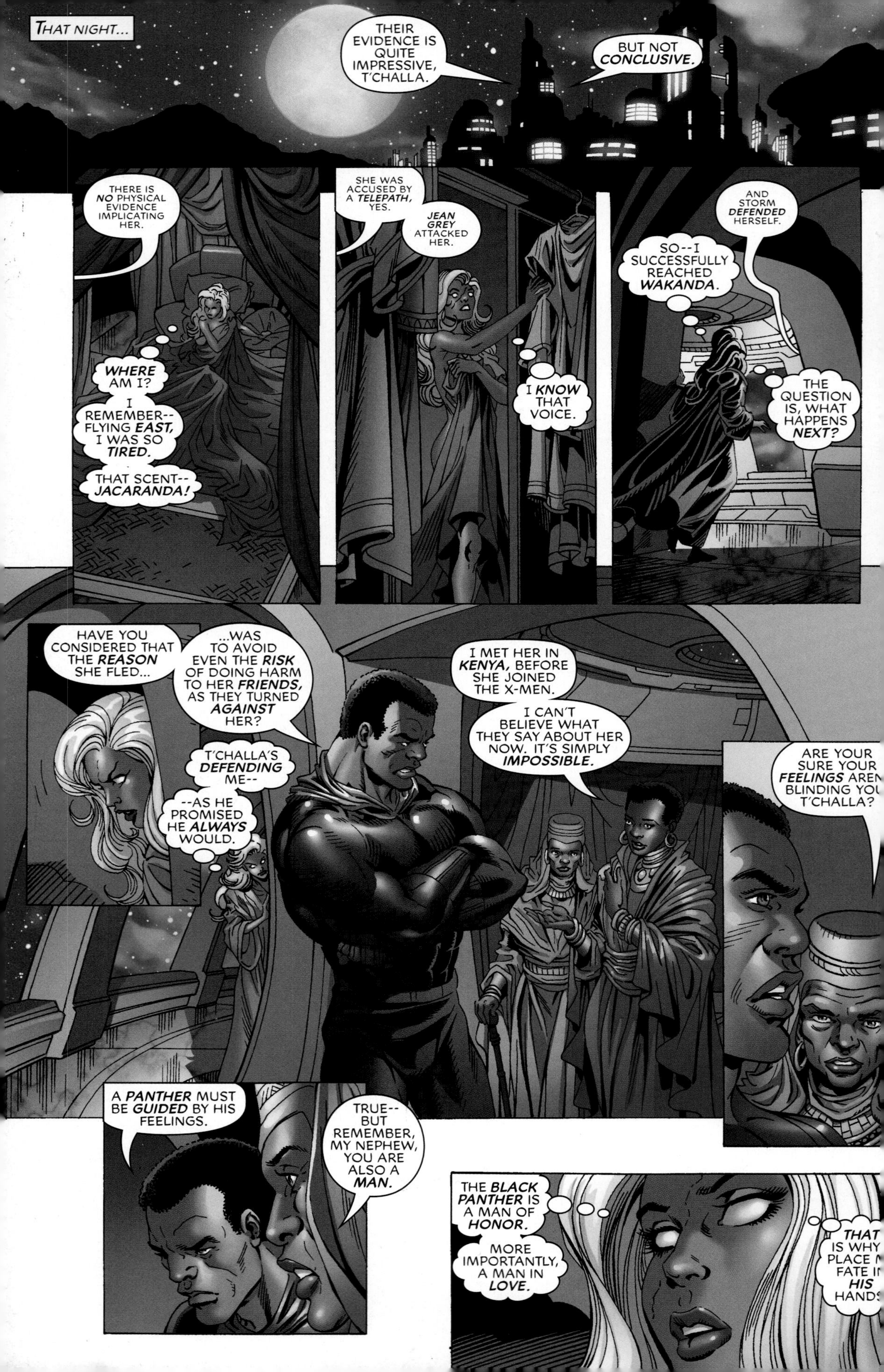
THAT NIGHT...
THEIR EVIDENCE IS QUITE IMPRESSIVE, T'CHALLA.
BUT NOT CONCLUSIVE.
THERE IS NO PHYSICAL EVIDENCE IMPLICATING HER.
WHERE AM I?
I REMEMBER-- FLYING EAST, I WAS SO TIRED.
THAT SCENT-- JACARANDA!
SHE WAS ACCUSED BY A TELEPATH, YES.
JEAN GREY ATTACKED HER.
I KNOW THAT VOICE.
AND STORM DEFENDED HERSELF.
SO--I SUCCESSFULLY REACHED WAKANDA.
THE QUESTION IS, WHAT HAPPENS NEXT?
HAVE YOU CONSIDERED THAT THE REASON SHE FLED...
...WAS TO AVOID EVEN THE RISK OF DOING HARM TO HER FRIENDS, AS THEY TURNED AGAINST HER?
T'CHALLA'S DEFENDING ME--
--AS HE PROMISED HE ALWAYS WOULD.
I MET HER IN KENYA, BEFORE SHE JOINED THE X-MEN.
I CAN'T BELIEVE WHAT THEY SAY ABOUT HER NOW. IT'S SIMPLY IMPOSSIBLE.
ARE YOUR SURE YOUR FEELINGS AREN BLINDING YOU T'CHALLA?
A PANTHER MUST BE GUIDED BY HIS FEELINGS.
TRUE-- BUT REMEMBER, MY NEPHEW, YOU ARE ALSO A MAN.
THE BLACK PANTHER IS A MAN OF HONOR.
MORE IMPORTANTLY, A MAN IN LOVE.
THAT IS WHY PLACE FATE I HIS HANDS

THE **RULES** T'CHALLA LAID DOWN WERE SIMPLE: STORM WAS GIVEN SANCTUARY AND NAMED A WARD OF THE CROWN. BUT HER FREEDOM WAS RESTRICTED TO THE BORDERS OF **WAKANDA**.

BEYOND THAT, A GLOBAL FUGITIVE WARRANT WAS IN EFFECT.

STORM DIDN'T SEEM TO MIND.

OVER TIME, SHE SETTLED QUICKLY AND NATURALLY INTO THE LIFE OF THE LAND, AS THOUGH SHE HAD BEEN BORN THERE.

ONCE MORE, SHE FELL INTO THE PATTERNS OF HER DAYS FARTHER NORTH, FROM BEFORE SHE WAS RECRUITED BY CHARLES XAVIER TO HELP THE X-MEN PROTECT THE WORLD.

SHE **CARED** FOR THE REALM.

SHE CARED FOR THE **PEOPLE** OF HER NEW HOME.

PROTECTING THEM FROM THE ELEMENTS THAT ARE BEYOND THEIR CONTROL.

AND FROM THOSE AMONG THEM WHO SEE THEMSELVES AS **PREDATORS**.

YOU WERE WARNED, **KILLMONGER.**

NOW YOU FACE A LIFE IN **PRISON**.

YOU SHOULD HAVE **KILLED** ME, T'CHALLA.

THAT'S A **MISTAKE** I GUARANTEE YOU'LL LIVE TO **REGRET**.

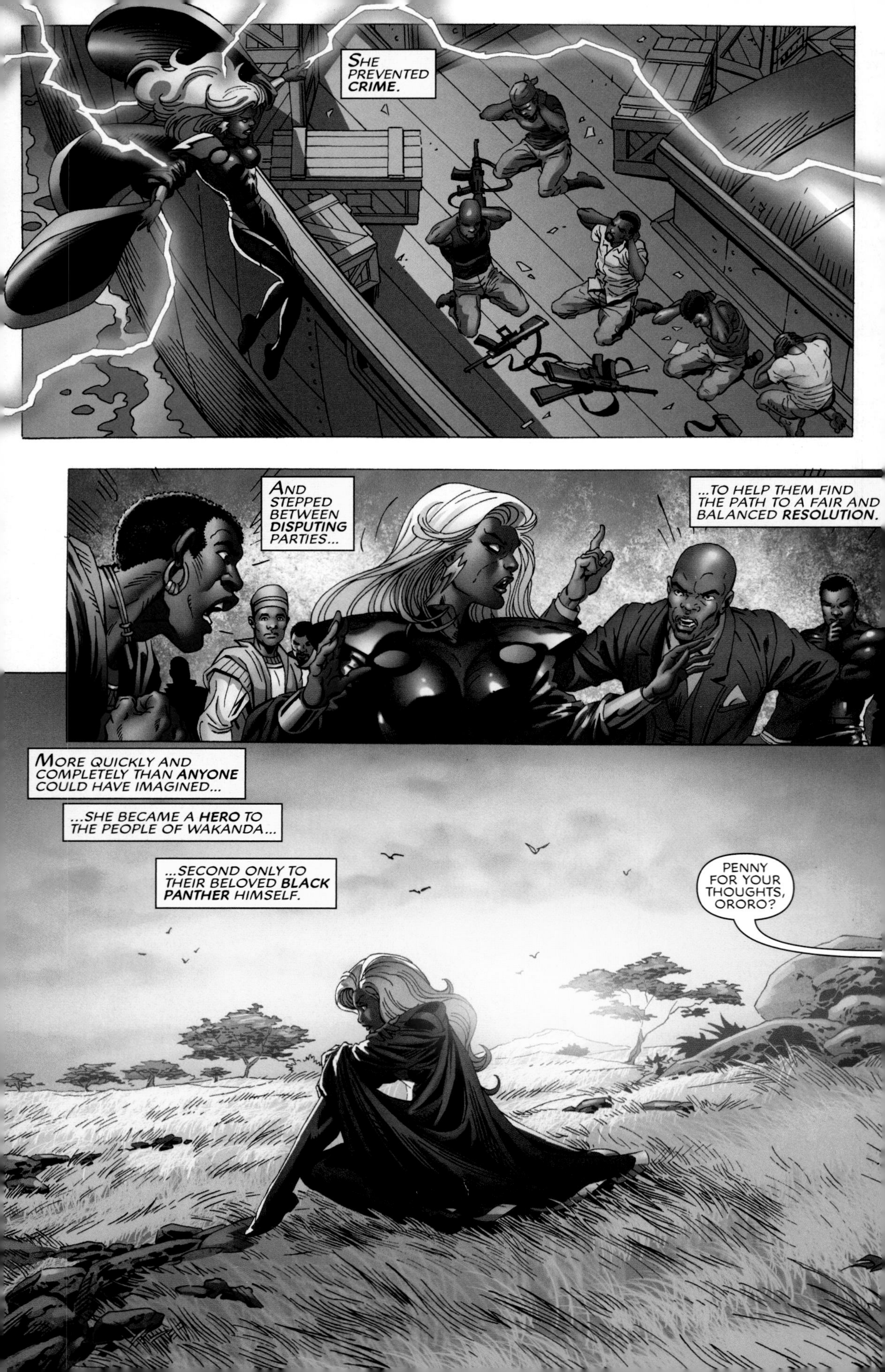
SHE PREVENTED CRIME.
AND STEPPED BETWEEN DISPUTING PARTIES...
...TO HELP THEM FIND THE PATH TO A FAIR AND BALANCED RESOLUTION.
MORE QUICKLY AND COMPLETELY THAN ANYONE COULD HAVE IMAGINED...
...SHE BECAME A HERO TO THE PEOPLE OF WAKANDA...
...SECOND ONLY TO THEIR BELOVED BLACK PANTHER HIMSELF.
PENNY FOR YOUR THOUGHTS, ORORO?

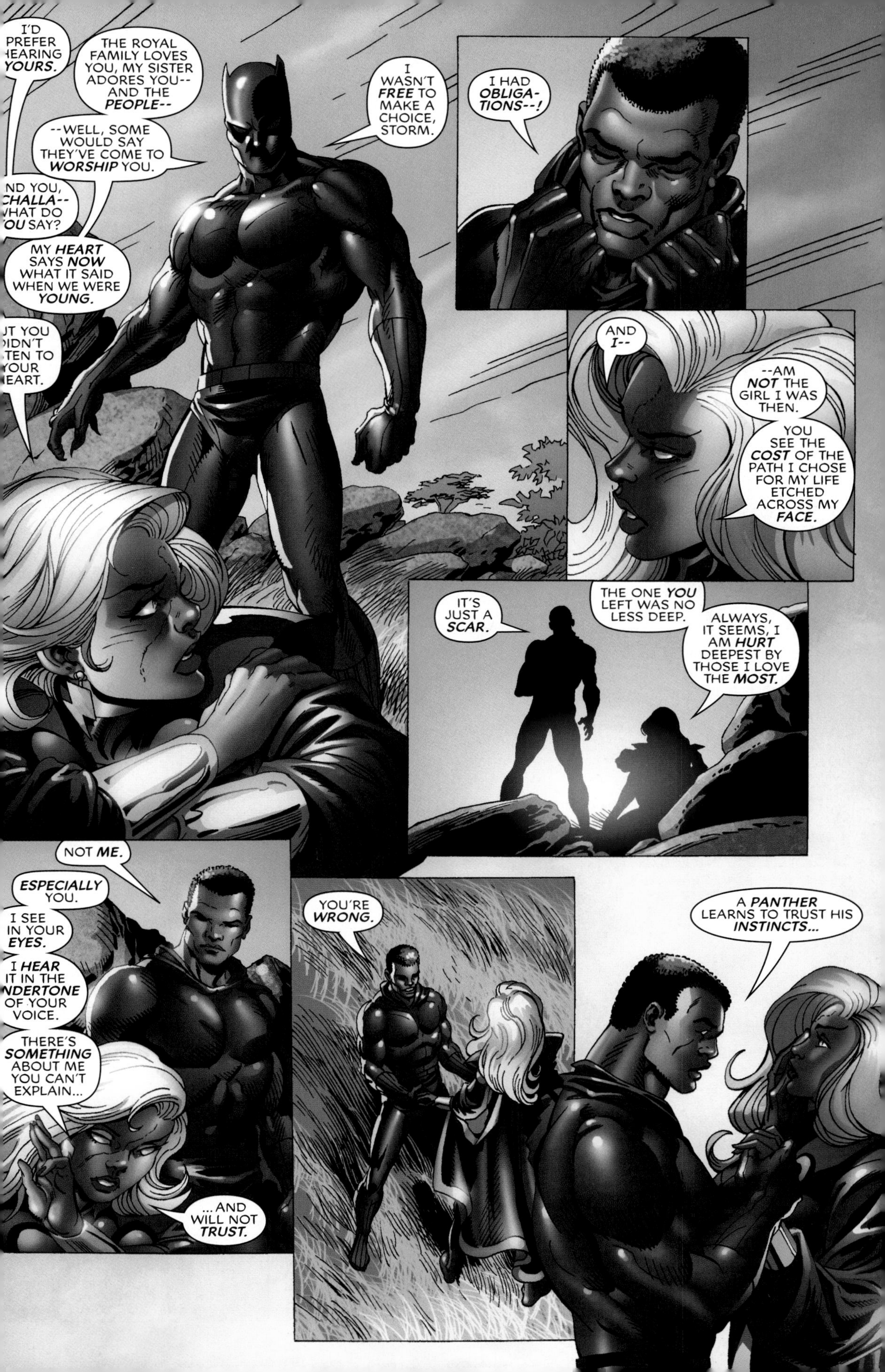

I'D PREFER HEARING YOURS.
THE ROYAL FAMILY LOVES YOU, MY SISTER ADORES YOU-- AND THE PEOPLE--
--WELL, SOME WOULD SAY THEY'VE COME TO WORSHIP YOU.
ND YOU, CHALLA-- WHAT DO YOU SAY?
MY HEART SAYS NOW WHAT IT SAID WHEN WE WERE YOUNG.
UT YOU IDN'T TEN TO YOUR EART.
I WASN'T FREE TO MAKE A CHOICE, STORM.
I HAD OBLIGA- TIONS--!
AND I--
--AM NOT THE GIRL I WAS THEN.
YOU SEE THE COST OF THE PATH I CHOSE FOR MY LIFE ETCHED ACROSS MY FACE.
IT'S JUST A SCAR.
THE ONE YOU LEFT WAS NO LESS DEEP.
ALWAYS, IT SEEMS, I AM HURT DEEPEST BY THOSE I LOVE THE MOST.
NOT ME.
ESPECIALLY YOU.
I SEE IN YOUR EYES.
I HEAR IT IN THE NDERTONE OF YOUR VOICE.
THERE'S SOMETHING ABOUT ME YOU CAN'T EXPLAIN...
...AND WILL NOT TRUST.
YOU'RE WRONG.
A PANTHER LEARNS TO TRUST HIS INSTINCTS...

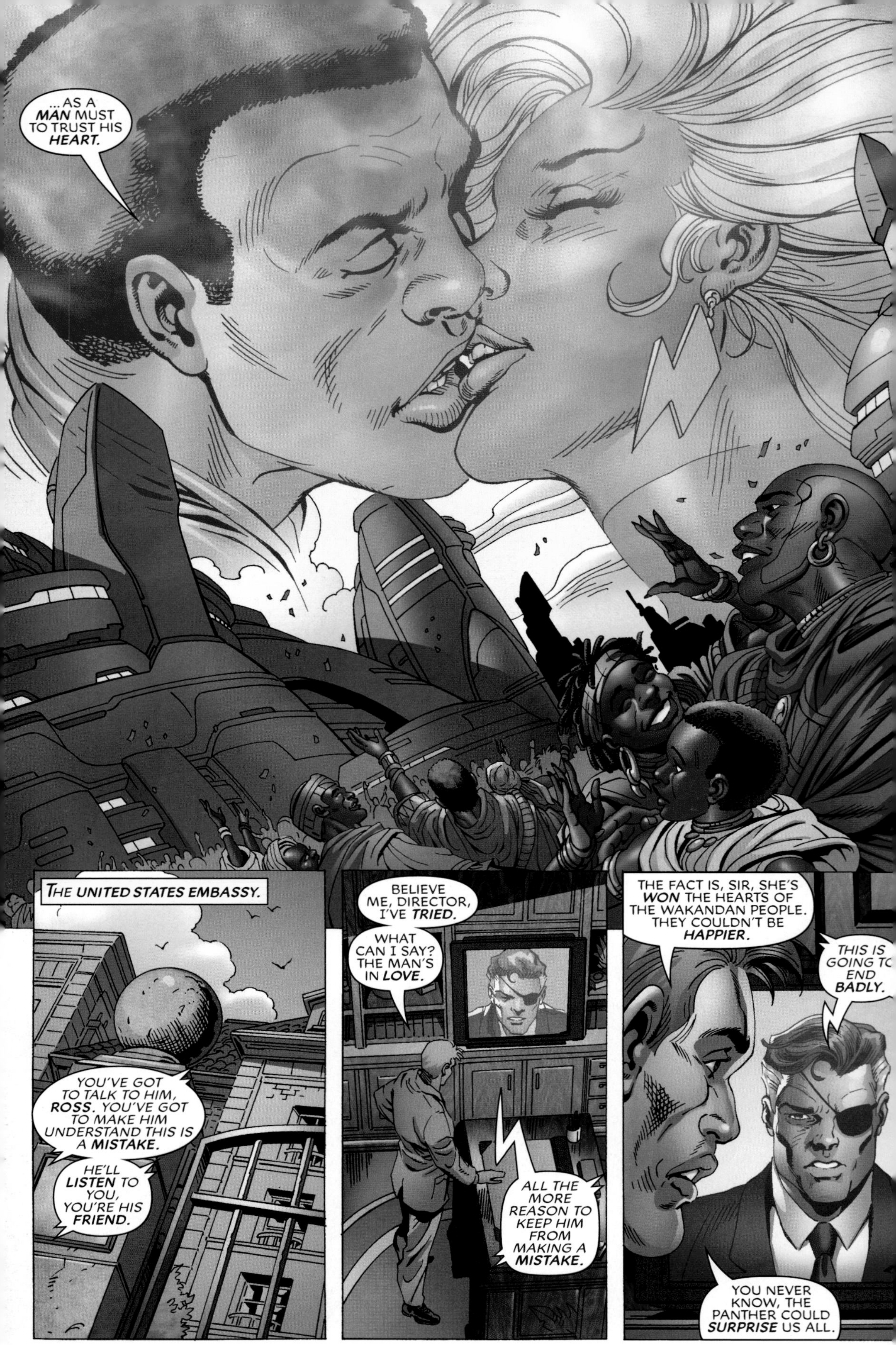
...AS A MAN MUST TO TRUST HIS HEART.
THE UNITED STATES EMBASSY.
YOU'VE GOT TO TALK TO HIM, ROSS. YOU'VE GOT TO MAKE HIM UNDERSTAND THIS IS A MISTAKE.
HE'LL LISTEN TO YOU, YOU'RE HIS FRIEND.
BELIEVE ME, DIRECTOR, I'VE TRIED.
WHAT CAN I SAY? THE MAN'S IN LOVE.
ALL THE MORE REASON TO KEEP HIM FROM MAKING A MISTAKE.
THE FACT IS, SIR, SHE'S WON THE HEARTS OF THE WAKANDAN PEOPLE. THEY COULDN'T BE HAPPIER.
THIS IS GOING TO END BADLY.
YOU NEVER KNOW, THE PANTHER COULD SURPRISE US ALL.

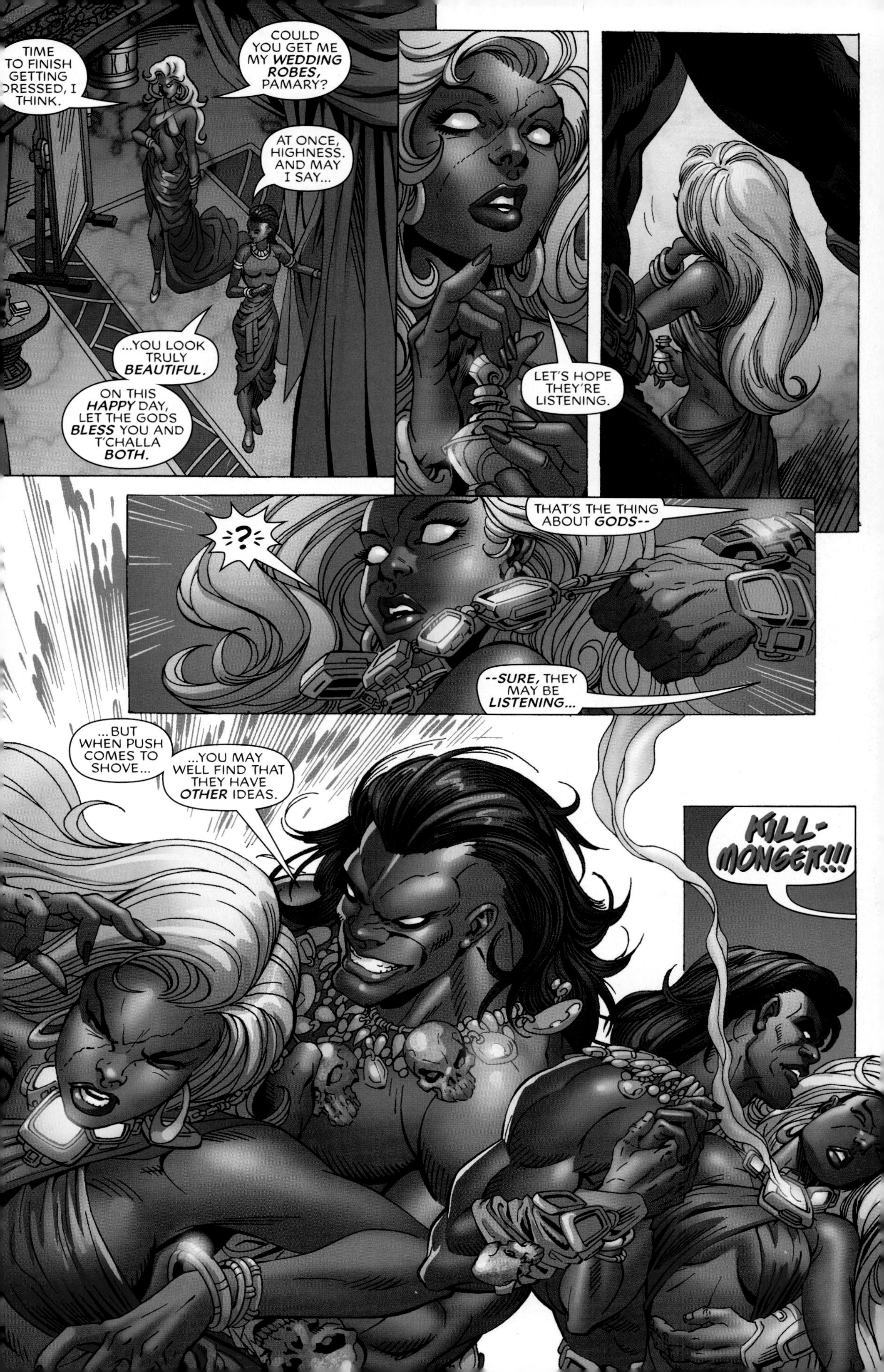
TIME TO FINISH GETTING DRESSED, I THINK.
COULD YOU GET ME MY WEDDING ROBES, PAMARY?
AT ONCE, HIGHNESS. AND MAY I SAY...
...YOU LOOK TRULY BEAUTIFUL.
ON THIS HAPPY DAY, LET THE GODS BLESS YOU AND T'CHALLA BOTH.
LET'S HOPE THEY'RE LISTENING.
?
THAT'S THE THING ABOUT GODS--
--SURE, THEY MAY BE LISTENING...
...BUT WHEN PUSH COMES TO SHOVE...
...YOU MAY WELL FIND THAT THEY HAVE OTHER IDEAS.
KILL-MONGER!!!

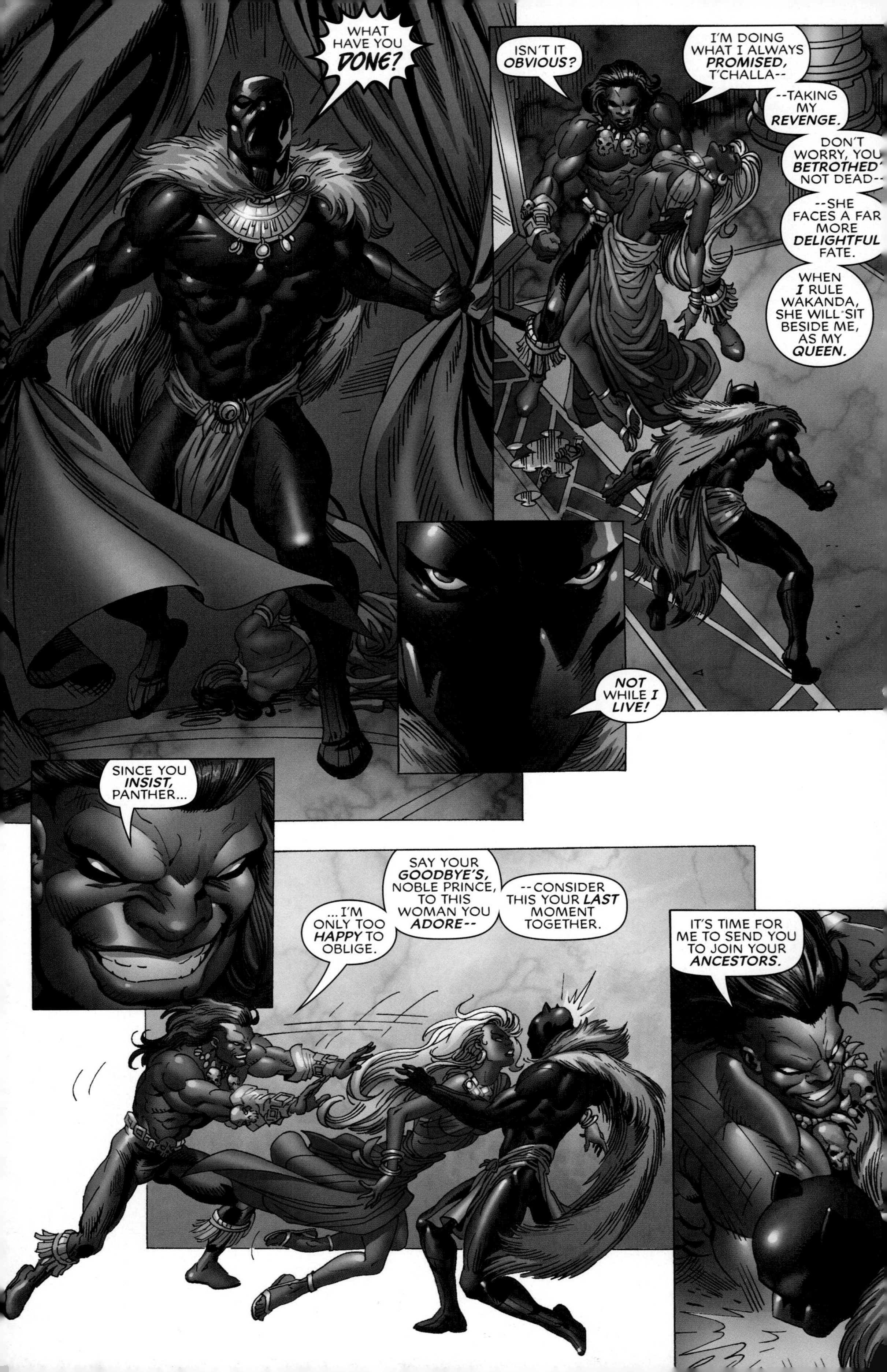
WHAT HAVE YOU DONE?
ISN'T IT OBVIOUS?
I'M DOING WHAT I ALWAYS PROMISED, T'CHALLA--
--TAKING MY REVENGE.
DON'T WORRY, YOU BETROTHED' NOT DEAD--
--SHE FACES A FAR MORE DELIGHTFUL FATE.
WHEN I RULE WAKANDA, SHE WILL SIT BESIDE ME, AS MY QUEEN.
NOT WHILE I LIVE!
SINCE YOU INSIST, PANTHER...
...I'M ONLY TOO HAPPY TO OBLIGE.
SAY YOUR GOODBYE'S, NOBLE PRINCE, TO THIS WOMAN YOU ADORE--
--CONSIDER THIS YOUR LAST MOMENT TOGETHER.
IT'S TIME FOR ME TO SEND YOU TO JOIN YOUR ANCESTORS.

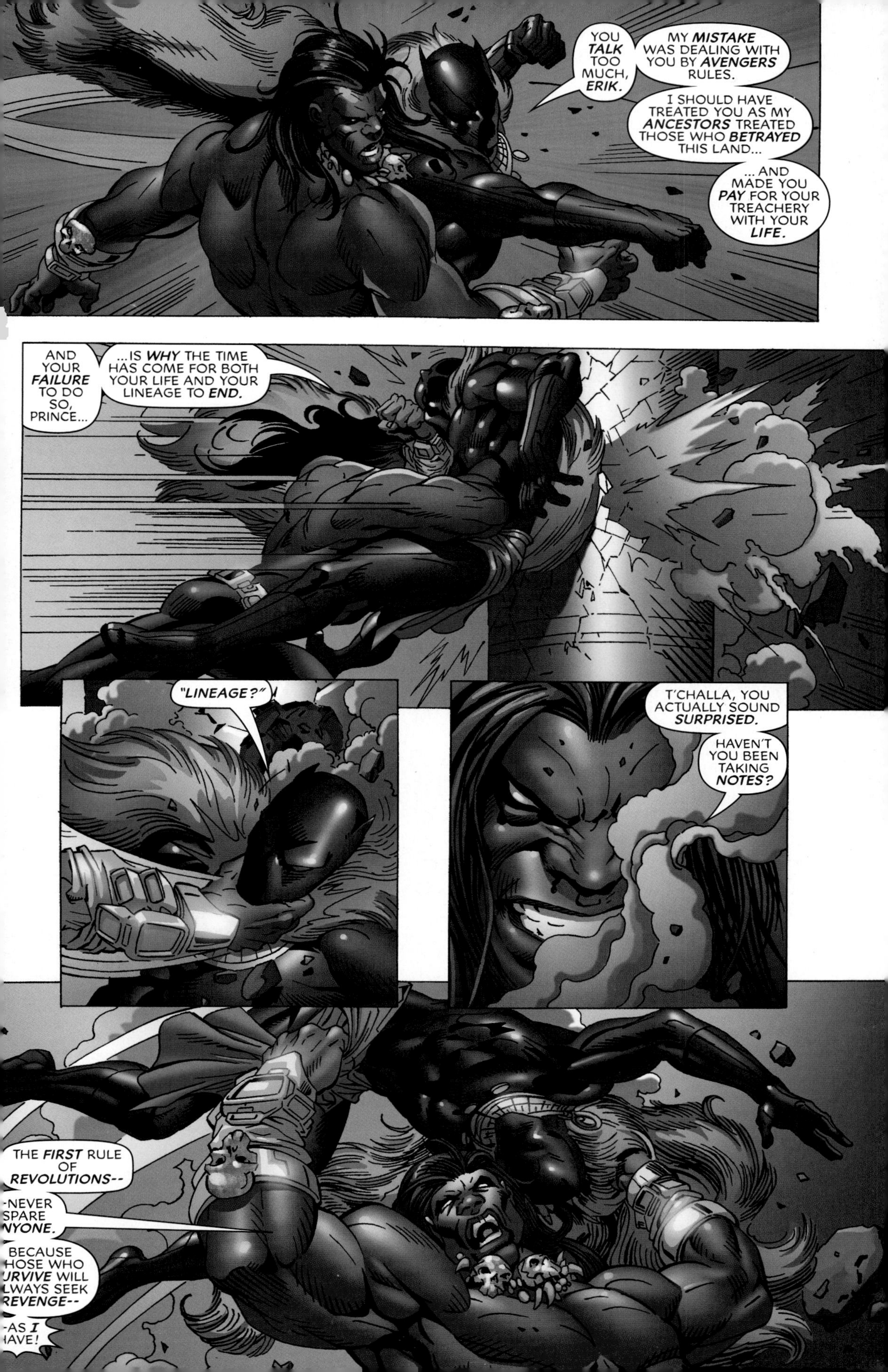

YOU TALK TOO MUCH, ERIK.
MY MISTAKE WAS DEALING WITH YOU BY AVENGERS RULES.
I SHOULD HAVE TREATED YOU AS MY ANCESTORS TREATED THOSE WHO BETRAYED THIS LAND...
... AND MADE YOU PAY FOR YOUR TREACHERY WITH YOUR LIFE.
AND YOUR FAILURE TO DO SO, PRINCE...
...IS WHY THE TIME HAS COME FOR BOTH YOUR LIFE AND YOUR LINEAGE TO END.
"LINEAGE?"
T'CHALLA, YOU ACTUALLY SOUND SURPRISED.
HAVEN'T YOU BEEN TAKING NOTES?
THE FIRST RULE OF REVOLUTIONS--
-NEVER SPARE NYONE.
BECAUSE HOSE WHO URVIVE WILL LWAYS SEEK REVENGE--
-AS I AVE!

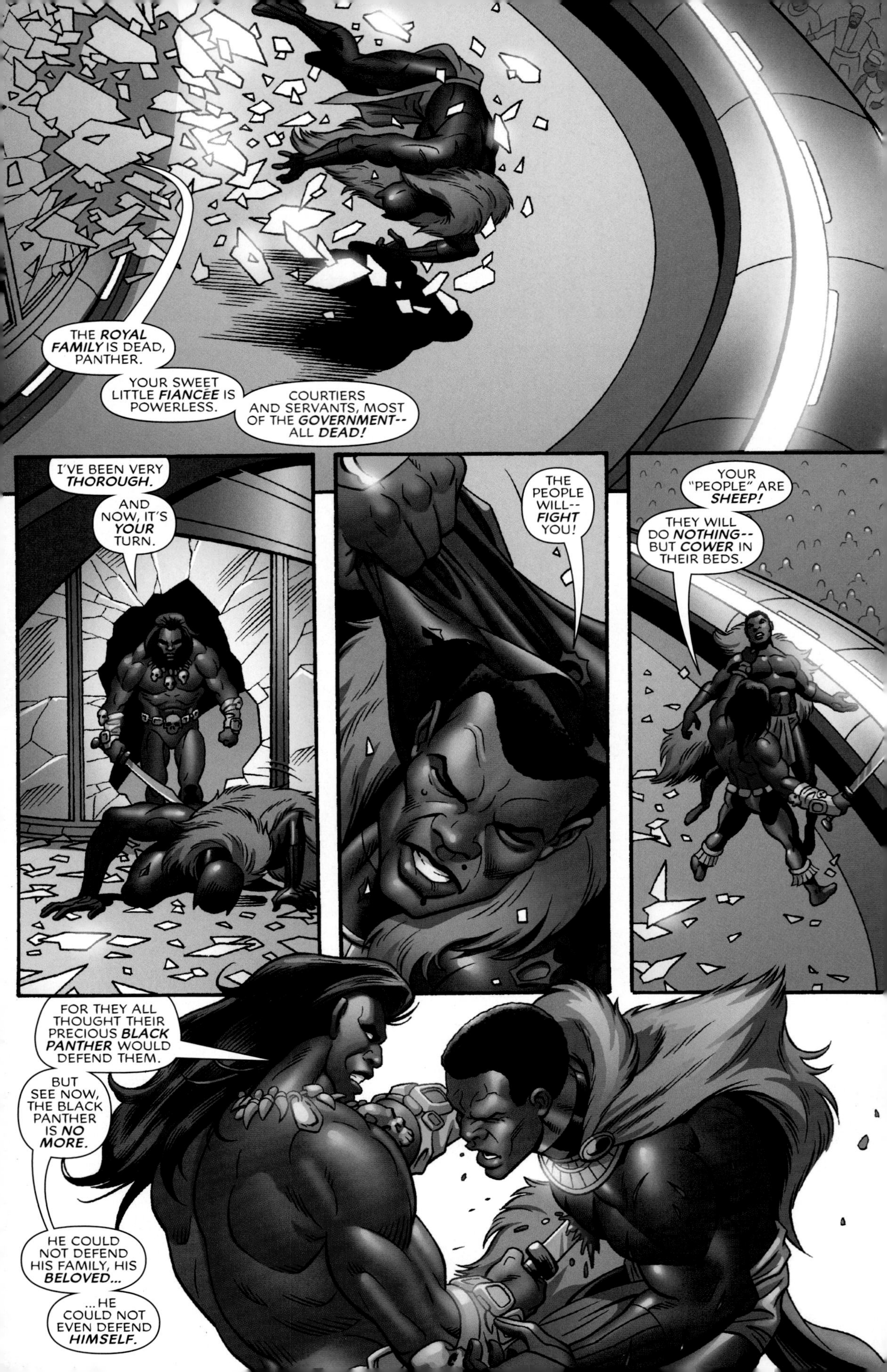
THE ROYAL FAMILY IS DEAD, PANTHER.
YOUR SWEET LITTLE FIANCÉE IS POWERLESS.
COURTIERS AND SERVANTS, MOST OF THE GOVERNMENT-- ALL DEAD!
I'VE BEEN VERY THOROUGH.
AND NOW, IT'S YOUR TURN.
THE PEOPLE WILL-- FIGHT YOU!
YOUR "PEOPLE" ARE SHEEP!
THEY WILL DO NOTHING-- BUT COWER IN THEIR BEDS.
FOR THEY ALL THOUGHT THEIR PRECIOUS BLACK PANTHER WOULD DEFEND THEM.
BUT SEE NOW, THE BLACK PANTHER IS NO MORE.
HE COULD NOT DEFEND HIS FAMILY, HIS BELOVED...
...HE COULD NOT EVEN DEFEND HIMSELF.

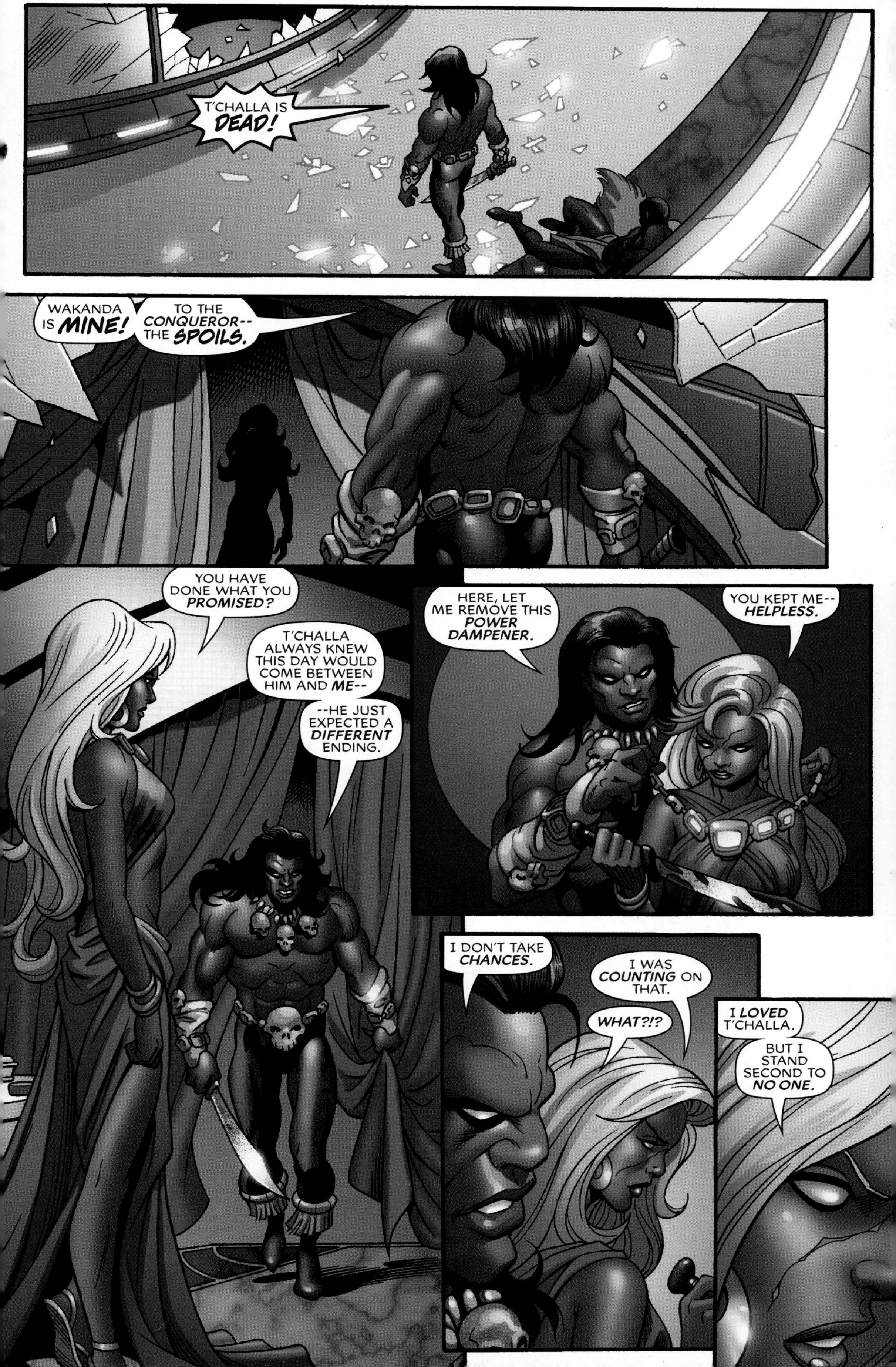

T'CHALLA IS DEAD!
WAKANDA IS MINE!
TO THE CONQUEROR-- THE SPOILS.
YOU HAVE DONE WHAT YOU PROMISED?
T'CHALLA ALWAYS KNEW THIS DAY WOULD COME BETWEEN HIM AND ME--
--HE JUST EXPECTED A DIFFERENT ENDING.
HERE, LET ME REMOVE THIS POWER DAMPENER.
YOU KEPT ME-- HELPLESS.
I DON'T TAKE CHANCES.
I WAS COUNTING ON THAT.
WHAT?!?
I LOVED T'CHALLA.
BUT I STAND SECOND TO NO ONE.

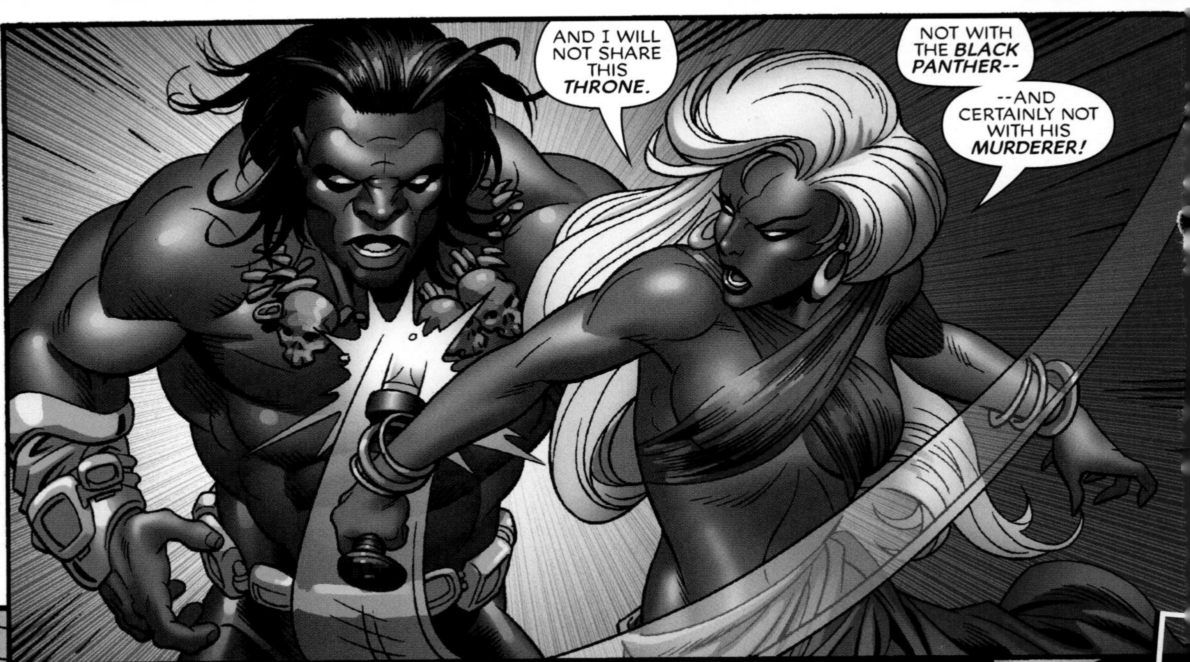
AND I WILL NOT SHARE THIS *THRONE.*
NOT WITH THE *BLACK PANTHER*--
--AND CERTAINLY NOT WITH HIS *MURDERER!*

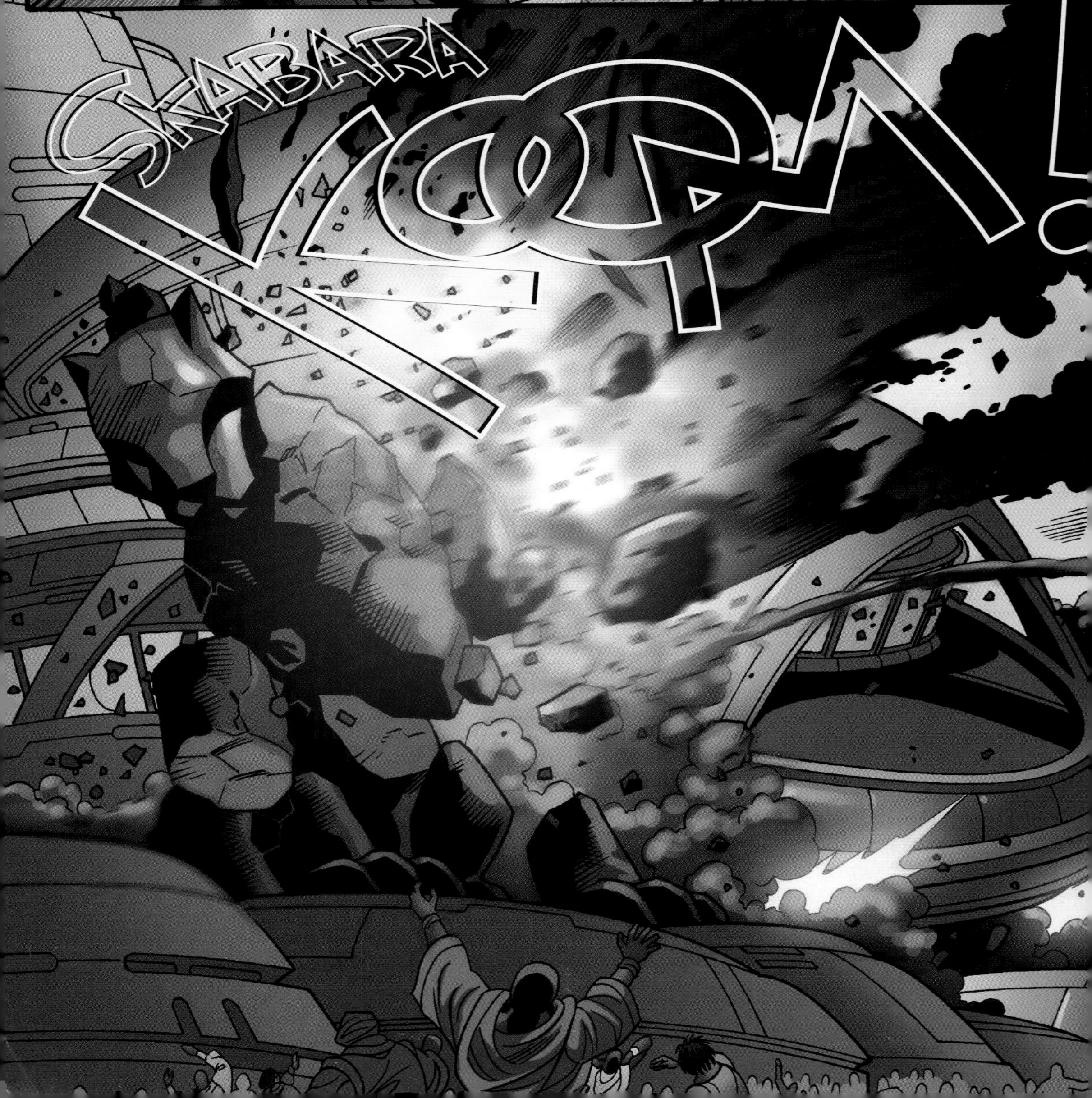
SKABARA

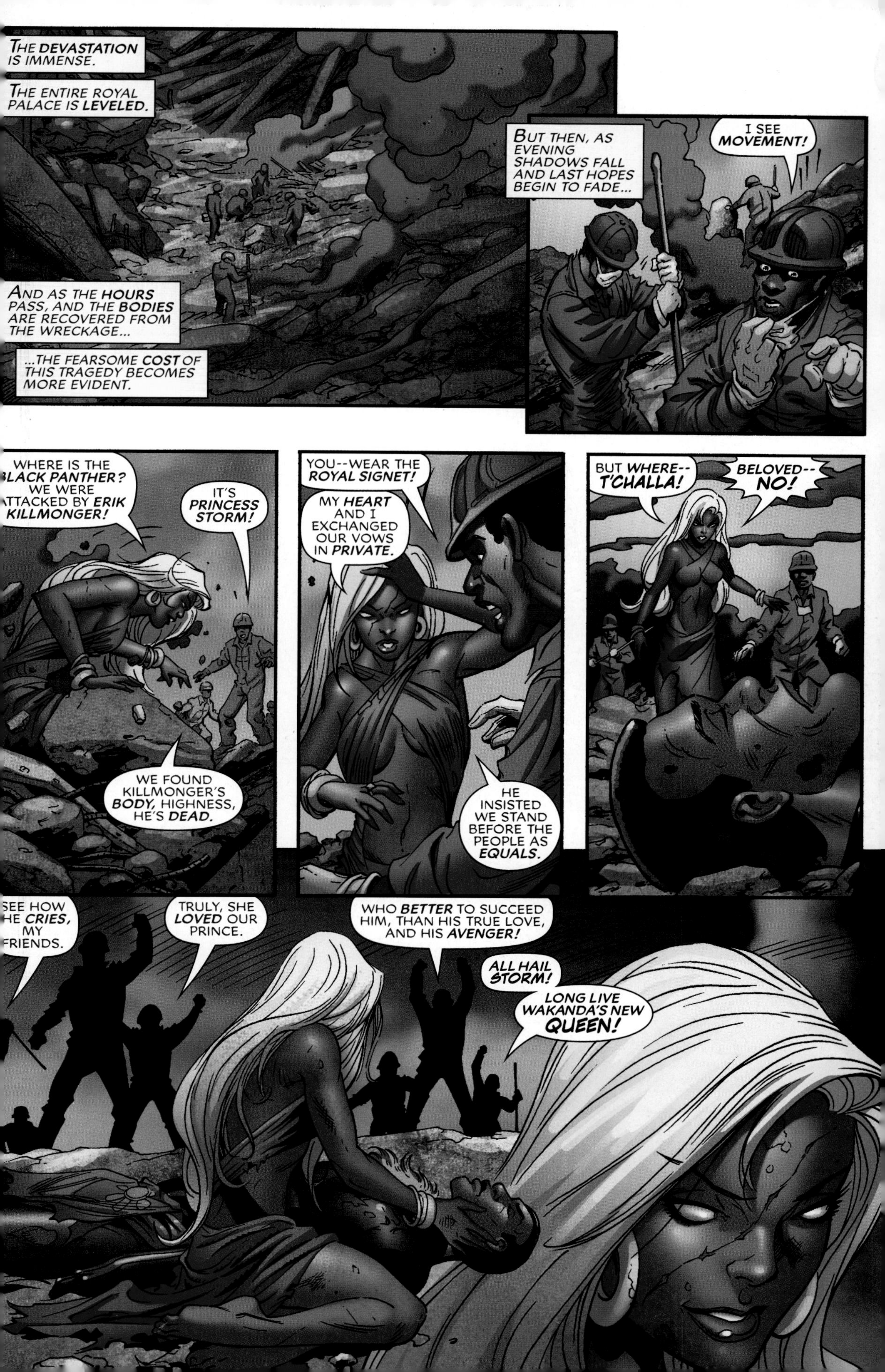
THE DEVASTATION IS IMMENSE.
THE ENTIRE ROYAL PALACE IS LEVELED.
AND AS THE HOURS PASS, AND THE BODIES ARE RECOVERED FROM THE WRECKAGE...
...THE FEARSOME COST OF THIS TRAGEDY BECOMES MORE EVIDENT.
BUT THEN, AS EVENING SHADOWS FALL AND LAST HOPES BEGIN TO FADE...
I SEE MOVEMENT!
WHERE IS THE BLACK PANTHER? WE WERE ATTACKED BY ERIK KILLMONGER!
IT'S PRINCESS STORM!
WE FOUND KILLMONGER'S BODY, HIGHNESS, HE'S DEAD.
YOU--WEAR THE ROYAL SIGNET!
MY HEART AND I EXCHANGED OUR VOWS IN PRIVATE.
HE INSISTED WE STAND BEFORE THE PEOPLE AS EQUALS.
BUT WHERE-- T'CHALLA!
BELOVED-- NO!
SEE HOW HE CRIES, MY FRIENDS.
TRULY, SHE LOVED OUR PRINCE.
WHO BETTER TO SUCCEED HIM, THAN HIS TRUE LOVE, AND HIS AVENGER!
ALL HAIL STORM!
LONG LIVE WAKANDA'S NEW QUEEN!

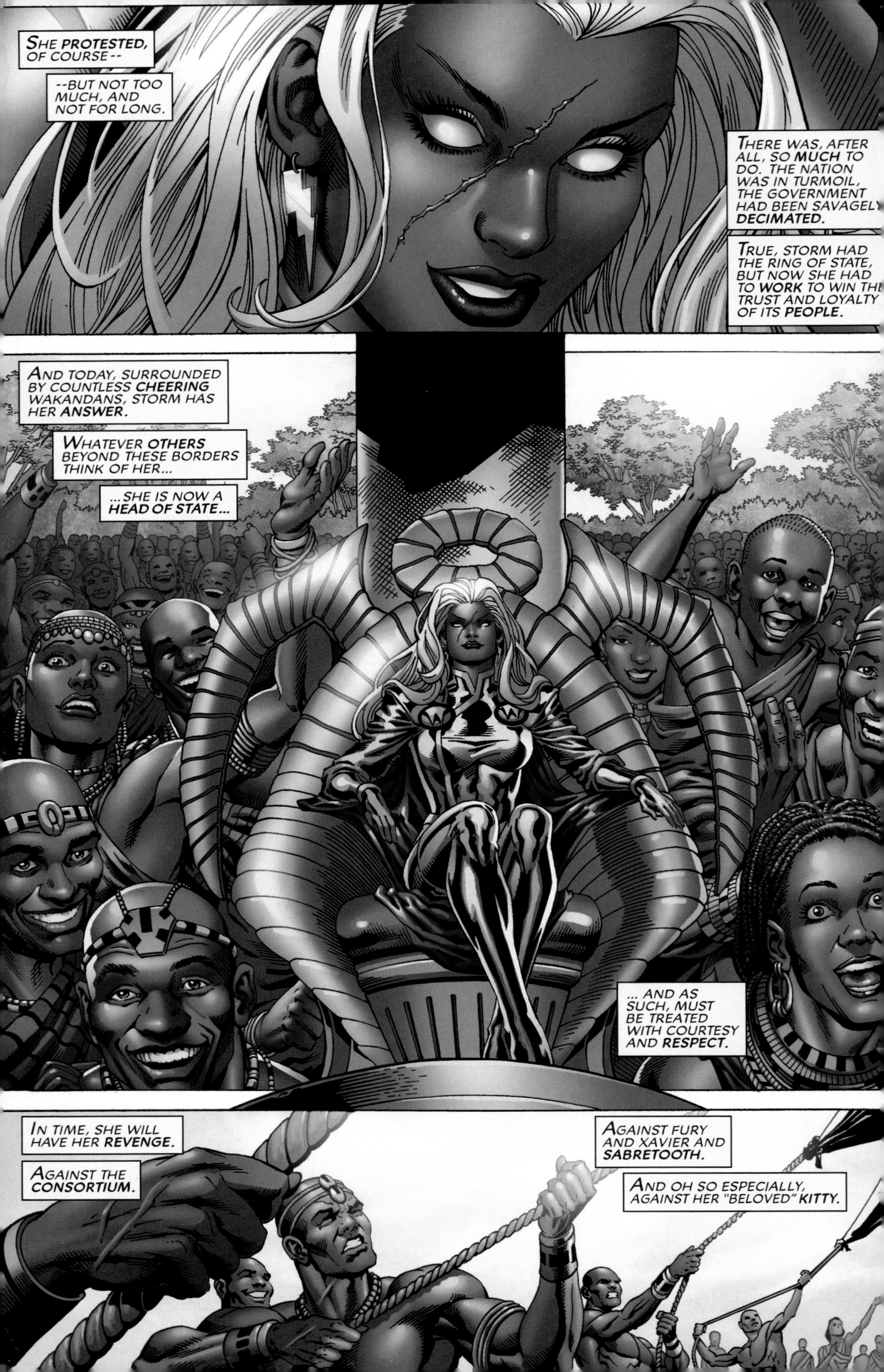
SHE PROTESTED, OF COURSE--
--BUT NOT TOO MUCH, AND NOT FOR LONG.
THERE WAS, AFTER ALL, SO MUCH TO DO. THE NATION WAS IN TURMOIL, THE GOVERNMENT HAD BEEN SAVAGELY DECIMATED.
TRUE, STORM HAD THE RING OF STATE, BUT NOW SHE HAD TO WORK TO WIN THE TRUST AND LOYALTY OF ITS PEOPLE.
AND TODAY, SURROUNDED BY COUNTLESS CHEERING WAKANDANS, STORM HAS HER ANSWER.
WHATEVER OTHERS BEYOND THESE BORDERS THINK OF HER...
...SHE IS NOW A HEAD OF STATE...
... AND AS SUCH, MUST BE TREATED WITH COURTESY AND RESPECT.
IN TIME, SHE WILL HAVE HER REVENGE.
AGAINST THE CONSORTIUM.
AGAINST FURY AND XAVIER AND SABRETOOTH.
AND OH SO ESPECIALLY, AGAINST HER "BELOVED" KITTY.

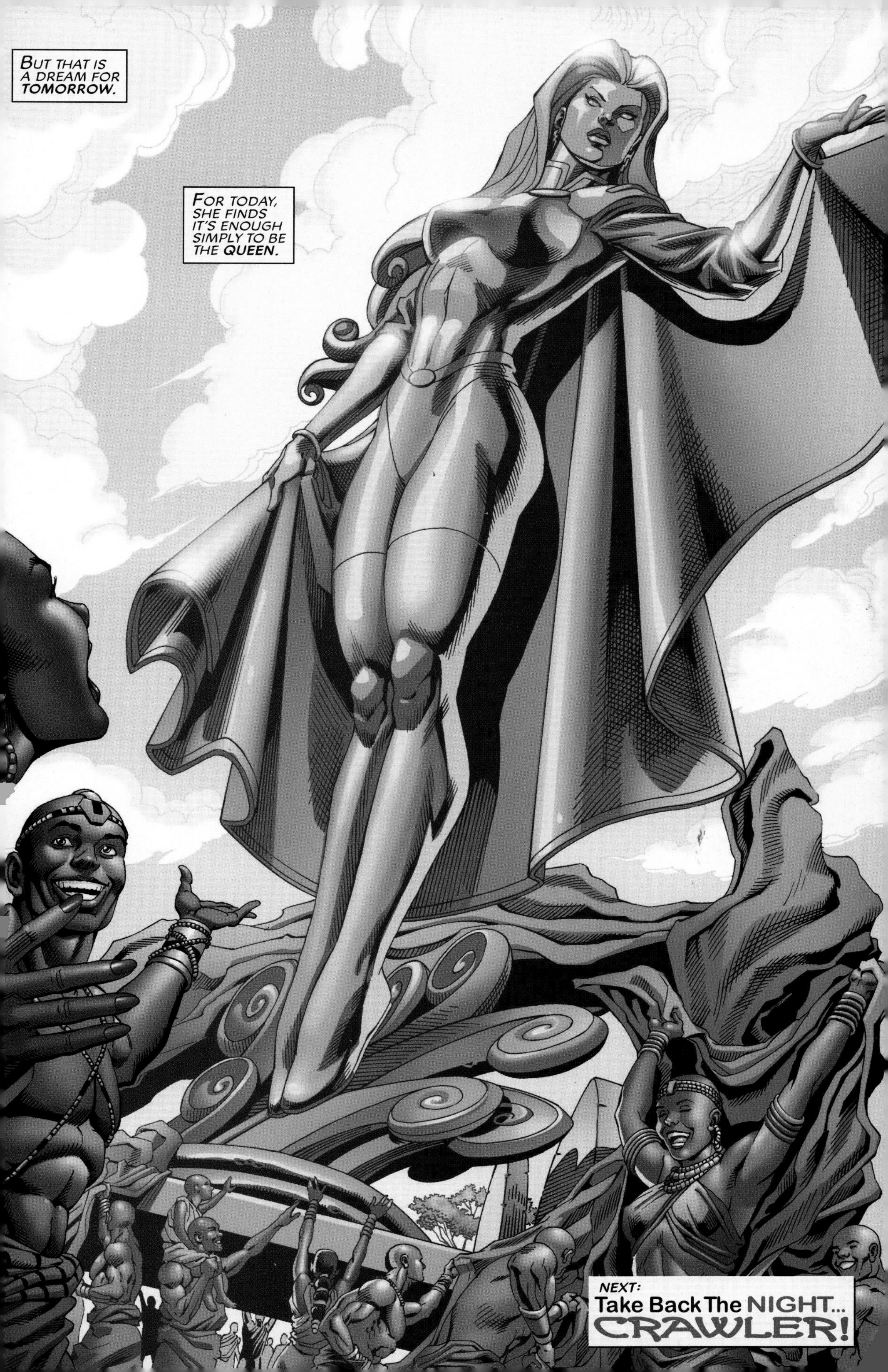
BUT THAT IS A DREAM FOR TOMORROW.
FOR TODAY, SHE FINDS IT'S ENOUGH SIMPLY TO BE THE QUEEN.
NEXT:
Take Back The NIGHT...
CRAWLER!